# Mediating Politics

## Newspapers, Radio, Television and the Internet

*Neil Washbourne*

 Open University Press

Open University Press
McGraw-Hill Education
McGraw-Hill House
Shoppenhangers Road
Maidenhead
Berkshire
England
SL6 2QL

email: enquiries@openup.co.uk
world wide web: www.openup.co.uk

and Two Penn Plaza, New York, NY 10121-2289, USA

First published 2010

A catalogue record of this book is available from the British Library

ISBN13: 978 0 335 21759 5 (pb)   978 0 335 21760 1 (hb)
ISBN10: 0 335 21759 1 (pb)   0 335 21760 5 (hb)

*Library of Congress Cataloging-in-Publication Data*
CIP data applied for

Typeset by RefineCatch Limited, Bungay, Suffolk
Printed in the UK by Bell and Bain Ltd, Glasgow

Fictitious names of companies, products, people, characters and/or data that may be used herein (in case studies or in examples) are not intended to represent any real individual, company, product or event.

**Mixed Sources**
Product group from well-managed
forests and other controlled sources
www.fsc.org  Cert no. TT-COC-002769
© 1996 Forest Stewardship Council

*The McGraw·Hill Companies*

# Contents

# Acknowledgements

I would like to acknowledge the School of Cultural Studies at Leeds Metropolitan University for research leave during the first semester of 2006, during which time I did most of the research for Chapters 2–4. More generally, I would like to thank full-time colleagues teaching on the BA (Hons) Media and Popular Culture and the MA in Screen Media Cultures degrees, because through their enthusiasm and dedication they make teaching, curriculum development and research, in an expanded and under-resourced university sector, bearable. To one such colleague, Dan Laughey, I give special thanks since we shared an office very amicably. Some of the ideas in the book have been tested out in papers given to the Media and Politics and the Political Marketing subgroups of the Political Studies Association, at the CRESC Conference on Media and Social Change and at the Cultural Studies Annual Conference. I would like to thank Stephen Cushion of the University of Cardiff for generously sending me some of his publications on which I draw in Chapter 5. To my editors and their staff – in particular Chris Cudmore, Melanie Havelock, Jack Fray and Stephanie Frosch – I offer thanks for their patience and timely interventions. Most of all I would like to acknowledge the very great help of Kate Nash, who read Chapters 1–5 closely (and some more than once), and enthusiastically and critically supported the whole project. For all remaining infelicities of expression or approach, I take sole blame (or credit).

*Neil Washbourne*

# Introduction

This book explores the way that contemporary democratic politics is mediated – both by media of communication and by political institutions – in the UK and USA, and through examples from liberal democratic countries and across the world. The title uses the processual 'mediating' since part of the argument of the book is that how we 'cover' (media of communication) and 'make' (political institutions) politics is dynamic, open-ended and, in part, 'up for grabs'. The book argues against all-too-common pessimistic scenarios that assert that we are witnessing the 'end of politics'. Instead, it suggests that such narratives ignore or greatly neglect the profound changes brought by broadcast media forms in the 1920s to 1980s and new media since then. Contemporary politics is *necessarily* built upon the expanded mediated social relationships provided by mainstream and alternative media.

Proper exploration of 'mediated' public life requires forgoing nostalgia and belief in a golden age of the face-to-face politics of yesteryear – a yesteryear we might indict as much as we celebrate. Instead, the book explores the 'complex democracy' we inhabit (Baker 2007). Concretely, the book examines mediated politics and the multiple contemporary practices of *mediating* politics in the following chapters.

The first chapter situates the debate over the perceived 'crisis of public communications' and the idea that it has been caused by television and the Internet, which sideline the ideal of democratic politics (and the *proper* role of media within it). It argues, instead, that we must situate the rise and expansion of mediated politics in the broad context of changes in society, politics and media at national and global scales. The chapter explores the claims that media coverage since the 1980s has grown increasingly trivial, and the common assertion that citizens or audiences are 'apathetic' and have withdrawn from public life. The chapter explores and criticises Habermas's conception of the public sphere as profoundly neglectful both of the role of media and political representations, which form necessary parts of democratic public activity. It uses Thompson and Craig's developments of Habermas's work to articulate an alternative model of mediated public life, which, precisely, gives a central and positive place to those media and political representations. The chapter further suggests that the sense of crisis of public life is produced by changing scales and intensity of interaction of the national political community with global processes: media commercialism, cultural complexity and political complexity, rather than any 'end of politics' per se. The chapter asserts that we need to create a fuller understanding of mediated public life, its contemporary conditions and what democracy means in its context.

Chapter 2 investigates the changing role of political parties and candidates as they increasingly use professional communication techniques to aid them in managing mediated debate and their connection to audiences/voters. It situates these changes in relation to the emergence of new forms of political party activity and competing theories for why contemporary politics depends upon political leaders. First, it explores the explanation of the focus on leaders provided by the (electoral) market-orientated party theory, which prioritises parties' attempts to poll the people and seek to satisfy their political concerns and demands. Second, it investigates the presidentialisation theory, which argues that increasing concentration of executive power and leaders' monopolisation of the sites of international politics explain the focus on the leader. Third, it examines the model of expressive politics, which focuses on the, often positive, dominance of popular culture in contemporary mediated public life, which ensures that celebrity politicians take centre stage in their capacity to create expressive political connections with voters. Finally, the chapter explores the ambiguous consequences for public trust in politics of its focus on a narrow range of political leaders.

Chapter 3 considers how well the media inform the public about contemporary political issues in the context of the development of the press and broadcasting in the twentieth century and since. The early decisions made (constitutive choices) in the development of press and broadcast media systems in different countries have important effects on the way public life is mediated. In spite of a shared experience of media commercialisation, media continue to serve the public need for information differently in each country. Further, the chapter explores the value for public life of contemporary forms of popularised television news programming, reality TV shows, and sensationalised press, radio and television. It suggest that these so-called 'trivial' forms do contribute to people's engagement with public life even if they do not particularly aid in sustained analysis of complex issues of public concern. The chapter concludes by suggesting that some features of the commercialisation of media lead to potentially significant loss of a sound journalistic basis for news and that some degree of revalorisation of public service or public interest media might be necessary.

Chapter 4 investigates changes in the way 'governing' goes on within nations and between nations in the rise of 'governance'. No longer does (or can) a single central government issue all policies and instructions but rather governments become an, albeit important, part of a wider system of relations between public, semi-public and private organisations involved in rule in contemporary societies. The shift to governance does not mark the end of national politics though it is certainly its complication. The rise of a series of governance structures within nations (e.g. devolved powers, quangos) and between nations (e.g. European Union, United Nations) causes difficulties for the democratic accountability of institutions and their perception as representative of interests and opinions within national societies. These difficulties are only partially addressed via media since though national media have been supplemented by transnational and global media in recent times the national societies that need to be represented are more complex, culturally and organisationally, and the supplemented media only partially match the new and emergent geographies of politics and demands of complex public life.

Chapter 5 explores how audiences make sense of politics both in the narrower sense of state institutions and, more particularly, in relation to politics as concerning collective decisions or activities of everyday life. It uses the active audience model, which it updates in relation to the extended audiences of contemporary multiple and complex access to media content (television, new media and mobile devices). Youth audiences are the key focus as likely to presage the future of all extended media audiences. The chapter questions the common belief that young people have no interest in politics in exploring their alienated relation to mainstream politics yet their active involvement in other aspects of public life. Extended youth involvement in the self-organised UK anti-Iraq War protests of 2003 is analysed in order to understand the media consumption, political thinking and collective political action involved. Extended youth involvement through social networking in Barack Obama's US Presidential campaign of 2008 is explored in order to illuminate some conditions likely to mobilise young people.

Chapter 6 puts the focus on uses of the Internet to benefit contemporary political and public life. It explores the Internet as both a product of, and as contributing change to, society, culture and politics. The chapter investigates the relationship between the Internet and consumerism, the fragmentation of society and politics, the way information is provided, and the making of global public life. The chapter continues to explore the complex, uneven way that people gain access to the Internet and ways they have used its multiple affordances for a variety of political and public life purposes. It concludes that the Internet has contributed to the expansion of the boundaries of mainstream politics through circulating alternative ideas, through presenting politics in popular cultural formats, and in allowing experimentation in mainstream political institutions. The Internet has an open future through which democratic public life might become more adequately updated or more systematically displaced.

# 1 The end of democratic politics?

> Within an immensely expanded sphere of publicity the mediatized
> public is called upon more frequently . . . for the purposes of public
> acclamation; at the same time it is so remote from the processes of
> the exercise . . . of power that their rational justification can scarcely
> be demanded, let alone accomplished any longer, by the principle of
> publicity.
>
> (Habermas 1989: 180)

> . . . media are the sites where politics and public life are played out,
> the sites where the meanings of public life are generated, debated and
> evaluated.
>
> (Craig 2004: 4)

## Introduction

Democratic politics depend upon the fulfilment of particular conditions or
requirements. These conditions include transparent government decision
making; regular, free, fair and equally accessible elections; and upholding of
the rule of law – in particular the defence of people's rights. They also include
open communication from parties and candidates; and the provision of full
and diverse media coverage of politics and public affairs. Media coverage has
to be adequate to both make the political system intelligible and accountable
to voters, and interesting enough to encourage voters of different social and
cultural backgrounds to fulfil their democratic duties. The conditions necessary for democracy receive their legitimacy or their broad acceptability from
two of their features. First, democratic conditions afford voters influence over
the political agenda. Second, democratic requirements allow the political
process and its institutions to be held to account by voters in relation to
their interests, values and needs. Democratic politics should aid in the

establishment of a politics identifying and serving public, collective – rather than merely private or individual – interests (Dahl 1998: 38).

Each aspect of these democratic requirements plays its role in this legitimacy and accountability. The regularity of elections defends political systems against elective dictatorship; fairness of elections provides that each vote cast will be counted; and equality of access to elections ensures that all relevant members of the political community can effectively become members of the electorate. The rule of law should protect citizens – and non-citizens who are also resident in the jurisdiction of the state – from arbitrary treatment by the state, and should allow for the defence of minorities against the assertion of majority power. Transparency of decision making, and the openness of communication of parties and candidates, should ensure that there is no secretive hoarding of relevant information at the level of party or the state, which should be revealed during the electoral process (cf. for the two paragraphs above, Dahl 1989, 1998; Beetham 2005: 31–6).

The democratic conditions of transparency, just elections, rule of law, parties' openness and adequate media coverage we might call ideals. These ideals are not easily realised – in fact nowhere have they ever been perfectly realised. Furthermore, perceptions of a decline in their level of realisation since the 1980s have led to fears of the end, altogether, of democratic politics (cf. Bauman 1999; Boggs 2000). Accompanying these fears is a powerful and persistent concern that there exists, across the world, a crisis in the way politics is publicly communicated, which has arisen in the dynamic combination of the growing apathy of voters and the trivialisation of media content (Postman 1988; Blumler and Gurevitch 1995; Franklin 2004).

These fears of a crisis in public communications have their material basis in the fact that adequate media coverage is the cornerstone of elections in contemporary wealthy democracies. Media circulate information necessary to inform large-scale audiences about contemporary politics. Media link voters to the institutions and practice of democratic politics and the public information necessary to voters. For example, media coverage of politics allows voters to know the important political contexts within which they are making their voting decision, and the competing policies of candidates of major and minor parties. Media are cornerstones of democracy, further, because free and adequate media may be necessary in order to address potential neglect of the democratic conditions of transparency, regularity and fairness of elections, or failures in the rule of law or the lack of openness of parties or candidates (Crick 2003; Craig 2004: 18–22). Media – press, electronic media and the Internet – make up the key *informational resources* and *communicational spaces* for the voting public.

Media are particularly important in democracy since the democratic political system of contemporary societies is a *representative* one. The voters very rarely vote on specific political decisions themselves – though referenda are becoming more common across the world – but rather contribute to the *selection* of those people who will make decisions: their representatives. Voters thereby contribute to the selection of a few people to represent the values, opinions and interests of the many. On a continuous basis, representatives have to perform to their citizens, via media, as representers of the relevant values and interests.

Because of this double importance of media – to both the represented and the representatives – media coverage of politics grants a great deal of influence to media outlets in terms of their use of specific modes and levels of discussion of policies, parties and governments. Such influence of media has grown since the 1970s with some authors arguing that media have been taking control over the public political agenda away from specifically political bodies such as parties and governments (Lloyd 2004; Stanyer 2007). Moreover, parties and governments increasingly recognise the influence of media (Barnett and Gabor 2001; Franklin 2004). As a result, parties increasingly use the services of professional communication consultants, known as 'spin doctors', and strategies of media management in attempting to maximise positive and minimise negative coverage of their policies and leaders (Lees-Marshment 2001, 2008; Street 2001a). This response of political bodies to contemporary media conditions involves full recognition of the importance and the power of media.

The major focus of the book is, therefore, exploration of the mediating, or media coverage, of representative democratic politics, as well as broader forms of political activity, through the dominant forms of communication in contemporary society. The nature, quality and quantity of that mediation has – as we have begun to see – crucial implications for the quality of democratic political practice. Some see the importance of contemporary media as so central as to involve us in a transformation to a new world of 'mediated politics' (Thompson 1995, 2000).

This book, therefore, is predominantly concerned with how the media of communication are inextricably intertwined with democratic politics. In order to explore this question further, it also gives attention to the democratic role of the particular practices and procedures of different *political systems*. The particularities of these institutions and procedures 'make' politics what they are – they, too, *mediate* politics. These political practices and procedures also differ significantly from country to country. Features of political arrangements such as the voting systems (proportional or majoritarian), the size of political constituencies, the roles of political parties, and the federal or unitary nature of the state, and so on, may be crucial to the development and flourishing or diminution and retardation of democracy. The way that the political systems organise politics can make it difficult or easier for the voters – independently of questions of the adequacy of media coverage – to contribute to policy development or to making governments accountable. These difficulties are called democratic deficits.

One of the most important factors today in creating democratic deficits is the dependency of national politics on global developments. Globalisation – as processes that break down barriers to economic transactions, the movement of populations, the spread of information, and anything produced by or embodied in people (cf. Scruton 2007: 277) – disturbs many of the settled political and media verities that national societies have relied upon in earlier periods. This *interdependence* in politics, media and economy also exacerbates fears of a crisis of public communication, intensifies current difficulties, and challenges the capacity to maintain the predominant – national – political community of democracy. Furthermore, globalisation seems particularly challenging to national democracy not merely by disturbing prior practices but also by inculcating anxious awareness of the risk inherent in current (and sometimes merely projected) global developments (Beck 1992). The nation-state seems unable to control 'risky' flows across its national borders such as those of international media programming, capital, migration, drugs, terrorism and pornography (Castells 2001). The concern is that the political decisions made through elected representatives in legislative bodies and executives decreasingly affect the arenas where important decisions are made. For example, national representation may be sidelined by the rise and secure institutionalisation of intergovernmental and supranational organisations such as the United Nations and European Union, which increasingly influence national democracies in order to manage global issues that states appear not to be able to resolve. Those institutions are rarely completely transparent or open to effective control through duly elected representatives. Thus, globalisation can lead to both real and perceived procedural and mediated democratic difficulties – democratic deficits.

Of especial importance to contemporary global developments is the rise of 'global' media. Since the 1980s, global media ownership and programming have developed extensively (Hafez 2007; Straubhaar 2007). For example, the global ownership of media takes national interests in media, and the fate of the nation and the media corporation in different directions. The development of global media programming gives less attention to specifically national needs and often imposes more highly commercialised and consumer-orientated media values in the place of the public service values of national media. These concerns are followed up later in this chapter and assessed in Chapter 3.

In the following sections of this chapter, three topics are introduced that are especially relevant to the practice of contemporary mediated democracy. First, we consider the criticism that the media of communication fall far short of the democratic ideal in support for democratic politics. Second, we will explore the 'public' as an important space and identity crucial to democratic politics. We are particularly concerned with how to make sense of the contemporary *mediated* public rather than depend upon an understanding of 'the public' built on face-to-face relations. Further, we are concerned with the argument that public interests – which are central to democracy – are being increasingly neglected in the pursuit of private interests. The existence of a vibrant public is crucial if genuinely public interests are to be forged and articulated in the political agenda. Only in this way will it prove possible to influence the political agenda or hold the government to account in the light of public, rather than particular and private, interests. Third, we will look at globalisation as processes that constrain the actions of national democracies thereby threatening to make irrelevant the publicly accountable decisions made there.

## The end of democratic politics: what do the media have to do with it?

In this section we introduce three ways in which media may contribute to difficulties with – or even threaten to put an end to – democratic politics. They are the trivialisation of media, and the contribution media make both to the rise of political apathy and to the erosion in trust in democratic politics.

### Trivialisation of the media

One significant aspect in which media have been increasingly criticised is in offering media content that falls short of the ideals of democratic politics. These democratic ideals require, as we saw in the Introduction, the public or voters to contribute to the creation of the political agenda and to make political institutions accountable to their interests or opinions. One keenly contested argument concerns the extent to which, in particular in the last decade or so, media have become trivialised. Critics of trivialisation claim that media output has become too frivolous – concerned with the activities of entertainment celebrities and expressed in human-interest stories – to aid the important activity of setting the agenda of politics and holding governments to account. The trivialisation argument has been made in relation to three main themes.

The first of these is that entertainment values take precedence over information values in contemporary media. It is argued that entertainment shows have large and growing budgets, and news and current affairs programmes smaller and diminishing ones (McNair 2003; Franklin 2004; Bennett 2005). The latter then may be so inadequately funded that they are unable to fulfil the purpose of providing the information needed by public and voters *as* public and voters (Mosley 2000). However, these questions are always complicated by the fact that no simple and widely accepted measure of informational needs of the public exists (cf. Graber 2001, 2004; Street 2001a). How long should television news be to encourage stories that are more detailed: half an hour, an hour, two hours? Which non-trivial stories should be covered: a speech from Parliament, reports from an intergovernmental conference on global warming, a detailed analysis of the factors behind a rail disaster? We could continue the list of non-trivial stories almost without end because the type and level of knowledge required of citizens/voters/public is extremely unclear. A further set of claims about entertainment programming is that new show formats, in particular so-called reality television, have become dominant and popular in many liberal democracies yet may promote anti-political values (Frith 2000; Barkin 2003; Crick 2003).

The second theme of the trivialisation debate asserts that the news and current affairs programmes supposedly dedicated to fulfilling ideals of democratic politics increasingly use entertainment styles of presentation. These styles, such as human-interest stories, the use of celebrity presenters and sensationalised forms of reporting, have become common where they are – or may appear – inappropriate for consideration of the serious subject matter concerned (van Zoonen 1998; Barkin 2003). They may, for example, focus attention on the celebrity presenter rather than the subject matter presented. The human-interest story, rather than exemplifying a more general experience or dilemma, may articulate merely a very specific or personal matter; the sensationalised style of reporting might overstate a danger or simply mislead the audience about the known facts of an issue.

The third theme of the trivialisation argument suggests that the content of news may become diluted – be less serious and informed – in order to maintain an audience level keyed in to advertisers' and broadcasters' interests rather than to articulate the public interest. The concern is that dilution of news or current affairs content might seriously affect the level of detail of discussion or exposition of public political issues – for example, the news magazine programme that has tended to replace the documentary format in television; it gives much less detailed information and a greater level of repetition of information, and thus is less able to explore complex themes (Kilborn and Izod 1997; Lindley 2002; Paletz 2002: 377; Craig 2004: 94; Holland 2006).

Taking all the three themes of trivialisation together, some argue that media simply do not give serious public political issues an informed and sustained airing to the majority (or even a large minority) of the population. One key argument about why all three aspects of media trivialisation may be occurring is the increasing influence of commercial and consumption values in contemporary society to which media coverage is beholden. We investigate and assess such claims concerning media trivialisation and possible links to the intensification of commercial values in the UK, USA and India in Chapter 3.

## Media contribution to political apathy

There have been widely reported and researched declines in levels of voting, party membership and partisan commitment to political parties across the world in liberal democracies since the 1980s (Stoker 2006: 32–46). Some commentators have interpreted these as evidence of a broader apathy, or fundamental lack of feeling, for politics and public life (Bauman 1999; Gamble 2000). Some have aired suspicions that media are – at least in part – responsible for this decline. Arguments have suggested that the following features of media coverage of politics have reinforced, and possibly given the public grounds for, apathy. First, that politics is covered in media predominantly in relation to cynical or self-interested aspects of political activity. For example, election campaign coverage reports on a 'horse race' between candidates, highlighting their political and media strategies rather than the details of their policies or political ideals. This can reinforce popular beliefs that politicians are in politics to win and thereby benefit financially, or to serve their vanity rather than public interests. Second, media coverage of politics does not give the public a model of being an active citizen (Lewis 2002; Lewis, Inthorn and Wahl-Jorgensen 2005). Instead, media coverage of politics represents voters as minimally interested in politics, with only residual attention given to expectations of their responsibility to vote. The idea that politics could be concerned with how we organise ourselves collectively as local, regional, national or global political constituencies and create conditions for our mutual creative co-existence is rarely the object of media coverage. In spite of the lack of models of active citizenship in programming, those who consume more news and current affairs programming appear to be more engaged and less apathetic – so the media coverage itself cannot simply be a determining factor (Norris 2001; Pew 2007).

## Media and the decline of public trust in politics

Some argue that the idea that the public have become apathetic about politics marks out a decline in trust in democratic politics and its institutions and procedures. To be trusted is to be believed in, to be considered responsible. A trusted figure or institution will be concerned with the accuracy and relevance of the information they give. Trust is strongly related to the ability to make (and fulfil) promises, whether those promises are specific and explicit or general and implicit (Hetherington 2005; Scruton 2007: 703–5). For example, it is often thought that parties make increasingly lavish campaign promises, but cannot once elected into government deliver on them. Public 'experience' of promise inflation during election campaigns, and the consequent inability of governments to make good on promises, can break or erode trust (Jamieson 2000: 19–36). Thus trust in parties, and even the political system as a whole, may decline (Stoker 2006: 119–21). Such decline in trust has a media dimension. Some *explicit* media criticism of politicians' untrustworthiness is apparent in the types and levels of detail of stories provided. For example, media coverage increasingly focuses on politicians' attempts to manage media rather than on their policy initiatives, or may focus policy discussion on political 'corruption'. However, it is even more common that *implicit* criticism of politicians and public institutions becomes embedded in media output and attitudes. In contrast, however, to arguments about the contribution of media to the decline of trust in politics and public affairs, media have even been cited as the last line against a widespread erosion of trust or fundamental belief – or legitimation crisis as some have named it – in the political system (Lloyd 2004; Arsenault and Castells 2006; Stanyer 2007). For example, accountable and trustworthy media are relied upon to connect publics both to media and other institutions even if other media may undercut trust in both as public resources. Further, the level of trust people have in media may vary over time and may be something they have to re-establish after a 'crisis of trust' (Blumler and Gurevitch 1995; Stanyer 2007).

The serious and trusted media coverage that stimulates citizen engagement presupposes a public that engages with the ideas, images and information contained in media. The public, then, can use that media coverage as an informational and perspectival resource for holding public authorities to account. The next section explores the concept of the public. It considers the public sphere in both its historical rise and as a normative ideal in the work of Habermas (1989). Habermas's conception of public sphere has been, and remains, very influential yet is also fraught with difficulties such as its neglect of media and its evident and powerful distrust of (political and symbolic) representation. We therefore also explore the idea of the 'public' further in its relation to media and both forms of representation through the work of Thompson (1995) and Craig (2004), developing the notion of mediated public life.

## Conceptions of 'the public'

The idea of the public is crucial to the ideal conception of politics with which we opened the book – the interconnected operation of fair elections, open government and the rule of law. The public – ideally – performs the tasks necessary to holding politicians and political institutions to account from outside the professionalised political system itself. Such accountability can be difficult to understand, however, since the public is rather a complex idea and reality. There are four main aspects or features of 'publicness' – it is associational, spatial, involves visibility and is concerned with values. First, the public is a kind of 'gathering' of people or an *association*, which has an important relationship to the state as a mechanism for the realisation of common goods. Second, the public is a kind of *space* potentially accessed by all, and certainly meant to be universally accessible. Third, 'public' refers to those things open to *visibility* or general scrutiny. The range of things that are visible, in large part, depends upon the operation of media of communications in any society. Media, then, are crucial since they have greatly extended the associations of the public, the range and content of what the public sees and, potentially, how it debates them. Fourth, the public is concerned with *values* such as the promotion and defence of goods held in common rather than (merely) privately consumed goods (cf. Craig 2004: 42–4 for the above).

## Habermas's ideal of the public sphere

By far the most influential thinking about the nature of the public and public sphere is that of Jurgen Habermas (Calhoun 1994; Crossley and Roberts 2004; Goode 2005). In his book *The Structural Transformation of the Public Sphere* (1989), Habermas articulates both a historical analysis of the rise and development of the public sphere and a claim for it as a normative ideal crucial for the realisation of democracy. The normative ideal is the public sphere as a place (or set of places) where private individuals come together for dialogue. These individuals, ideally, put aside their own private interests and seek to establish – through disinterested argument – a rational consensus of public opinion on where the public interest lies. This is a consensus unforced by power relations but, rather, established by reason through the influence of the best argument. Habermas expects that there would be a singular answer to where the public interest lies if rational critical debate takes place. The members of the public sphere, thereafter, raise that public opinion and interest as criticism of a particular state policy. Through this criticism, members of the public sphere thereby demand present and future accountability of the state to the interests of the public *as* public. The ideal of the public sphere, therefore, asserts that rational argument, rather than the greatest concentration of power or money, should decide the outcome of the discussion. Habermas thereby defines the political function of the public sphere as 'subjecting the affairs that it [i.e. the activity of the public sphere] made public to the control of a critical public' (1989: 140).

According to Habermas's historical analysis, the public sphere arose from the seventeenth century as autocratic European rulers – both monarchs and tyrants – were no longer able to treat the state and administration as *personal* possessions. Rulers had previously put on shows of 'representative publicness' *before* the people rather than on *behalf* of them, in order to advertise the legitimacy and splendour of their 'god-given' rule (Goode 2005: 4). Coincident with the rise of new social classes, came the idea that the state should constitute, rather, an *impersonal*, public authority (Habermas 1989: 24). Such impersonal authority should operate on behalf of the people as a public. It should be possible to discover public interests in the way the state administers society. The merely personal interests of the monarchs or leaders were seen no longer to legitimate state policy but nor could the aggregation of merely private interests of the population point the way to selecting particular policies – those private interests being divergent. Divergent and distinctive private interests grew in line with the shift from a feudal to an emerging, dynamic capitalist economic order based on private ownership of business firms. The rising order of new social classes – a bourgeois social order – expanded both the possibilities for creating public spaces and intensified the potential for divergent individual material interests. In order that the state should serve the public interest, therefore, its administration should be open to rational-critical public scrutiny. The rise of the public sphere, therefore, was defined in relation to state and (latterly) corporate power. It involved the public's rational challenge to the exercise of both forms of power.

For Habermas (1989: 32, 39–41) the public sphere was a place open to the participation of citizens. Pamphlets and newspapers as important resources for debate supported that participation. The public sphere was built upon the participation of individuals already formed by an education in individuality through their engagement with what Habermas calls the literary public sphere. This is the world of novels, plays and poetry (1989: 34, 49–50). Media therefore form an important part of Habermas's notion of public sphere. Yet Habermas understands media as *merely supportive* resources for what he sees as the fundamentally *face-to-face* activity of public discussion. In Europe in the eighteenth century, the public sphere found its institutional space, in particular, in the coffee houses of Great Britain. In the coffee houses, private, educated individuals met to discuss common concerns and offer criticism of state policy. Media provided a resource for such activity with particular intensity after the first quarter of the eighteenth century as news-sheets and newspapers circulated publicly important information. These print sources contained social information and surveillance of the activities of the state, examples of appropriate styles of argument and, in the letters page, a space to contribute to published discussion.

According to Habermas, the health of the public sphere as a contribution to critical debate depends both upon the *quality* of discourse (1989: 37, 41) and the aforementioned *universality* (openness) of participation. Much criticism of Habermas's notion of public sphere has centred on the historical exclusion of women and working-class men from the supposed universality of public debate (Fraser 1994). These groups were excluded because of contemporary cultural definitions of who constituted a rational, publicly orientated person. It was generally assumed that such a person must be a property-owning, educated man. In spite of these exclusions it can be argued – which Habermas does – that forms of public debate did take place that put individual material interests to one side in the attempt to explore critically what was in the interests of all (but see Schudson's (1994) counter-argument).

The historical public sphere, as understood by Habermas, formed a crucial place for democratic debate and values. As well as a *historical reality* the idea of a public sphere also expresses a powerful yet difficult – some say impossible – to realise *normative ideal*. Unless participation in debate is qualitatively high then we cannot fully speak of the existence of the public sphere. If the quality of discourse declines then the public sphere may no longer provide a critical distance from state and corporate interests. Habermas asserts that the formerly clear boundaries between individuals and the organised forms of state and corporation have been eroded leading to negative consequences for the articulation of a public sphere. Thus, the role of individuals gathering to hold the activity of the state to critical account has been sidelined by political and structural developments. This account of the public in terminal decline is not unique to Habermas but rather forms perhaps the most common storyline in discussions of the recent history of the public (Jensen 1990; Schudson 1994; Gamble 2000; Silverstone 2007).

We will focus on Habermas's account of two crucial developments: one concerned with the political sphere and other with the dominant form of economic organisation. First, the public sphere declined because of the manipulative use of publicity by increasingly organised politicians and mass parties. The manipulative use of publicity contributed to bypassing the public's rational-critical analysis of policy since it created political spectacle rather than the time and space for participation in debate. Second, the late nineteenth-century rise and twentieth-century development of the welfare state and corporate capitalism blurred the relationships between private individuals, the state and capital, thereby disrupting the activity of the public sphere as *private* individuals coming together to rationally debate. The rise of larger-scale capitalist and state institutions seemed to necessitate *managing* people rather than *involving them in debate*. Instead of a public sphere critically examining policy these political and economic developments have resulted, Habermas asserts, in a managed and manipulated society, whose organisation elides the formerly important distinction between public and private domains. Thus does Habermas gesture towards an end of democratic politics in what he calls the 'refeudalisation' of the public sphere; here old-style 'representative publicity' as a show of the kind medieval monarchs used to put on in front of the 'people' is revamped in contemporary society. The dominance of 'representative publicity' edges out any debate (Habermas 1989: 142). Such changes, according to Habermas, not only close down the *spaces* of the public sphere, they also disrupt the *forms of subjectivity* formerly underscoring involvement in rational-critical debate.

Three main features of Habermas's analysis can be criticised from the perspective of the potential role of the public in contemporary society: his disdainful treatment of political representation, his distrust of symbolic representation and his limited analysis of the role of media.

First, we need to consider his suspicion of political representation. Political representation has already been discussed in this chapter. It is the system of choosing, in elections, representatives or delegates: the few who 'stand in for', or represent, the interests and perspectives of the many. The suspicions of representation as embodied in Habermas's work are based on his belief that representation typically dilutes the rational and critical potential of the public sphere (Peters 1993; Goode 2005). Giving too much of a role in the public debate to representatives disrupts what Habermas pictures as the value of the public sphere – that issues are *freely and fully* discussed by *private individuals* (Habermas 1989: 203, 204). Habermas discusses the role of political representatives in the public sphere and asserts that their role is legitimate only so long as they are given no special advantages versus other private individuals in that public rational debate. It is crucial, for Habermas, that members of the public sphere *participate* and do not opt out of their role in this debate and delegate their activity to others. Such delegation of debate will only narrow the range of lines of argument pursued and automatically give greater weight to some members in the debate – those to whom others have delegated their role. Even in the political institutions rather than the public sphere per se, the public-sphere role of political representative may close down debate. For example, elected political representatives often come to decisions by voting according to instructions from party leaders, rather than on the basis of full and open, rational inquiry. This, then, would provide little aid in discovery of the public interest; it might only – Habermas argues – contribute to destroying the process whereby the public interest might be discovered. For Habermas, political representation, on the immense scale that it occurs in modern national political systems, is a form of political bargaining over myriad private interests rather than a system built on, and able to guarantee, public rational consensus.

However, Habermas's position disallowing elected political representatives any special standing in public debate neglects the important reasons for which representatives are elected in the first place: to allow for division of labour in public life. We allow some politicians to speak for us, in particular in areas of specialised knowledge or where the sheer amount of time necessary to keep abreast of contemporary issues might require a form of professionalised politics. Habermas discusses the famous mandate-delegate debate (for that debate see Pitkin 1967; Judge 1999). The debate concerns a fundamental dispute about the nature of the position of representatives and their relationship to those they represent. Are representatives elected thereafter to freely give their opinion on all issues of policy, or are they delegates, dependent on directives seen to be issued by those who voted for them? Habermas asserts that independence of the representatives does not mean the former; rather he argues that such independence was meant to function only as a 'guarantee of the parity in standing' of the representative as merely one 'among *all* private people within the public' (Habermas 1989: 204). Such independence rather, was 'only supposed to prevent the status of representative from becoming underprivileged *because of* delegation' (1989: 204, my italics). Such a narrow (and historically inaccurate) view of representatives, however, invalidates the roles for which we do elect them: to debate and make political decisions for which they will be accountable to electorates. Chapter 4 explores the often positive consequences of the expanding range of representative relations in existence in contemporary complex society.

Second, Habermas shows a powerful disdain for the various symbolic representations through which contemporary political discussion and debate is necessarily conducted. Symbolic representation refers to the codes through which people, values and claims are symbolised in words, pictures or narratives. Media content consists of symbolic representations. For example, the images at the start of television news programmes – of the places of national political life, the typical membership of the nation and the activities of its people – are designed to 'stand in' for the nation (or region) being represented. Such symbolic representations were given a definite if quite limited role by Habermas in the historical development of literary and interpretative practices of individuals as they read novels and developed their sympathetic and critical faculties. Instead of developing this line of argument further in the present, however, Habermas focuses on the great negative potential that is established by 'substituting' images and spectacular forms of representation, which operate on the emotional and 'irrational' register, for the sober, rational consideration of a policy or topic. It is the performative, 'showy pomp' (Habermas 1989: 195) of some forms of representation that form the basis of Habermas's concern. As Peters argues (1993: 562), 'Habermas prizes conversation, reading and plain speaking as worthy forms of discourse for a democratic culture and is frankly hostile to theatre, courtly forms, ceremony, the visual and to rhetoric more generally.' However, debate also requires rhetoric and aesthetic or symbolic forms. This is true even of rational-critical debate in the public sphere.

Since rhetoric appears necessary to any form of debate and our contemporary public politics depends so overwhelmingly on both political, and a variety of forms of symbolic, representation, we need to find grounds for the hope that some form of the public is compatible with the full flourishing of relations of symbolic (and political) representation (Peters 1993: 565). This is not to be blasé about the consequences of any particular uses of symbolic representations. We might need, also, to understand and fully appreciate the limitations representative relations might impose. Yet it is upon those limitations that, overwhelmingly, Habermas focuses.

Third, though – as we have seen – Habermas gives attention to the role of eighteenth-century print sources in originally creating and sustaining the public sphere, his is *not* a model of mediated social relations. Rather, Habermas thinks of the public sphere as overwhelmingly based on face-to-face relations, merely supplemented by printed sources: 'the periodical articles of the *Tatler, Spectator*, and *Guardian*, he contends, were merely *conversation by other means*' (Saccamano 1991: 694, my italics). Peters (1993: 564) also notes that Habermas considers such printed texts 'an *immediate* part of coffee house discussions' (Habermas 1989: 42, my italics) precisely missing out the *mediating role* of such *mediated* forms (Garnham 1994; Schudson 1994; Goode 2005).

Further, Habermas has a quite a negative account of the role of specific media such as nineteenth-century newspapers and, more recently, television. For example, he argues that television, in particular, contributes to the political manipulation of individuals and closing down of debate (Habermas 1989: 171–2). However, media necessarily play a larger role in contemporary society than in the past. In wealthy societies and regions, there is very widespread access to radio, television and the Internet in addition to printed sources of information. Further, we need to recognise the intensified role of contemporary media in taking into consideration that media create *visibility* – they open up issues and concerns to public scrutiny – thereby making them 'public' (Thompson 1995, 2000). In making issues public, media play a profound role in making people aware of the world around them (cf. McNair 2000: 1). Media, therefore, can also structure the understanding of that world in quite significant ways. Therefore, we need a much more sustained understanding of the role of media and mediation in public life than Habermas's approach can offer us.

### Thompson and mediated publicness

Thompson, unlike Habermas, treats media not merely as a resource for the public sphere and the development of public opinion but as part of the framework crucially necessary for the large-scale *forms of social relationship* on which contemporary politics is based. He gives emphasis to the *constitutive* role of media (cf. Thompson 1995: 119–48). Media are considered fundamental as placeless 'spaces' for public discussion, and as crucial resources (and the main institutions) by which people acquire information and encounter different points of view on matters about which they then form judgements (Thompson 1995: 40–1, 256).

For Thompson the constitutive role of media highlights media power to shape significantly our perspectives on the world precisely because media relations are *not* face-to-face relations. Thompson calls this form of contemporary publicness 'mediated publicness' – a publicness of *openness* and *visibility* rather than, as with Habermas's ideal of the public sphere, the sharing of a common physical meeting place or locale. For example, broadcast media that emerged in liberal democracies from the 1920s greatly expanded forms of 'mediated visibility' metaphorically via the sounds of radio and, literally, via television. They opened up this visibility to audiences of tens, and then hundreds, of millions of people. These new spaces of the visible, though, are very different from the public sphere as a specific physical place. Mediated visibility constitutes a non-localised, non-dialogical, open-ended space of the visible. The mediated symbolic forms of the radio and television pro-gramming, for example, are transmitted to a plurality of non-present and 'unknown' others (Thompson 1995: 245). Mediated publicness involves a non-dialogic media relationship – unlike the dialogue that can potentially occur with face-to-face interlocutors. We can only read the paper or listen to the radio news and think about what it is we read or hear. We may – of course, this is extremely common – talk about what we have seen and heard with our family, workmates, friends or neighbours. What the context of the mediated public itself does not allow for, however, is a dialogue with those – newspaper editors and radio broadcasters – giving us the information on which we are likely, thereafter, to base our opinions. It is only through a modification of the basic operation of large-scale media that they have attempted, in the last few decades, to overcome the non-dialogic nature of large-scale communications by becoming interactive and offering something 'like-a-dialogue' through phone-ins, 'talk backs' and right to reply programmes (Livingstone and Lunt 1994; Higgins 2008: 92–111). In Chapter 6, we explore the possibility that Internet and digital media may significantly contribute to changing these features of 'mass media'.

Therefore, for Thompson, the contemporary mediated context of the public is very different from Habermas's public sphere, where physical meeting between people took place in actual 'places' such as coffee houses. The 'non-localisation' effect of large-scale media, however, can also create dif-ficulties. For example, it makes it easier for a decline of trust to set in when relationships are stretched across space and time, requiring faith in the contents provided often by unknown actors. These mediated features make the role of the media context of contemporary politics very different from Habermas's account of media's negative role in 'refeudalisation'. As Thompson argues:

> [T]he showiness characteristic of mediated politics today and its concern to cultivate personal aura rather than to stimulate critical debate may seem, *at first glance*, to resemble the kind of 'representa-tive publicness' typical of the middle ages [as Habermas argues]. But the similarity is more apparent than real ... the development of communication media has created *new forms of interaction, new kinds of visibility* and *new networks of information diffusion* in the modern world, all of which have altered the symbolic character of social

> life today so profoundly that any comparison . . . is *superficial* at best
> . . . we need to think again about what 'publicness' means today in a
> world permeated by new forms of communication and information
> diffusion, where individuals are able to interact with others and
> observe persons and events *without ever encountering them in the same
> spatial-temporal locale.*
>
> (1995: 75, my italics)

The contents of contemporary media, Thompson argues, against Habermas, can aid members of the public in fruitful deliberation over a range of issues of public concern if the media contents are of sufficient diversity and accessibility (Thompson 1995: 257). Such wide accessibility ensures (the potential for) a wide range of participation with mediated public deliberation, and diversity of media contents should ensure that various perspectives are explored. The extent of such accessibility, actual access and the range of diversity of media contents, then, are crucial considerations in the contemporary health of mediated public life. They will be considered in Chapter 3 in comparing the democratic and public, 'health' of the UK, US and Indian media systems.

Thompson argues that the scale of contemporary representative politics means that the public-sphere ideal of *face-to-face* dialogical politics cannot work as the key way of regulating political power in the modern state (Thompson 1995: 258, 261). Rather, public involvement in democracy can at best aim at securing some high degree and quality of accountability of rulers to the electors. Such rulers or leaders are elected as representatives of the electorate, and consideration of their rule requires the electorate's deliberation over alternatives, reasons and arguments as articulated in media. Thus, Thompson asserts, against Habermas, precisely that it is *representative* democracy that forms the basis (and is likely to continue to form the basis) of the democratic role of mediated publicness in contemporary society. It is an aid to representative democracy that those institutional boundaries of politics are not fixed and constant but, rather, are being constantly, and fruitfully, challenged, extended and refreshed by 'extra parliamentary social movements and pressure groups' (Thompson 1995: 252). Chapter 4 explores the institutionalisation and contemporary dynamic developments in political and symbolic representation in our changing world of representative governance.

In addition, with regard to questions of symbolic representation, Thompson argues against Habermas's views, that watching a television programme or reading a book may be as conducive to *deliberation* as face-to-face conversation with others (Thompson 1995: 256). What Thompson does share with Habermas is the idea that something like the formation of reasoned judgements is a central and crucial activity of the democratic role of the public. 'Reasoning' for both occurs in the consideration and comparison of different points of view in relation to public debates. Where Thompson differs from Habermas, though, is in the belief that deliberation may be accomplished in individual 'self-reflection'. Thompson even speculates that in some contexts 'citizen assemblies obstruct rather than facilitate the process of reasoned . . . deliberation' since they may not benefit the careful weighing of alternatives and may give rise to uncontrolled passions (Thompson 1995: 256). For Habermas, as we have seen, critical reasoning depends upon interaction, upon face-to-face dialogue (Thompson 1995: 296, n. 19). The form of interaction Habermas foregrounds is 'argumentative speech' in which 'good reasons or grounds' are required to convince the interlocutors in the debate and in which the existence of the other interlocutors is crucial in that they 'broaden[s] [the] limited perspectives' that each individual brings with them to the debate (Thompson 1985: 208, 212; Outhwaite 1994: 70). A further condition for individual engagement with the symbolic representations contained in television programmes or books to contribute to deliberation, for Thompson, is that such reasoning must not merely 'idle' – individual judgements must be systematically incorporated into collective decision-making processes (Thompson 1995: 255). Whether such 'self-reflective' reasoning is widespread and whether it is systematically fed back into decision making, therefore, forms a crucial element in the health of mediated democracy.

## Mediated public life and symbolic representations

Craig (2004: 65) draws on the work of Thompson (1995, 2000) in arguing that 'public life' – as Craig prefers to refer to the domain of the public – has a communicative basis. He asserts that the 'media are the sites where politics and public life are played out, the sites where the meanings of public life are generated, debated and evaluated' (Craig 2004: 4). Craig uses the phrase 'mediated public life' to capture Thompson's idea that the media, in part, *constitute* public life and provide a space or environment for debates, and may, therefore, even be able to significantly structure the kind of debates that take place. Focus on the constitutive role of media highlights the new forms and 'the kinds of social relationships [developed] between public figures and the public' (Craig 2004: 4) in mediated public life. For example, it is quite common that politicians and even rock stars, who are so 'well known' by citizens and consumers through an array of media representations, function as types of 'political celebrity', and the public connect to them and use them as complex symbols of political or ethical perspectives (Street 2004; Street, Hague and Savigny 2008).

Additionally, Craig's notion of mediated public life is concerned with the details of the symbolic representations so neglected by Habermas's approach. Craig, rather, 'highlights the textual basis of public life' (2004: 4). The focus on the symbolic representations contained in media is present in Thompson's work. Craig takes it further by suggesting that the *reasoning* embedded in media texts, and thereafter reflected upon by the public, is only one aspect of media content that is relevant for the democratic role of the public. Rather, he suggests that a whole range of types of media contents may benefit public life. Those contents might refer variously to emotional states, identities, aspirations and performances in addition to specifically 'rational' claims, and may include visual images as well as written forms, yet play important and positive roles in democratic politics. In short, Craig focuses his understanding of mediated public life on the widest range of media contents, not merely the more 'serious' end of news and political or current affairs media forms. This compares to what seems a fixed assumption of the Habermasian position that writing should be automatically coded as *rational*, therefore valuable for democracy, and, for example, visual representations coded as *non-rational*, therefore forming impediments for the public debate (Craig 2004: 22).

The practical implication of Craig's exploration of a variety of media textual contents is that the publicness of public life, as Craig conceives it, includes consideration of kinds of previously 'private' concerns such as personal finance, sexuality and the consumption of consumer goods, in addition to traditionally public concerns such as taxation and public services. Consideration of such concerns is in tension with the Habermasian serious consideration, by private individuals, of solidly public concerns. For example, discussions of gender, racial and ethnic, labour, legal and international relations in contemporary mediated public life may take place through a range of media forms (press, radio, television, online) devoted to all kinds of mixes of entertainment and informational perspectives. This expanded conception of mediated public life includes consideration of topics where the particular object of attention actually represents broader concerns that engage with collective rather than merely individual considerations (Craig 2004: 179–80). For Habermas's public sphere account, these issues and the nature of their discussion – for the most part – are likely to fall spectacularly short of rational, disinterested dialogue on important public concerns. For instance, Habermas would think consideration of female celebrity lifestyles as dealing with distracting forms of publicity rather than having the potential to contribute to debates in the public sphere about the changing role of gender in society in relation to the shifting boundaries of public and private. Further, consideration of the ethnic or racial make-up of national sporting teams, Habermas might suspect, would be likely to draw on what 'the public' merely happens to be interested *in*, defined by an aggregate of *private* consumption decisions and the needs of commercial subscription media, rather than a rationally derived unitary public interest in the issues involved.

In the mediated public life perspective, none of these examples of public life is considered intrinsically worthless or merely a matter of private concern. Rather, each mix of media contents requires close consideration before judgements of worth are made. We need to consider the contexts and contents of the symbolic representations and considerations involved in each case, in order to make judgements of their value in and for public life (see Street 2001b; Jones 2005; van Zoonen 2005; Reigert 2007). Media have a role in public life as providers of written, visual and audio resources for vibrant and varied public awareness and discussion. The media are also seen, in this perspective, as arenas in which discussion, and struggles over representation, take place. For example, access to media by excluded groups may be crucial to their adequate representation, yet they might have to organise and protest in order to access media.

Craig's conception of public life is plural and contested, whereas Habermas's tends to be unitary and 'placid'. The domain of debate called 'the public sphere' is presented by Habermas as capable of producing an unforced, rational consensus on a single definition of principles of public interest. For Craig, in comparison, contemporary society is too complex for any simple unities to be likely to be formed. Drawing on perspectives such as Nancy Fraser's (1994), Craig explores mediated public life as comprising overlapping and intersecting sub-spheres of engagement with media contents (2004: 65). Furthermore, such a perspective also recognises that public life is the product of contestation. In such contestation, excluded groups organise themselves and seek or demand recognition in public life. The make-up of mediated public life is, for Craig, a product both of the interlocking relations of multiple publics – what Fraser calls 'interpublic relations' (1994: 66) – and struggles over what issues, vocabularies and perspectives are given primacy. Craig believes that the fragmentary and contested nature of public life is a *desirable* characteristic allowing a richer comprehension of the contemporary public rather than a forlorn search for a unitary public interest (2004: 65).

So what difference does a mediated public life approach make to how we analyse media? The issues and opportunities raised by Craig's consideration of a wide range of symbolic media representations can be fruitfully explored in contemporary public life in considering the symbolic audio-visual representations of television and other media 'performances' of political leaders. For example, in contemporary political discussion the television political interview forms a particularly interesting combination of forms of symbolic representation with the *potential* for a much greater, more detailed, level of political accountability of leader to the public (cf. Clayman and Heritage 2002; Craig 2004: 99). Viewing members of the public judge not only *what* the leader says but *how* the leader says it (including all the communication via the body of which the leader is neither entirely conscious nor in, full, control). Further, such television performances allow the public to be drawn in to the discussion since it allows space for an emotional basis for the connection between 'public figures and their constituency' (Craig 2004: 120). Further, we should acknowledge the function of the political interviewer as the people's 'representative' questioning the people's 'other' *political* representative (the political leader) and the complex judgements of meaning and trust made by the viewing public (Craig 2004: 101). The consideration of a wide range of symbolic representations does not deny the possibility of support for public concerns, since judgements can be made concerning the public benefit or implications of policies outlined or discussed (and also in establishment of the grounds for belief in the promises made by the politician) as well as merely private interests. In consideration of the political leader's claims during the television interview, members of the viewing public are making complex symbolic and political judgements of emotions and their truthfulness and sincerity, the interview performance as well as reasons proffered, by the politician, for the administrative or legislative decisions made (Livingstone and Lunt 1994; Street 2001a; van Zoonen 2005; Gill 2007: 167).

How, then, is this plural mediated public life *public*? Craig asserts that it is public because it offers a particular kind of value. It 'fosters a particular ethico-political orientation towards others', which differs from merely private orientations (Craig 2004: 47). As a public, as distinct from an audience, for example, we have more of a sense of agency: that our proper role involves *doing* something, *making* things happen, and *making decisions*. Craig gives, as examples of public decisions, such things as 'which government to elect, which values inform our identity, and how we should punish wrongdoers' (2004: 61). However, the boundary between public and private is neither unambiguous nor fixed. For example, Craig argues that the view that individualised lifestyle media might be growing at the expense of more traditional (public) political journalism is a legitimate concern, however 'anxiety about a *clearcut* [sic] division between the two forms of media is misplaced' (2004: 198, my italics). The boundary between public and audiences is 'blurred' (2004: 65). Like the distinction between media focused on individual lifestyles and decisions and those focused on collective or public decisions, the difference between the public and private does not, however, exist in some essential way. Rather, public and private are defined in *relation* to each other *in debate* (Craig 2004: 47). Making, and reflecting on, such distinctions, Craig argues, 'helps us to focus on the civic identity of publics and our activities and relations with others through membership of a public' (2004: 65).

However, before we endorse Craig's model of mediated public life completely, we must consider that the models of the public we have been discussing so far have been developed with national systems very much to the fore. These models of the public therefore tend to have embedded in them hidden and, perhaps unwarranted, assumptions of national centred-ness (Law 2001; Craig 2004: 61–2). However, in the contemporary world, actions, processes and relationships from elsewhere in the world increasingly affect the national public context, causing problems with both the changing reality and the idea of national public and its role in democratic politics. This means that models of the public must be extended in order to understand global relations.

In the next section, we explore the effects of these global, boundary-spanning processes and relations – in short globalisation – on national public life, and their contribution to real and perceived democratic deficits in national politics.

## Globalisation and challenges to mediated national public life

Three key aspects of processes and relationships that span national boundaries challenge the national and public focus of contemporary political life. These processes and relationships create interdependencies affecting the organisation of national publics. We call these interdependencies globalisation (Albrow 1996; Held and McGrew 2002, 2007; Lechner and Boli 2008). First, we investigate the impact of economic globalisation on media provision, because of the way it increases emphasis on commercial and market motives in the ownership and content of media (Hafez 2007: 158–66). Such commercial and market motives, it is feared, lead to sidelining of *public interest* motives and a consequent decline in media support for the distinctive requirements of public life. Second, we explore the impacts of cultural globalisation on the unity of the national public in relation to the growth and transformation of migration and the maintenance, by migrant individuals and groups, of diasporic and transnational links across national borders (Cohen and Rai 2000; Levitt 2001; Fortier 2005). Such groups gain support for their ethnic and national identities from global and diasporic media, which therefore contribute to more *plural* and *culturally complex* national societies (Hannerz 1992, 1996; Couldry 2000). Societies in receipt of inward migration may find it challenging to maintain the coherent national identities that contribute to a strong sense of *national public life* and shared *political community*. Third, we explore the impacts of political globalisation on the democratic status of national public life (Held and McGrew 2007: 157–8, 170–1). National public life is becoming increasingly complex organisationally, in part because of the complex tasks representative political systems undertake, but also because national public life is increasingly bound up with the international, supra-national and global organisation of politics.

### Public versus global commercial interests in media

The contemporary increase in the intensity of the commercialisation of media brings starkly to the fore consideration of the potential clash between private interests in profit derived from media and public interest values in media content or the mode of media provision. Economic globalisation is a complex of processes and opportunities by which national borders become much less important in the commercial organisation and operation of media (Stevenson

2003: 14–15). The increased intensity of media commercialism is very much tied up with processes of economic globalisation though these have, crucially, been underwritten by, and supported in, national and global political decision making (Freedman 2008).

The commercialisation of media has, in large part, resulted from media corporations' and conglomerates' globally co-ordinated plans to benefit from larger markets, economies of scale and increasing profits through expansion into new territories. Such expansion increases competition for national media. National – in particular, broadcast – media were developed within significant regulatory controls such as imposed limits on concentrated media ownership, restricted 'foreign' ownership and guaranteed support for public interests (Washbourne 2006, 2009; Freedman 2008). However, in the 1980s and 1990s, many wealthy governments developed policies that opened up their national media to overseas investment (McChesney 2007; Freedman 2008). Changes in national media regulations in the UK, USA and India, as we will see in detail in Chapter 3, for example, allowed for cable and satellite provision of multiple new television channels. They thus allowed competition for previously monopoly or near-monopoly national broadcasters. Such changes in regulation of both media ownership and content also allowed commercialisation by those national media and their new competitors (Doyle 2002; Hallin and Mancini 2004; Kelly, Mazzoleni and McQuail 2004). Regulatory changes allow and encourage a more economically dynamic 'competitive climate' in media, and the potential for new media oligopolies or monopolies to arise.

These new national media policies were typically motivated, and certainly justified, by the idea that inward investment in media would provide benefits for wider media choice for the 'public' or society, via the cabling of national societies for which public money and organisational capacity was thought lacking. The danger of commercialisation of media for public life is that media are provided to ensure profit maximisation or market control. They are correspondingly designed to appeal to the *individual desires* of consumer-audience members rather than to provide media content with particular value for *public needs* (Ang 1991). The dangers are even greater with some forms of global media since, for example, satellite and cable media can bypass national attempts to regulate both media *ownership* and *content*. How the public interest is to be defended, encouraged, or even where the public interest lies, however, is very much contested (Washbourne 2006, 2009).

### Cultural complexity and the national

Cultural globalisation is the phenomenon whereby culture and symbolic representations now flow readily between countries via media, travellers and migrants, and is increasingly taken up into people's senses of self with little regard for where the cultural or symbolic expression originated (Hannerz 1992:

218). Cultural globalisation has resulted in the increased cultural complexity of contemporary national societies with the effect that it may be more difficult to develop a coherent and shared sense of an overarching public addressing the state (Hannerz 1992, 1996; Couldry 2000; Huntingdon 2005). A strong sense of the 'national' was established and maintained as a notion of national identity and belonging through print and, increasingly importantly, broadcast media (Anderson 1991; Scannell and Cardiff 1991; Morley and Brunsdon 1999: 111–291; Starr 2004). That national identity, as a form of cultural identity, is being relativised and challenged in relation to the global migrations of the past few decades. The idea of the 'national public' has to come to terms with linguistic and ethnic diversity. Recent waves of migration form one source of that diversity. Migrants and their second- and third-generation offspring commonly take an interest in their country or region of 'origin' and its public life (Fortier 2005). They may feel connected to a diaspora – a loose transnational network of ethnically, or religiously, identified people – across borders. Such networks may articulate forms of 'identity politics' in which membership of a nation other than that in which a person is resident is the primary, sometimes 'essentially' defined form of cultural and political membership for that person. Members of such diasporic groups, typically, will use transnational or ethnic media, which supplement the mainstream national media of the state in which they are resident and give support to their distinctive identities (Anderson 1991; Gillespie 1996). In part in response to these changes brought about by migration and extra-national identifications, the national has been undergoing creative redefinition – in some countries, such as Canada and the United Kingdom, in terms of multicultural policies that allow for, or even encourage, recognition of difference and value pluralism (Modood 2007). In other countries – perhaps the best example is France – universal definitions of what it means to be a national citizen and what constitutes national public life is often defensively protected against difference. These ongoing debates over changing national identity have often been differentially and acrimoniously refracted in nostalgic, fear-laden and narrowly self-interested national media output. These debates have also led to a challenge to models of national identity, which suggests that the nation is 'pure' and in every part distinct from other nations, and to awareness that all identities are hybrid, complex and 'impure' (Bhabha 1989; Sen 2007). The unity of the national public is becoming increasingly problematic. National public life may be understood as either 'breaking up' or becoming complex and plural (Delanty 2000).

## Political globalisation, complexity and democratic deficits

Political globalisation – seen in the development and expansion of (global) intergovernmental and supranational political organisations such as the

United Nations, the World Trade Organization and the European Union – has contributed to the growing organisational complexity of contemporary life. Intergovernmental organisations are bodies established by multilateral agreement between states, but that remain subservient to member states' interests and perspectives in negotiations with each other (Scruton 2007: 342). Supranational organisations – of that the European Union is the best and most developed example – are those that establish a new polity above – 'supra' – the level of the state. They make supranational laws, which provide constraints for member states and become supranational institutional actors in their own right (Christiansen 2005: 586; Hix 2008: 574). Paradoxically, supranational and intergovernmental organisations have been established very much to help manage increasing global complexity. However, such global organisational complexity has not been embodied in democratic organisational designs, and this has subsequently led both to problems of accountability of those institutions to national publics and consequent democratic deficits.

There are two main contexts for the growth in political globalisation. First, the key context is provided by the impact of processes of economic and cultural globalisation, which involve multiple scales of interaction and interdependence across cultural, social, economic and political boundaries (Held and McGrew 2007).

Second, political globalisation has arisen in order to manage the increased and interdependent organisational complexity of national societies in the decades following the Second World War (Held and McGrew 2007: 137–58). Organisational complexity relates in particular to the complex tasks governments have taken on since the 1950s often to benefit national public life (similar increases in complexity can also be found in business and non-governmental organisations). The new tasks governments set themselves, for example, include controlling national economies in the attempt to establish steady economic growth, developing welfare states to ease the economic insecurity of being unemployed, creating national healthcare systems to ease the fears of illness, and maintaining military establishments in order to provide 'national security' in times of complex strife. Though there are quite variable attitudes across the world towards government expenditure – from a virulent strain of anti-federalism in some parts of the United States to very pro-government attitudes in Scandinavian consensus democracies – governments of all representative democracies, nevertheless, spend between 35 and 55 per cent of gross domestic product (GDP) in order to fund these complex tasks.

How do we understand the problems produced for democratic accountability by this increased organisational complexity? We have clues from the work of Robert Michels (1964) who, in the early twentieth century, already saw the challenge of complexity arising from the vastly increased scale and elaborate technical requirements of modern society, in his classic, and pessimistic, study of oligarchical barriers to democracy. Michels argued that such scale and complexity were the key factors which meant the ordinary people would never be able to control the political agenda as required by democratic theory. He argued, therefore, that complexity in itself was bound to produce profound democratic deficits, especially since complexity also gave advantages to culturally and organisationally knowledgeable insiders, which advantages could not be matched by ordinary members or publics. The non-democratic, oligarchical structure appears common in the case of many global interstate organisations. This occurs for two key reasons. First, global interstate organisa-tions are not subject to the surveillance of effective public knowledge or adequate media coverage of their activities. Second, there is no effective public sanction should the interstate organisation prove incompetent, ineffective or corrupt. We explore the implications of intergovernmental organisations for democratic public life further in Chapter 4.

As we have seen, the complex organisational complexity of contemporary political globalisation creates problems for representative politics. Only par-tially and with great difficulty can we hold to account the intergovernmental institutions that deliver goods and services, manage risk and create frame-works for science, education and health policy. Yet accountability is crucial not only to democracy but also to the quality of the global public goods provided by intergovernmental institutions. Further, the complexity both increases the need for accountability yet makes it increasingly difficult to establish the conditions for public involvement in, or adequate media support for, governmental accountability (cf. Beetham 2005: 31–6). With the full set of overlapping global political relations factored in, complexity levels increase, systems of accountability become less secure or non-existent, and the con-trol of national political community over its activities seems deficient. The representative systems and forms of mediated public life thereby fall short in making sense of where power and influence really are and making it democratically accountable; in short, profound democratic deficits appear.

## Conclusion

The ideal of politics implies both adequate media support necessary for audiences to make national political power accountable to them as voters and citizens, and political institutions and procedures that are likewise open to inspection and influence. The quality, quantity and relevance of media, and the democratic deficits in political institutions, seem to put the fulfilment of this ideal under tremendous tension. Transformation and, as some argue, trivialisation of the media may make their contents inadequate to that ideal task. The public sphere idea set the bar of that ideal of political accountability very high, and though this chapter argues for a more flexible ideal of mediated public life, it still finds that mediated public life is undergoing powerful transformations that are difficult to comprehend and negotiate. These trans-formations distort the possibilities of democratic politics. Further, these trans-formations come at least as much from outside as inside the national polity. Called globalisation, they have dynamised market-orientated media, which contribute to the displacement of public values in media provision. These processes of change also include multiplication of non-national identities within the national polity, making it more difficult to establish conclusively where national mediated public concerns lie. Nations are increasingly part of transnational governance structures whose membership muddies the waters of accountability and may dilute democratic representative politics. The change from a relatively easy to comprehend national political order through media, cultural and political dynamics renders national polities fearful, unsure and without clear forms of accountability of politics to citizens/voters.

## Further reading

Craig, G. (2004) *The Media, Politics and Public Life*. Crows Nest: Allen & Unwin.

Gamble, A. (2000) *Politics and Fate*. Cambridge: Polity.

Higgins, M. (2008) *Media and their Publics*. Maidenhead: Open University Press.

Lechner, F.J. and Boli, J. (eds) (2008) *The Globalization Reader* (3rd edn). Oxford: Blackwell.

Stoker, G. (2006) *Why Politics Matters: Making Democracy Work*. London: Palgrave Macmillan.

## 2 On the media marketing of parties and leaders: emergence and consequences

... party behaviour has changed. Political parties no longer pursue grand ideologies, fervently arguing for what they believe in and trying to persuade the masses to follow them. They increasingly follow the people.

(Lees-Marshment 2001: 1)

Presidentialization . . . is . . . a set of parallel and interrelated processes, which . . . serve to enhance the centrality of national political leaders.

(Webb and Poguntke 2005: 347, 348)

Through a mediated public performance, politicians try to demonstrate certain political qualities and connect them to political values.

(Street 2004: 446)

### Introduction

This chapter explores the contemporary role of political parties in democracies as the key organisations linking voters, elections and parliaments or presidents. The roles that parties undertake in most liberal democracies include the promotion of candidates, the creation of distinctive policy choices for the electorate, a reference point for supporters and voters, and competing for votes in elections in order to become representatives and, thereafter, form governments (Haynes 2005: 25). With regard to the latter, parties compete with each other in order to access political power through their ideological reputations, their programmes of policies and their images in media (Webb 2000).

The roles listed above have been undertaken by parties in most wealthy, liberal representative democracies since the existence of the mass-membership political party, which emerged and became dominant between the years 1880 and 1950 (Haynes 2005: 26; Newton and van Deth 2005: 222). The mass parties were built around the major structural fault-lines in industrial society – principally class but also religion. Those fault-lines were represented in the policies and political ideologies, such as support for the interests of workers, in such mass parties as the British Labour Party, the Swedish Social-Democratic Workers' Party and the Spanish PSOE (Caramani 2008: 321). Religious parties arose in Belgium, Germany, Switzerland, Italy, France and Austria (2008: 323). The mass party became a social as well as a political reference for its mass membership – commonly measured in hundreds of thousands or even millions – across Western Europe and in Canada, New Zealand and Australia. US parties differ in significant ways from those of other liberal democracies. In the USA, the two highly dominant parties – Republicans and Democrats – are business parties rather than those with a specific class or religious basis. US political parties are also much less centralised than those in other liberal democracies, and play a less prominent role – in particular in creating policy choices – sharing that role with single-interest groups, business lobbyists and specialist policy organisations (Katz 2007).

An overwhelmingly important aspect of contemporary changes in the relation between parties and media is what has been called the 'rise of the political marketplace' (Denver 2003). A political marketplace has arisen because the mass party can no longer guarantee either the level or intensity of support that it previously relied upon from members and followers. Changes in the class (and religious) composition of society from the 1950s, and with increasing intensity from the 1970s, make the mass party redundant as mass party in satisfying the needs and desires of the electorate. Because the political marketplace arose out of changes in the constitution of the electorate, it has also been referred to as the 'rise of the political consumer' (Scammell 2003). The claim is that the 'political consumer' is no longer satisfied by the messages and policies of the mass party because the aspirations of voters have changed. Changes in levels and intensity of commitment to mass parties have caused profound difficulties for the practices associated with mass parties. These changes have also led to a greater focus on the need for media access on the part of parties and politicians, in order to get their message to a variety of different groups since this is necessary to winning an election. Further, this has been seen to necessitate the employment of political consultants. In exploring change in politics, this chapter gives particular emphasis to exploring why it is increasingly focused on political leaders.

Social and political change, including changes in the media, has led to the reform of both the mediated and institutional roles of parties outlined above. One area of reform has been the employment of political consultants as experts in market research and communication. They are employed by parties to plan campaigns to influence the transformed electorate. This has been seen to negate some of the social and political functions parties had for their mass membership. For instance, validating expert knowledge sidelines party members.

Change has been so widespread as to lead to a dominant contemporary view that parties now lack principle, and connect to the public by manipulating opinion (Lees-Marshment 2001). This has led to concerns that parties and politicians can no longer be trusted. One aspect of the role of political consultants more than any other has captured the imagination and has raised these concerns about trust and the manipulation of opinion: the party promotional phenomenon called 'spin doctoring'. It functions, according to many authors, to the detriment of political debate (Pitcher 2002; Lloyd 2004). Critics claim that it is the secret plotting of 'spin doctors' that has led to trivial aspects of the behaviour of leaders being given undue attention while important facts are sidelined. Concerns over manipulation and trivialisation of mediated politics raise difficulties for democratic ideals of politics and public life based on the ideas of public control over the political agenda or accountability of representatives to their public, as we saw in Chapter 1.

This chapter, rather, suggests that the view that what 'spin doctors' do is merely manipulative is far too narrow an understanding of their activities, which need to be grasped within larger changes in parties, their leaders and their relationship to voters. Public life itself has been changing, especially in relation to the rise of widely 'consumed' broadcast forms of *mediation* and their increasing centrality to public political life, as we saw in Chapter 1 and will explore further in Chapter 3. We situate party change in relation both to the mediated public and to the emergence of a dynamic political marketplace.

Within the context for party change since the 1950s, including the use of political consultants, the professionalisation of parties and the steeply rising costs of election campaigns in the new political marketplace, the chapter then explores three key theories seeking to explain and explore perhaps the key change in contemporary parties: their increasing focus on leaders. The theories seek to explain parties' increasing emphasis on 'promotion' of their leaders, which raises what some have called the problem of the 'personalisation of politics'. First, the chapter analyses market-orientated party theory, which is concerned with an economic understanding of politics and how parties since the 1990s have been prepared to change most aspects of their behaviour if they should cause consistent impediments to electoral popularity, in conditions of a leader-friendly, emergent political marketplace. Second, it explores the presidentialisation theory, which is concerned with how both political complexity, and the international scale of contemporary executive political action gives leaders increased power and autonomy from their party or government. The presidentialisation theory, therefore, extends the debate introduced in Chapter 1 concerning the effects of globalisation on national democracy. Third, the chapter explores the expressive theory that foregrounds voting and participation in politics as meaningful, expressive acts to which neither the economic nor institutional theories of politics give due attention. The expressive politics theory has recently been used to focus on the way citizens and voters, in contemporary conditions, connect through popular cultural forms to celebrity politicians. Finally, the chapter explores how we should assess this focus on the leader. We see reasons to believe that leadership-focused politics may be able contribute to forging more trusting relationships between public, leaders and parties, and we explore evidence for this in both the expressive and the market-orientated party theory. Contemporary developments might also contribute to unstable or declining levels of public trust in democratic politics, to the detriment of public life. The presidentialisation theory gives us examples of the latter, including anti-democratic developments. The concluding section of the chapter seeks to provide an overall assessment of the effect of the focus on leaders on the issue of levels of public trust in politics.

## Political consultancy as an indicator of the new political context

Political consultants, often called 'spin doctors', have been employed by politicians with increasing intensity, and with a much wider range of responsibilities for the policies of parties and candidates and their communication, since the late 1980s. Political consultants perform a whole range of tasks for parties and leaders – though some specialise in only one or two of the areas. These tasks include setting the strategy and tactics of political campaigns, polling, information gathering and processing, and image making for politicians. They also include activities such as the creation of pseudo-events, leaking information to journalists, giving and arranging press interviews, planting stories with friendly columnists, planning TV news coverage, coining slogans and soundbites, and aiding in the planning of political advertising (Street 2001b: 147–51; Sussman 2005: 18, 21, 54). Political consultancy has expanded across the world largely because of changing and converging political and media conditions in different countries, but also in relation to the advisory role of American political consultants in other countries (Sussman 2005: 134–45). No simple global standardisation of practices has occurred, however, since there is significant variation in electoral systems, media systems and political culture between countries (Esser and Pfetsch 2004: 391). The activity of political consultants has received a great deal of – often negative – attention in media coverage of electoral campaigns and in the daily activities of parties. The rise of 'political spin' is best understood as the appropriation and development of communication techniques to greatly changed contexts. These changed contexts include that of the existence both of a new political marketplace and of a much wider variety of media outlets, platforms and formats through which to connect to voters and audiences (Washbourne 2006, 2009).

In 'spin doctoring', the writing of speeches is a key practice that attempts to structure political discussion by identifying politicians positively with the nation, party or modernity, and identifying political opponents as incompetent, feckless and distant from the people. In this case, the role of spin is to ensure that the message of the party or politician is clearly expressed, as often as necessary, to the appropriate audiences.

What has been *newly created* in contemporary mass-mediated and mass-party politics is the ongoing 'media management' tasks that such ambitious goals and the contemporary context create. These media management requirements are *much more than* the construction of politicians' identities. In contemporary politics, therefore, the roles of spin doctors are both of enormous importance and form a part of the continuous activity of parties and leaders – as the cliché has it, '24/7'. Elections have become less distinctively important times for the creation and circulation of party and leader messages since governing requires so very much more ongoing media management than before. These activities raise the problems of the 'management of visibility', which was discussed in Chapter 1 (Thompson 1995, 2000). Why has 'spin' arisen as an apparently unavoidable aspect of contemporary politics? It is because parties, and the contexts of society and media within which they work, have changed. We explore a broader approach to understanding its rise below in considering spin in the context of a range of crucial specific recent changes in political parties, and focus on the difficulties in contemporary life of parties accessing the changing political marketplace.

## Explaining contemporary change in parties

How have parties changed? In most liberal democracies in the second half of the twentieth century, mass parties have either changed or been replaced by those seeking to capture the broader middle grounds of the electorate. This has required the de-emphasising or jettisoning of ideological inheritances in their messages and policies (Lees-Marshment 2001: 12; Katz 2008: 303–4). Parties have become more complex and professionalised in order better to compete in contemporary complex and mediated society. Part of this professionalisation arises as parties have acquired a more expansive and continuous relationship to media as well as employing political consultants in strategic positions; they increasingly closely co-ordinate the activity of politicians and members, and they create dynamic national campaigns based on quick responses to a 24-hour-a-day media cycle (Norris 2001). Professional political consultants use a wide variety of techniques to find out what the electorate think or feel on certain issues, such as polling and tracking surveys, focus groups and opinion polls. They also use a variety of means to communicate the party or leader's message such as broadcast TV, cable and satellite TV, direct-mail videos, voice broadcasting, electronic messaging and varied uses of the Internet (Sussman

2005: 88–97). We will explore two key areas of change from the 1950s onwards that have raised the level of importance of the media as an environment for the sustained activity of parties and the need to know what the electorate are thinking and feeling.

There are two main kinds of reasons articulated for the rise of the 'political marketplace'. The first, which was introduced earlier, is the decline of political identification based on class alignment and partisan alignment (Denver 2003). The argument is that mass parties have had to change or face inevitable decline in electoral popularity. For example, left-wing political parties, which had been created around the great (mostly class) divisions of industrial society, had been able to rely upon the great of majority of manual workers, as a matter of family and neighbourhood tradition, for the 'labour' party. Such workers, typically, were aligned with, and regularly voted for, that party and maintained that alignment with intensity of commitment, a phenomenon that can be seen, albeit with some variation, across Europe. Likewise, right-wing parties representing business and middle-class interests could rely upon their committed core vote. However, changes in the structure of employment such as the transformation from the industrial to the post-industrial, or infor-mation, society from the 1950s and with greater intensity from the 1970s, have made manual workers a minority rather than a majority of Western populations, and created a new and dynamic social structure (Castells 1998–2004, 2009; Bell 1999).

The second key reason for the creation of the political marketplace is the rise of television. Television became an almost universally available domestic medium in wealthy countries between the 1950s and 1970s, and the dominant medium for political engagement and persuasion of the large-scale audience. Television challenged the partiality typical of the old-style mass-party press, which supported the party with vehemence and an unquestioning attitude. Television, instead, covers politics based on 'objectivity' rather than partisan-ship. I put 'objectivity' in scare quotes to distinguish 'objectivity' as part of the professional credo of non-partisan journalism from objectivity as access to truth. There are two main elements to the 'objectivity' encouraged by televi-sion. First, there is the 'objectivity' of the professional detachment of a televi-sion journalist or presenter whose role it is to explain, 'impartially', political developments and policies to a national audience made up both of politically committed and uncommitted viewers. Second, there is the 'objectivity' as dis-passion seen to be required of media communications that will be received in the domestic context of family life. With regard to the first aspect of objectiv-ity, television broadcasters did their best to hide their own political beliefs and commitments and, instead, to focus on the content of political speeches and party manifestos. With regard to the second feature of objectivity, television constructed the domestic domain as requiring dispassionate forms of com-munication. It, therefore, put political leaders under the close-up dispassionate scrutiny of the home audience and increased the likelihood of them being seen more 'objectively' than would be the case if the audiences were present at live speeches at party conferences witnessed by a committed audience.

These two main conditions – the changing social structure and television 'objectivity' – have led to the rise of a highly competitive political marketplace and, subsequently, electorates targeted as political consumers. This creates the context for increased volatility in politics as parties compete for the attention and votes of the uncommitted, called 'switch voters' in the USA and 'swing voters' in the UK. This can lead to parties creating policies and campaigns to attempt to appeal to emerging subsections of 'the public'. In the USA, 'soccer moms' and 'NASCAR dads' have been the recipients of such attention, as has 'Worcester woman' and 'Mondeo man' in UK politics. These phrases attempt to capture emergent forms of family and work structure, and give some sense of the values and commitments of this new target 'audience'. Television and other media are especially important in order for parties to access audiences – and the target audiences in particular – when a small number of votes in only a few constituencies may swing an entire national election.

## Why do parties focus on leaders?

Parties increasingly focus both their electoral campaigning and day-to-day activities on their leaders. The focus on political leaders in politics is not a completely new phenomenon. Thinking about the necessity for leadership was common in the undemocratic Ancient world (Gardner 1974). In mass parties in the late nineteenth and early twentieth centuries, leaders would be feted and exert a great deal of control over the party. To the sociologist Roberto Michels, writing a little before the First World War, it seemed apposite to argue that an 'Iron Law of Oligarchy' operated in parties, allowing control by a few leaders rather than democratic control by the mass membership (Michels 1964; Washbourne 1999, 2001). However, the contemporary focus on political leaders arises in new ways, with a greater intensity and in a new context. This section of the chapter focuses on political leaders for two reasons. First, perhaps the greatest consequence of the changes in political parties we explored above is that their identities, reputations and activities are increasingly embodied in, and tied to the role of party leaders. The foregrounding of the leader is the most important general consequence of the rise of the dynamic political marketplace. Second, the focus on leaders reveals certain features of the contemporary personalisation of both politics and media that are at the heart of debates about the status of contemporary mediated politics and anxieties about distortion and manipulation. Some have argued that personalisation is a form of the trivialisation of media and politics, that it is a limited framework for exploring political debate, ideas and policies. We explore, below, three key theories that offer competing explorations and explanations for the focus of attention on leaders.

## Leaders and the market-orientated party

The market-orientated party idea is a theory precisely seeking to explain major changes in party *behaviour*. The behaviour of parties has changed, especially since the 1990s, in relation to the dynamic political marketplace and mediated publics. The theory uses concepts from the marketing of consumer goods in order to analyse party change. It argues that a new form of political party – the (political) market-orientated party (MOP) – has arisen across the world (Lees-Marshment 2001, 2004, 2008; Lilliker and Lees-Marshment 2005a; Lees-Marshment, Rudd and Stromback, forthcoming). MOPs are competing for votes in a changing situation, employing political consultants and public opinion techniques in order to find out about the electorate, modifying party policy and, thereafter, using a range of media to communicate the party policy to them (Lees-Marshment 2001: 1).

Lees-Marshment (2001, 2004, 2008) has called her approach to understanding the changing form of party 'comprehensive political marketing' (CPM), to distinguish it from other approaches that treat marketing predominantly as a form of selling (Newman 1999; Scammell 2003). The distinction between comprehensive political marketing and selling is important. 'Selling' parties and candidates has been common since the 1950s in permissive regulatory structures such as that of US politics that allow paid television advertising spots for parties and candidates (Jamieson 1988). Politicians and parties are inventively 'sold' in films extolling their virtues – their policies, parties or their candidature (Diamond and Bates 1992; Jamieson and Campbell 2006). Such selling has also occurred in less permissive paid TV message environments, such as the UK, since the 1960s (Cockerell 1989). Nevertheless, these ventures demonstrate little evidence of other changes in party or candidate *behaviour* in order to attract votes. For Lees-Marshment, what is distinctive about the market-orientated party is that it may change any or all of its behaviour – its policies, how it communicates with voters, its leadership, its membership rules, its internal structures, its sources of funding, etc. – in order to build a connection to the electorate in the changing political marketplace (Lees-Marshment 2001: 2).

The contemporary 'classic' example of the MOP is Tony Blair's 'New' Labour party, which changed its name and its left-wing policies on the economy and taxation in response to four consecutive general election defeats between 1979 and 1992 (Foley 2001, 2008; Lees-Marshment 2001; Lilleker and Lees-Marshment 2005a). The choice of Tony Blair as Labour party leader in 1994 was also greatly influenced by the need to change the image of the party since he could most adequately symbolise and communicate the 'new' party.

Market-orientated parties are, thus, crucially different from those in the past. The mass parties that dominated the 1880–1950 period are characterised by Lees-Marshment and others as product-orientated parties (POPs). The POP is a party orientated to a principled political position or ideology, which then determines its policies and behaviour. According to theorists of the MOP, POPs became very unpopular because they proved inflexible, resisting reviewing their principled policies in relation to changing contexts (Lees-Marshment 2001: 95). Lees-Marshment argues that the attitude of POPs was that if people did not 'buy' their 'product' (i.e. vote for them) then the people were wrong (2001: 131). Between the 1950s and 1980s, as television arose as a dominant medium, the POP had been required to modify itself in order to win elections. However, what it did – as we have seen – though it seemed to involve a great deal of change to the way the party conducted itself, was only to change the way it communicated and 'sold' its 'product.' Such parties did not alter the 'product' itself. Thus between the 1950s and 1980s POPs tended to become sales-orientated parties (SOPs), using sophisticated selling techniques in a variety of media of communication in order to sell their principled party ideas.

The idea of the MOP is, thus, very different from that of either the POP or the SOP. The MOP starts by asking what voters want, and answers that question through the use of market research to discover voters' aspirations and desires rather than commencing with a distinctive founding philosophy or 'product'. The MOP, thereafter, seeks to build policies that are based on the aspirations and desires of 'the people' as found through market research. The MOP then uses opinion polls and focus groups to test prospective policies against voters' perceptions. A hugely important finding of such market research is that the leadership of the party plays a very large role in the way the party is identified and understood (e.g. Lees-Marshment 2001: 130, 213–14, 228; 2004: 26, 33–4, 238; 2009: 135–7). The political success of New Labour – it won three consecutive general elections (1997, 2001 and 2005) – seemed to require the main opposition party in British national politics – the Conservatives – to change its party in line with voters' desires (found via market research.) Such changes included a series of failed attempts to promote a media-friendly new leader before, in 2006, electing David Cameron.

Why has attention been particularly given to the leader rather than other aspects of party behaviour such as its other elected politicians, the mass membership and their characteristics, the staff, the party's symbols, its constitution and its policies? The answer from the theorists of MOPs is that MOPs respond to the desires and demands of the political marketplace, and that the electorate focuses on party leaders and continually draws upon conclusions about the competence, trustworthiness and likeability of leaders in their assessment of parties. Therefore, parties increasingly must focus some or a great deal of their opinion polling and focus group information collection on the electorate's perception of their leaders in order to inform their 'marketing' of the leader. In addition, leaders help identify parties and their policies in an information-rich world in which the electorate have little time to research complex and dynamically developing issues. For example, the leader clearly links both the presentation and the nature of a party's 'product'. This is because the leader is crucial to the presentation of party policy – s/he will be called upon to explain its meaning and implications. The leader will also function as a very important part of the product of the party. Leaders, in short, operate as summaries of what parties are, what they do, where they have come from and where they may go. Furthermore, the media through which the electorate derive most of their information gives attention to leaders *even* if actually discussing broader topics. This media effect has been called 'personalistic encapsulation' (Johnson-Cartee 2005: 266). The leaders of parties seeking to orientate themselves fully to the political marketplace are key aspects of how the party communicates to the public; leaders give speeches, are at the centre of publicity material and photo opportunities, and (help to) create and defend policies and aid the 'spin doctors' in framing the public debate. However, there exist internal limits or difficulties for leaders because voters may want contradictory things from leaders – such as clear and strong leadership *and* voter involvement in political discussion and decision, for example – which often cannot be rationally satisfied (Lees-Marshment 2001: 228; Foley 2008).

Although the New Labour party is considered exemplary of the MOP, comparative research has discovered that the MOP is also flourishing outside the UK in such diverse societies as Brazil, Peru, the United States, Germany, Ireland and Austria (Cotrim-Macieria 2005; Galindo 2005; Knuckey and Lees-Marshment 2005; Lederer, Plasser and Scheucher 2005; Lees 2005; McGough 2005; Lees-Marshment, Rudd and Stromback, forthcoming). It seems that the MOP idea and practices, in part drawing upon the UK example, have been exported widely around the world as an attempted solution to common problems for parties and leaders. In the USA, this led to both Republicans – with George W. Bush – and Democrats – with Al Gore – operating as MOPs. Competition between two MOPs seems to have resulted in a focus of '*credibility*' or *trust* in the candidates (Lilleker and Lees-Marshment 2005b: 213) in their attempts to reframe the political debate in terms of Candidate and party *values* rather than specific policies (Lakoff 2004: xi). The MOP-influenced debates over the Democratic nomination of the candidate for Presidential election of 2008 were largely built around who could best embody the Democrat electorate's known – through polling and focus groups – desire for political and social change: Senator Hillary Clinton or (then) Senator, Barack Obama (Thomas 2009). For the latter, what needs to change in America is the balance between general ideals of American life: 'self-interest and community, markets and democracy, the concentration of wealth and power and the opening up of opportunity' (Obama 2008: 193).

## Presidentialisation and the power and autonomy of leaders

The theory of presidentialisation is a supplementary – rather than fully competing – theory to that of MOP since 'presidentialisation' also recognises the importance of the rise of the political marketplace and the role of television as the dominant medium for contemporary public life (Poguntke and Webb 2005: 14–17). However, theorists of presidentialisation are most concerned with the *institutional grounds* for the focus on political leaders in complex societies (Price 1997; Foley 2001; Poguntke and Webb 2005: esp. 13–17; Webb and Poguntke 2005: 348; Foley 2008; de Wijs 2008). They argue that three main changes since the 1980s have produced a presidentialisation of party, and governmental, politics. First, the increasing centralisation of power in the executive – the branch of government that implements domestic and foreign policy and applies law – gives power to those leaders who control the executive, and it thereby gives them freedom of action, or autonomy from, parties and legislatures. Second, leaders have been empowered as international politics becomes more important and visible. Third, the media focus on individual leaders – 'personalistic encapsulation' – built into television, radio and press coverage gives the electorate the lead on how they should think of politics. It also gives the electorate concrete aid with considering politics, parties and government in terms of the focus on one or a few leaders who are thereby made 'presidential'. Simultaneously 'personalistic encapsulation' emphasises and reinforces the resources of leaders' access to the electorate. Becoming 'presidential' means leaders gaining distinctive access to power resources, the space for autonomy from both parliament and party, and media access to the public (Poguntke and Webb 2005: 5).

There are two main types of political system known in liberal democracies: presidential and parliamentary. Presidents in traditional presidential systems are directly elected (by the people) leaders of the executive branch of government. They are typically invested with substantial powers in national constitutions (those founding national political documents that describe the main political institutions and the scope of each). However, typically, the other branches of government (the legislature – the law-making bodies; the judiciary – the law-administering bodies) have large scope for constitutional action and veto over executive powers. In the development of the US Presidency, for example, presidential power was intended to be limited and balanced by the powers of Congress and Supreme Court (Jones, C.O. 2007: 21–2). Parliamentary systems involve voting for political candidates to become members of legislative assemblies. Dominant parties in those assemblies appoint their party leader as prime minister. The prime minister then heads the executive. The presidentialisation theory argues that 'presidentialisation' is occurring in *both* main types of political system: presidential and parliamentary. It occurs both in political systems in which *direct voting* for a leader is possible (the USA) and in parliamentary systems in which leaders are voted for *indirectly* by the public (for example, in the UK, Germany and Australia) (Poguntke and Webb 2005: 1–2).

As we saw earlier, the two key reasons for the rise of presidentialisation are the growth and centralisation of the state and the internationalisation of polit-ics over the last half-century (Poguntke and Webb 2005: 13–14; Hix 2008; Kersbergen and Manow 2008). Both state centralisation and the international-isation of politics put the focus on individual increasingly empowered and autonomous political leaders, giving those greatly magnified resources and international arenas in which to act where they have no national political competitors.

The centralisation of control within national politics brought by presiden-tialisation allows political leaders to evade some important aspects of their former accountability to both parties and parliaments, and gives the leaders greater direct access to the electorate through media. Presidentialisation, therefore, empowers leaders – though leaders have very great difficulties in spite of their access to resources when they get into political difficulties (Foley 2008). Sometimes it may even be the case that access to the potential released by the centralisation of power generated by presidentialisation gives incen-tives for leaders, even of democracies, to fight wars, since executive power is even less constrained in times of emergency than in peacetime. For example, the divided nature of the US political system – which is built around a great number of institutionalised veto points – can make everyday Presidential pol-icy making and political delivery fraught (Poguntke and Webb 2005: 11; Jones, C.O. 2007: 115, 118). In response to this, leaders can act as President George W. Bush did, by making the most of 'a radical transformation of the inter-national environment [which] created the conditions [also] for presidential leadership to re-emerge domestically' (Fabbrini 2005: 329).

In addition to their increased political power, leaders of parties that have won control of the executive also have access to a wide variety of resources for influencing media, including controlling media access to the leader as a valuable media-political asset. Opposition party leaders attempt, but struggle, to manage media because they have access to lesser resources. For example, national election regulation differences play a very important role in how far money may buy media access. In political systems where broadcast political advertising is closely regulated and cannot be bought – this includes Belgium, Demark, France, Ireland, Norway and the UK – a large part of the job of oppos-ition parties is to creatively maintain access to media via leader-led stunts, policy launches and (often sensational) criticism of government action and policy. If opposition parties prove successful in some strategies, gain high opinion poll ratings, and thereafter seem likely to become the next govern-ment, their non-financial resources tend to increase in value and influence.

In summary, then, the level of presidentialisation, the autonomy of leaders with regard to control by party or 'parliament' and the concentration of power resources in the hands of the leaders, manifest in any polity is affected by the form of the political system. It is also affected by how the leader negotiates the differences built into these systems and by the precise access to media the leader is granted by the media system (Poguntke and Webb 2005: 11–12). In the UK, media access for leaders is high and leads to a situation where 'party leaders play an evermore prominent role in governing and electioneering' (Heffernan and Webb 2005: 55). In Portugal, such presidentialisation has occurred especially in relation to deepening European integration, which has made the leader less accountable to the national parliament (Lobo 2005: 284). Furthermore, all of the national studies in liberal democracies suggested that some level of presidentialisation had taken place since the 1990s. Many cases evidenced significant levels of presidentialisation in the executive, in relation to parties and in relation to the electorate (for example, Belgium, Canada, Italy, the UK, the USA, Sweden, Finland, France, Portugal and Germany) (Webb and Poguntke 2005: 338–9).

### Expressive politics and leaders as political celebrities

Our third theory of the focus on leadership emphasises the expanding world of media, specifically its popular cultural contents, provided by the dominance of television since the 1960s. Instead, the expressive politics theory is based upon a critical rejection of the economic model of politics on which the MOP theory is based. The expressive theory starts from the idea that politics is fundamentally expressive – that it concerns the values, perspectives and emotional attachments people have to politics (Street 1997, 2004: 443; Street *et al.* 2008; Castells 2009: 382). It therefore rejects economic models of politics, which are built on individual interest maximisation, as a reason for voting. Such models have found it impossible to explain why people vote at all since it is so very unlikely that their vote will ever make a difference to either a constituency or general election. Expressive theories presume that people vote because they connect to a candidate, identify with him or her, or feel a duty to vote regardless of their influence on the outcome. In short, expressive theories suggest that voting *expresses* the political perspectives and values of voters through their involvement in campaigning and elections.

The expressive model of politics encourages us to explore the focus on party leaders as embodiments of the meanings of political views, perspectives and communities. Media and popular cultural forms of expression are crucial here as sources of ideas and images of the leader through which people may make identifications. The foregrounding of the political leader as embodying the views, opinions and identities of her/his political supporters gives priority to those who are especially skilled at communicating via media. These skilled communicators include both 'telegenic' politicians such as Bill Clinton and

Tony Blair, and figures from entertainment, show business and sport who later become politicians.

To those who have taken both routes into politics, Street gives the title 'celebrity politician' (2004: 437). What both sets of leaders have in common is that they use 'celebrity' styles of communication 'to enhance their image and communicate their message' (2004: 437). This includes using photo opportunities to link entertainment stars with politicians, and the exploit-ation of non-traditional platforms or formats to promote the politician. Important examples include Bill Clinton playing the saxophone on the *Arsenio Hall Show* (Street 1997, 2001a, 2004: 437), Tony Blair appearing both on *The Simpsons* and the Des O'Connor entertainment show (Street 2001a), and John McCain's failure to appear on the Letterman show and the mockery resulting from his 'pretend' illness (Thomas 2009: 133). Further, celebrity politicians may also benefit from the use of the techniques and knowledge of those who market celebrities, such as film directors making political broadcasts or celeb-rity consultants advising politicians on television self-presentation.

Street (2004: 439–40, 2008) argues for the careful consideration of the expressive meanings of such performances. Rather than labelling them unserious or trivial, and thereby ignoring their potential for contemporary political engagement, he suggests properly analysing such performances and appropriately valuing the expertise that celebrity politicians possess (2004: 441). He calls for an analysis of the nature of the link made between celeb-rity politicians and their audience, built as it is upon both political process and a cultural performance (2001a, 2004: 442, 443). The political process involves voting and campaigning; the cultural performance involves the way politicians make connections to ordinary people through the way they speak and present themselves. Such an approach suggests that 'political appear-ance' is not merely a superficial and degraded matter but, rather, may stand as a proxy for the 'character and competences' of politicians or even for their 'policy coherence, political skilfulness or ideological consistency' (2004: 444). The appropriate use of political appearance will therefore depend upon the full development among citizens of methods of 'reading' or understand-ing appearance. The development and use of such methods will put the focus on the creative, performative acts of celebrity politicians in stylising political reality in new ways. For example, Barack Obama attempts, at the same time, to *discuss* and *manifest* political and cultural change. He attempts the former through thematising change in his speeches and writings. He attempts the latter through his distinctive combined ethnic, national, religious and racial heritage. In Street's perspective the relationship between politician, party and voter is constituted and experienced 'aesthetically' and therefore must be understood through such a strategy of skilled reading of aesthetic performances (2004: 445, 449). These perspectives suggest that we understand the politician–voter relationship as 'not just *analogous* with other forms of popular performance' but rather as *'derived from it'* (2004: 447, my italics).

Any celebrity politician can of course fail in their attempt to convey the values and qualities in their use of gestures and devices. Any politician may be judged as successful or a failure in their performance. However, this perspective suggests that *all* contemporary politicians are celebrity politicians; it is 'only [that] some are more convincing, more "authentic" than others' (Street 2004: 447). This implies that a full and proper acknowledgement and development of this celebrity politician form is necessary to understand and even enhance contemporary politics.

## Assessing the focus on leaders: public trust in politics

As we saw in the Introduction to this chapter, the greatly expanded role of political consultants in politics has produced a great deal of anxiety, in particular fears of the manipulation of politics. These fears symbolise, represent and contribute to the decline of trust in the political system. Lack of trust in politics is a widespread concern – it has been raised in public debate in countries as wide-ranging as the UK, USA, Japan, India, France, Germany and Australia (Ginsborg 2008: 26–7). Further, trust in politicians in many countries of the world is extremely low and this provides a context for politicians' attempts to articulate trust, and show how institutions may become trustworthy again. For example, the British Conservative party, under their telegenic leader David Cameron, felt the need to research the reasons for a decline in trust and released the results of that research in 2008. Their 'Trust in Politics' report elaborates a wide-ranging 'programme for restoring public respect for the political system' (Conservatives 2008: 1).

However, the work of political consultants seen as 'spin doctors' working to promote leaders, *may* actually produce the conditions for greater levels of distrust. This may be, in part, precisely because of the way that public knowledge of the activities of political consultants contributes to 'the popular denigration of politicians as fake or insincere' (Parry-Giles and Parry-Giles 2006: 33). The sincerity and authenticity of politics was a key feature of the mass party, whatever else its limitations. Thus, the focus on political leadership based on political consultants' expert knowledge of marketing and promotion, paradoxically, can contribute to the undercutting of trust in the very process in which leaders are seeking to interest the electorate. Contrarily, the leadership focus encouraged by political consultants may be able to contribute to easing the strained trust relations. We explore that possibility later in this section of the chapter when we consider the MOP and expressive theories of the focus on leaders. Whether the focus on leaders produced by 'spin doctors' leads to greater trust or heightened distrust is likely to relate to precisely how the political consultancy is conducted and used.

## What is trust?

Before going on to explore how the three leader theories analyse the role of political consultancy, and assess the overall consequences for public trust in politics of a focus on leaders, it is worth analysing further the phenomenon of trust. Generally trust can be referred to as the 'disposition to rely on another to behave openly, honestly and transparently towards his [sic] fellows' (Scruton 2007: 703). In that sense, we have various levels of trust in the people with which we engage in our daily lives. However, if we are an ordinary member of the electorate concerned with political leaders our situation is a different one. With regard to the former, we judge them on the concrete relation they bear to us and other people *we know*. We can watch over the actions of those we know in our everyday lives and directly discuss any lack of openness, honestly and transparency they manifest. With regard to political leaders, we judge them based on *knowing about* them, and their contexts of action, 'at a distance'. We *only* have access to *mediated* evidence of what they say, how they speak and how they act. In making sense of their saying, speaking and acting we have need to judge, in a continuous way, how much to trust to put in the various sources of information through which we know about them. In short, we are in a *complex mediated relation* to leaders – dependent not upon face-to-face contacts but rather on abstract systems, to know anything about them. Abstract systems are forms of organised knowledge and technology that we depend upon in order to carry on our daily lives. Giddens, in discussing the dependency of people in wealthy contemporary countries upon such abstract systems gives the following examples:

> [e]very time someone gets cash out of the bank or makes a deposit, casually turns on a light or tap, sends a letter or makes a call on the telephone, she or he implicitly recognises the *large areas of secure, coordinated actions and events* that make modern social life possible . . . hitches and breakdowns can also happen . . . [b]ut most of the time the taken-for-granted way in which everyday actions are geared into *abstract systems* bears witness to the effectiveness with which they operate.
>
> (Giddens 1990: 113, my italics)

This need not lead us to fundamental scepticism about knowing anything about leaders. However, it does require us to consider carefully the differences between face-to-face trust and trust via abstract systems in mediated public life.

Political systems in which leaders operate are forms of abstract system. Following Giddens, we can argue that it is not so much the leader in whom we trust but, rather, the background political arrangements, the abstract system, which the leader foregrounds in policies, speeches and media appearances (1990: 85). Those political arrangements themselves depend upon the ordinary, everyday activity of various abstract systems (for example, voting arrangements, newspapers, television programmes, systems of accountability and judicial processes) for which, in part, the leader stands as proxy. In contemporary politics, might distrust appear endemic in part since the leader seeks to represent trust but actually is the front for an incredibly complex array of 'backstage' activity?

Giddens' later work can also help us think about the electorate's changing relationship to trust. His work aids this in the use of the distinction between active and passive trust (Giddens 2007: 189–94). Passive trust was more relevant in the past – such as the time of the dominance of the mass party. In passive forms of trust, people naively accept without having the capability of judging how and why they should trust. They allow that an expert in the trust situation has privileged sources of knowledge. Giddens suggests that for many of us that is our relation and attitude, for example, to doctors, the military and the police. However, in a society that requires us to think about how we interact with abstract systems 'trust is less of a passive, taken-for-granted phenomenon' (Giddens 2007: 189). Instead, we question and challenge the authority and the claim to privileged knowledge, which some individuals and institutions seek to assert, since, as Giddens argues, '[e]ven the most reliable authorities can be trusted only "until further notice" ' (1990: 84). Giddens argues that the passive forms of trust are on the retreat everywhere in contemporary society since the 'doctor knows best' philosophy underpinning it is unsustainable (2007: 190). However, for Giddens, the decline of passive trust is not an end to trust altogether since people may yet be able to establish 'active trust'. Active trust is, however, more complex to sustain since it depends upon contingent relations and transactions. Communication, therefore, is much more central to active trust than passive trust. Some of the electorate's distrust in the abstract systems of politics, then, can be understood as an expression of the shift from the system's justification through unquestioning or passive trust to the need to justify it through active trust. We can find a great deal of evidence for this view (for example, Power 2006).

What does MOP theory suggest in terms of trust? Lees-Marshment asserts that the market orientation has the potential to 'restore trust' and even to improve 'democracy as a whole' since it institutionalises the ongoing activity of political consultants, which she argues makes the MOP respond and listen to voters through the findings of opinion polls and focus groups (Lees-Marshment 2001: 227, 231, 232, 2004: 239). In short, the electorate are present in contemporary political decision making since, Lees-Marshment asserts, the electorate's perspectives and wants are thereby present and it is on this basis that the MOP makes policy and chooses its leader.

We find suggestions, too, in the expressive theory, that this might benefit the electorate in encouraging and enabling them to connect to leaders. Street's (2001a, 2004; Street *et al.* 2008) defence of the role of celebrity politicians is aimed at asserting that 'in principle' reading celebrity politician performances has the potential to strengthen political representation. The celebrity politician possesses the potential to involve a wider range of the electorate in political debate. He or she is able to do so because they conduct themselves in debate through what Street argues is the common communicative culture of liberal democracies: popular culture. The celebrity leader thereby might aid in dispelling some forms and types of distrust. The success of these ventures depends upon their motives, skills and expertise, and how they use the advice of political consultants.

However, the presidentialisation theory suggests that quite negative 'implications for modern democracy' arise out of the centralisation of power and creation of zones of autonomous action for political leaders. Presidentialisation involves an amalgam of two prior models of democracy. The first is the elitist theory of Schumpeter, which puts the focus on 'the competitive struggle for power between rival political elites, the centrality of political leadership to this struggle and government, and the prescription of a relatively limited political role for citizens, as voters' (Webb and Poguntke 2005: 354). The second theory focuses on plebiscitary (of, or related to, popular participation) elements in politics. Contemporary politics, as we have seen, includes the common use, guided by political consultants, of such plebiscitary components as 'membership ballots, referenda, and the continuous tracking of leadership popularity through opinion polls' (2005: 354). Webb and Poguntke, unlike Lees-Marshment, do not see the use of these plebiscitary elements as grounds for the dissolution of distrust. Rather, they assert that these plebiscitary forms of 'direct democracy' produce conditions conducive to greater distrust in the way they are used since they are 'highly imperfect forms of democratic accountability, since they are at least partly susceptible to being *elite driven . . . initiated and controlled by leaders . . .* tend[ing] to *enhance*, rather than limit, *elite autonomy . . .* by bypass[ing] collective decision-making bodies' (Webb and Poguntke 2005: 354–5, my italics).

The feature of collective-decision-making bodies that is being bypassed is the deliberation based on the exploration of alternatives and weighing of evidence that is necessary to democracy, as we explored in Chapter 1. Leaders bypass collective decision making, as we have seen, through their strategic and tactical access to emergent forms of structural power and spaces of autonomy in centralised states and international politics.

How, then, are we to assess the consequences for public trust in politics of the focus on leaders? The focus on leaders can have seemingly *paradoxical consequences* for trust in politics, in part because leaders have roles both as figureheads for the electorate and as behind-the-scenes strategists. The former role, focused on plebiscitary forms, can be manipulatively used by elites as in the Webb and Poguntke example, or used to 'listen and respond' to the electorate as in the best-case scenario provided by Lees-Marshment and, in a more culturally elaborate way, by Street in the expressive theory. The latter role, of leader as strategist, foregrounded in the presidentialisation theory, depends, in part, upon secrecy and media invisibility, and can lead to severe erosion of the accountability of leaders. The strategic role of leaders, however, is little considered in the theories of the MOP and expressive politics.

Further, trust relies upon a rather deeper relationship of the electorate with the political system than merely listening and responding to polls can provide (or the powers of presidentialisation might allow). Taking our cue from Giddens' (2007) notion of active trust, we can assert that it is the quality and level of communication and involvement with leaders that is crucial to the creation of active trust. Active trust requires a two-way dialogue – it is contingent upon the nature of the transaction or communication taking place. Giddens suggests that plebiscitary measures – he cites the use of focus groups – may be valuable but, nevertheless, satisfy only one part of the conditions for active trust and therefore only form a 'halfway house' towards it (2007: 191). Giddens argues that what is needed for the plebiscitary forms – he adds citizens' juries, citizens' deliberative councils, e-dialogues and decision days to focus groups – to be more than forms of management is for them to be systematically involved with government and coherently related to the outcome of decisions. This conclusion implies that getting out of a situation of passive trust to one of active trust requires *systematic building* of the public's relation to leaders, parties and politics. Though the focus on leaders per se may very well be compatible with rebuilding those relationships, as they are currently constituted, they mostly contribute to difficulties with establishing *active trust*. Therefore, some structural changes in politics may well be necessary to rebuild those relationships. This will include increased accountability of leaders and the development of plebiscitary features within inbuilt rights for the electorate to contribute to policy (Ginsborg 2008). Giddens calls for the supplementation of representative democracy by deliberative forms and the provision of 'spaces in which issues of public concern can be openly debated in an informed way' (Giddens 2007: 190). Therefore, the generation of active trust in contemporary political leaders might also require updated forms of media responsibility since media form a crucial requirement for electorates' knowledge of leaders and policies.

The next chapter investigates media systems in three national contexts – the UK, the USA and India. It explores whether the media content of mainstream news and new media programming – such as popularised news formats, reality television programming and 'sensationalised' media – serves

# 3 Mediated public life in national democratic contexts: comparing newspapers, radio and television in the UK, USA and India

> Our democracy requires some space in our vast system of communications that is not controlled by the imperatives of power or profit.
>
> (Starr 2004: vii)

> Media coverage of politics *differs* between countries and political systems.
>
> (Street 2001b: 58, my italics)

## Introduction

The purpose of this chapter is to analyse the political and cultural frameworks governing the operation of media in three different national societies – the UK, the USA and India – and the implications of the organisation of media and the output provided for the fulfilment of the democratic ideals discussed in Chapter 1. Those democratic ideals require full and diverse coverage of news and public affairs to make political institutions, and public life more generally, intelligible and accountable to people, and interesting enough to encourage people to fulfil their 'democratic' duties. We analyse these frameworks in order to show how specific historic 'constitutive choices' continue to structure the options of respective media systems and media output. This will provide a grounded national context for the discussion of mediated politics initiated in Chapter 1 and further explored in relation to media management and party and leader use of media in Chapter 2. In short, this chapter recognises similarities and highlights differences between national contexts and media output. Further, this chapter considers the dominant idea that convergence is occurring – that national systems are becoming similar (in particular concerning commercialisation and the increased importance of media distribution technologies, such as cable and satellite) and less regulated. Commercialisation may compromise the democratic role of media both by encouraging an anti-democratic concentration of symbolic power in media and by fostering the wielding of great unchecked power by unaccountable individuals (Baker 2007: 5, 16). The chapter will concern itself mostly with news and current affairs as media content most closely tied to concerns of democracy and public life, though it also considers the public life credentials of a range of contemporary popularised news formats, reality television programming and sensationalised coverage.

This chapter, therefore, emphasises differences between national contexts and types of media. Discussions of mediated politics often tend to assume that the relations between media and politics as were raised in the first two chapters are broadly the same across national and regional differences. The focus on political and cultural frameworks and the 'fundamental decisions' or constitutive choices made in national histories over how media are to be organised and funded makes a further point clear. This is that neither technological determinism (that the media technology in and of itself explains the outcome of its uses in any social context) nor market determinism (the product of 'pure' market decisions by media companies and their relation to the sovereign public or audience) provide proper explanations of the structure of media. By 'constitutive choice' is meant those 'political' decisions made early in the development of press, radio and televisions, which structure the media institutions in distinctive ways thereafter. This includes whether the media are organised locally, regionally or nationally, are run by the state, for purposes of public service or for commercial gain, how media are paid for and what kind of broader regulation of media takes place in the society concerning programmes made and limits over media ownership. These 'choices' sometimes involve specific decisions made at one moment but also emerge over time. Once choices are made and instituted they often, thereafter, seem the natural and taken-for-granted way press, radio and television are (and should be) organised (Starr 2004).

This chapter explores the press, radio and television systems of the UK, USA and India as their solutions to, or constitutive choices over, provision of media and public discussion. With regard to broadcast history, this chapter explores choices foregrounding state (India), public service (UK) and commercial (USA) media. With regard to the press we have regional and local partisan (Indian), national commercial partisan (UK) and local and regional 'objective' commercial (USA) variants. We also analyse the subsequently enhanced policy support for commercial media in all three countries, and the impact of media commercialisation on mediated public life.

## Why these national histories?

The examples of the UK and USA are chosen because of strong links in their historical developments, including the long-term commitment of both countries to a democratic role for media. These links have led to scholars putting them in the same model of media system – the North Atlantic or Liberal model (Hallin and Mancini 2004). This asserts that there are greater similarities between the UK and US media than, for example, between the media of the UK and other European nations. Furthermore, a common argument exists that the commercial power of US media is imposing itself on other media systems and therefore they will increasingly grow to resemble the USA. Rather, we emphasise continuing differences between media in the UK and USA (cf. Preston 2009).

India is included for two reasons. First, India as the world's biggest democracy is emerging as a power economically, culturally, politically and militarily, and thus is increasingly being recognised as a place where the future of the world in the next 20 to 50 years is likely to be made (Friedman 2006). Second, India has been neglected in recent analysis of both media and broader history (Varma 2005), and this makes how Indian society has transformed its colonial media heritage and developed as the world's largest democracy of importance to media-political analysis. Thus the specific constitutive choices over media and how they have been made to work in a diverse and massive country whose elections involve over 600 million registered voters might not only illuminate India but also the models that have been applied to the UK and USA (Hallin and Mancini 2004: 306). Some have even suggested that with India we will find a country on a pathway to an alternate modernity (Manuel 1993; Mankekar 1999) rather than on the same path of development as the USA or 'West' (Lerner 1958).

## The emergence of the press in the UK, USA and India

The liberal model of media system into which both the UK and USA have been put by media scholars gives especial emphasis to the rise between the late eighteenth and late nineteenth centuries of widely read mass-commercial newspaper industry. In the USA, this industry was early conceived as 'the People's Tribune' – which spoke for a free, constitutionally governed people in which all men (barring slaves) had the vote. Such free men should have as wide as possible access to free (from government interference) newspapers, whose transportation was subsidised through specifically low postal service rates. The 'constitutive choice' that all people should have access to the postal service and that newspapers could be carried inexpensively expressed the values of the American revolution and constitutional conventions of 1787, which view was likewise embedded as 'Freedom of Speech' in the constitution. Such untrammelled circulation of views in the press contributed to the making of America as an 'imagined community' whereby people thought of themselves as Americans rather than merely 'Rhode Islanders' or 'Bostonians', for example. As Benedict Anderson has argued 'all communities larger than primordial villages of face-to-face contact (and perhaps even these) are *imagined*' (1991: 6, my italics). In the large-scale societies of the modern and contemporary worlds, media have played the role of the environment within which that imagining takes place.

The rise of a widely read mass-commercial industry in the UK was also tied into conceptions of the necessity of press to citizens carrying out their political duty. This arose more slowly in the UK, in part because it was not until 1885 that even the majority of men had the vote, and because of sustained government attempts to control the radical press between 1810s and the 1840s through taxes and the punishment of editors for 'sedition'. Court cases established limits to overweening governmental power in these areas (Wilson 2005).

In both countries, the great expansion of an increasingly commercial press and its associated national press agencies by the end of the nineteenth century required *demotic* forms of newspaper language, a broader treatment of news and supplementation of news with entertainment. In the geographically smaller United Kingdom the development of ownership that is more concentrated and a system of national, rather than regional or city, press was in train by that date. The requirements for a demotic media led to the creation of a 'new journalism', which consequently was able to conceive of the newspaper as able to *represent* the interests and concerns of 'the people'. From time to time, in raising contentious issues, the press grew able to construct their commercial status into an argument over citizens' or people's sovereignty.

The press in India started in the eighteenth century at a time when large parts of India were controlled by a commercial enterprise – the East India Company. British government rule over India as part of the British Empire did not formally commence until after the Indian Revolt (often known as a 'Mutiny') of 1857. At first, the press expressed and defended British Imperial viewpoints. An Indian press articulating alternatives to imperial rule slowly arose with the Congress movement by the 1880s, which argued for a national India to be run by educated Indians. The press, then, played important roles promoting the independence movement throughout that period to 1947 when independence was achieved. It often used English-language editions to communicate with British India and Indian language editions to articulate more contentiously expressed messages in favour of Indian home rule. This had the consequence that all newspapers were politically, rather than commercially, orientated and motivated. They were organised to argue a case to committed audiences. Once independence was achieved the Indian press continued in its political role of articulating varied views of what India should do with its independence rather than 'objectively' reporting the news of, and to, the emerging nation. The emergence of a commercially motivated press is, as we shall see, a development of little more than since the 1990s in India.

These 'constitutive choices' in press development have major impacts to this day. The US and UK systems are similar in being widely read (UK newspaper readership levels per capita are about twice that of the USA) and commercial. However, differences remain too. US conceptions of journalism as the people's tribune have encouraged papers to remain local and to continue to represent the 'local' or regional in structures of journalistic practice, as has the vast geographical scale of the USA. Therefore, US papers use press agencies much less than those of the UK, instead spending time and energy sourcing local stories, whereas the UK's smaller and more concentrated national market reinforces and encourages a national press drawing on national (and international) press agencies. US journalists are also more likely to have had journalism training and to have imbibed notions of 'journalistic objectivity.'

From the perspective of this 'objectivity', unlike with the UK press, it is often unclear what ideological viewpoint US papers represent. There might be only a handful of papers that call themselves liberal (in the UK this might be the equivalent of 'progressive' or 'left leaning'): the *Boston Globe*, the *Washington Post*, the *New York Times*, the *Detroit Free Press* and the *Miami Herald* have been suggested (Laufer 1995: 213). There are, also, only a few that are widely recognised as conservative: the *Chicago Tribune*, *USA Today* and the *Wall Street Journal* have been cited (Paletz 1999: 353). The national newspaper market of the UK is, unlike that of the USA, distinctively divided up among class-based national readerships with distinctively different styles of news presentation ('tabloid' and 'serious'). This phenomenon has had the consequence that UK papers' selection and reporting of stories – the telling of the news – is frequently marked by ideological or party orientation relative to their audience. 'Objectivity' is the reporting of news without the intervention of the attitudes or partisan viewpoints of journalist or editor. This means that, in the UK press, editorialising commonly spills over into news selection and the tone of reporting. This is especially the case with the UK's notorious tabloid press (Conboy 2002, 2006).

It needs to be understood, however, that 'objective' reporting does not simply lead to the most perfectly legitimate, or best, news coverage. As Bennett (2005: 182) has argued, although appearing neutral, 'objective reporting' tends to 'create the conditions that *systematically* favor the reporting of official [government, military, corporate] perspective', and gives the impression that 'the resulting news is the *best* available representation of reality' (my italics). Gans (2003: 151–2 n. 7) agrees that 'the fact that journalists have traditionally seen . . . through the eyes of public officials does not make that practice objective'. Both UK and US press have been criticised exactly for this – representing the official, sanctioned views of the already powerful. In the USA, the media management of the government and the acquiescence of the objective media have been analysed, for example, as part of 'the social production of misinformation' over the Iraq war (Arsenault and Castells 2006). What the UK press lacks, which the US press possesses, is an institutionalised ideology of objectivity in journalism to sanction this top-down practice of reporting (Friel and Falk 2004).

Indian newspapers, having played so large a part in the achievement of independence, were given formal guarantees of 'freedom of expression' in the Indian Constitution. However, the Indian press has been greatly regulated by the state and ruling parties. They have achieved this through such diverse actions as the application of obscenity laws, complex and opaque administration of the registration of newspapers, artificially created scarcities of newsprint and the application of security legislation – such as the Civil Defence Act of 1962 and the Defence of India Act 1971 – which has prohibited the printing of matters 'prejudicial to the defence of the country' (Kohli 2003: 52–3; Kasbekar 2006). For example, in the Emergency of 1975–77 the Prime Minister Indira Gandhi's Congress government used such powers to close down all newspapers (and used government control over radio and television) to closely sanction publicly expressed views, to the benefit of the government (Kasbekar 2006: 114–15). Since that time, however, governments have been more circumspect in controlling the press. However, emergency powers continue to exist in the constitution and governments could legally impose such restrictions again (Kundra 2005). These possibilities of governmental sanction increase *self-censorship* by publishers and editors anticipating state action as a routine phenomenon.

## The emergence of radio in the UK, USA and India

Radio inaugurated a co-ordinated, simultaneous national public where many millions might be listening in, knowing that all those others were listening in, too (Scannell 1996). In establishing radio broadcast systems governments were placed in a different situation than with that of newspapers, on whose conception of the nation or locality they served radio built, which often predate powerful organised states. Broadcasting, therefore, has been much more closely regulated by states than the press. Broadcasting emerged in the 1920s when states had grown more powerful and used to mobilising the wealth and populations of their countries, in particular during the First World War. Radio spectrum also appeared scarce and some means of regulating its use necessarily would need to be found. Thus, broadcasting was examined closely for the purposes it should play by governments conscious of their own influence on the economy and well-being of their populations. UK, Indian and US governments all regulate and license broadcast stations.

The governments and elites of each country, however, made different constitutive choices in how the broadcast system should operate. These constitutive choices gave different answers to questions about how radio should be financed: through advertising, licensing or state expenditure. Likewise, answers differed concerning how many radio stations there should be: a monopoly, competing stations in each locality, or a few stations around the country. They also gave different answers to who should provide the programming and whether any specific criteria of education or taste need be employed in deciding what types of programmes to make; and how politicians and pressure groups should access stations for purposes of political communication to the emergent national audience. These considerations were answered in the USA by the creation of the US commercial broadcasting system, funded by advertising, and friendly to network interests. In the UK arose a monopoly public service, the BBC, funded by a licence fee paid by all listeners. In India in 1947 was created the conditions for taking over the imperial state All-India Radio service to be funded, and run, as a state broadcaster, by Indian governments.

The USA is often viewed as having a commercial system of broadcasting as if that were a simple and natural outcome. It is neither (Smulyan 1994; Starr 2004). Stations can broadcast only because the Federal Communications Commission (FCC) has issued them with a broadcasting licence to a specific local area for a seven-year period. The grant of such a right is giving a publicly owned good – a section of broadcast frequency – for, in this case, purposes of commercial profit. As such, that grant creates obligations, which the broadcaster is required to fulfil: to broadcast in the 'public interest, convenience or necessity'. The FCC, however, has never explained the meaning of these requirements. However, they do imply that broadcasters cannot operate as the US press may and publish any claims they see fit, and thereafter, in their defence, invoke first amendment rights. Instead, broadcasters must have consideration for community standards, such as conceptions of obscenity, and for the period between 1949 and 1987, when the 'fairness doctrine' flourished, to make sure they broadcast *a range of views* on public topics likely to prove contentious.

The level and specificity of 'public interest' requirements laid on commercial broadcasters by US governments was the product of a series of negotiations conducted in the 1920s and 1930s between corporations, politicians, pressure groups and the public, culminating in the creation of the regulatory body the FCC in 1934. The FCC acknowledged that listeners' interests were more important than those of broadcasters' (Craig 2000: 67). However, this remit was interpreted to require the highest technical standards of radio broadcasting, in a time when poor reception was common. Such high, and costly to facilitate, technical standards forced out of operation most of the non-commercial stations. Further, special interest groups which ran radio stations, such as unions and churches, were treated as propagandists who should not be encouraged to compete with commercial stations. Commercial broadcasters were able to use these *interpretations* of public interest to expand their networks and dominate broadcasting. By 1940, 80 per cent of US homes had radio (Craig 2000: 12), and the ideologically and patriotically named 'American System of Broadcasting', funded by advertising and dominated by the networks of NBC and CBS, was firmly in place in spite of the fact that advertising had been greatly disliked and resisted during that period (Lazarsfeld and Field 1946: 13–37; Smulyan 1994).

Though some specifics of this American System of Broadcasting were open to challenge, the general form of US broadcasting was set in place. When television arose in the 1950s it did so on the basis of the working assumptions already laid down in this so-called American System of Broadcasting.

In the UK, the scarcity of broadcasting frequencies led to different conclusions about the future of radio and a stronger sense of the 'public' nature of radio. At the same time difficulties arose because the 'public interest' could easily be defined by ruling governments in ways favourable to them. When the BBC emerged as a monopoly broadcaster with a Royal Charter in 1927, it depended heavily upon its first Director General, John Reith, to espouse a clear conception of broadcasting as a national public service that guided the creation of programming and carved a space for independence from the state (Scannell and Cardiff 1991). Reith's conception of public service was that broadcasting should be universally available, should provide a wide variety of types of programming, which should educate more than entertain – building listeners' capacity to understand and enjoy complex news, discussion and music – and should be based upon all licence payers making an equal contribution. The licence fee meant that all householder-listeners contributed to paying for the service and therefore it could serve them rather than the interests, as in the US case, of advertisers. Both UK and US broadcasters and politicians were very aware of the existence of other ways of funding broadcasting. Each system discussed its advantages over alternate ones, with the USA claiming that the swirling cultural and regional diversity of US radio in the 1920s was properly representative of US society in the way that the BBC's 'one station' couldn't be (Craig 2000: 42).

A contentious relationship with the government, and pressure from the press industry, led to extreme caution by the BBC in developing a news service. It was not until the late 1930s that it felt established enough to give freedom to news gatherers and journalists to develop the depth of analysis and appropriate radio presence to begin to become an important source of news (Scannell and Cardiff 1991; Allan 1999, 2004; Chapman 2005: 156–9). In the USA, despite similar conflicts with the press in the early 1930s – though some US newspaper chains owned radio stations – news became a staple of radio though only a small proportion of radio time was spent on it – some 3 per cent in 1935 compared to 75 per cent for music and vaudeville (Craig 2000). Political crises in Europe in 1938 and competition from foreign radio stations broadcasting in English caused broadcasters in both the UK and USA to give news greater priority and invest more in independent news gathering. It was in this period that such political leaders as Franklin Roosevelt, Winston Churchill and Adolf Hitler exploited access to the national simultaneous radio public diversely. During the Second World War a fifth of all programming was news – the crises proving sufficient motivation for both production and consumption of much greater levels of news. By this period, the USA and the UK had institutionalised distinctive systems of national broadcasting that served their respective countries and peoples in the provision of news and discussion, as well as a range of entertainments: music, variety, comedy, drama and soap opera.

In India, All-India Radio (AIR) was established in 1930 (operating under that name only from 1936) as a service to support British official perspectives. In spite of its role in empire, AIR also had the effect of making it easier for Indians to think of themselves as members of an imagined national community. After Independence in 1947, AIR's job was reconceived as supporting the activities and perspectives of the Indian, modernising, state. The focus of government within this was to aid that modernising development – commercial, economic, agricultural, educational and cultural. Radio was conceived as a state system, and news and current affairs were closely controlled by the minister responsible for broadcasting (Viswanath and Karan 2000; Pendakur 2004). Although the Indian Constitution of 1950 protects 'freedom of expression' (Kundra 2005: 38–9, 144–5) this was not interpreted by government or the judiciary as a defence of the *public role* of media until an Indian Supreme Court decision in 1995. Public service ideals have been absent in Indian broadcasting and, therefore, there has been little intrinsic, principled and sustained support for opposition to manipulative uses of broadcasting by governments. Because of the state control over news and the proscriptive cultural choices offered (AIR stations played mainly Indian classical music) radio audiences often preferred to listen to radio from other South Asian countries – especially Radio Ceylon, which programmed Asian cinema and folk music and offered supplementary perspectives on the news (Poffenberger and Poffenberger 1971; Kasbekar 2006: 134).

The different frameworks established in these histories of radio (and broadcasting more generally) have been challenged and changed since then. Nevertheless, the way the challenges of new technology, the shifting expectations of audiences, and emergence (or change in) commercial competition have been managed and negotiated depended upon these prior, constitutive, choices. I explore these changes later, and consider the issues of democracy and public life that arise from them.

In the USA, radio diversified for a while between 1950 and 1970 and thereafter closed down into a heavily formatted form of radio, though, as we shall see, the rise of National Public Radio and alternative radio networks do make important contributions to US public life (Douglas 2004). In the UK, radio was diversified – in part in competition with foreign and pirate stations – but within limits of the predominance of BBC national radio stations. The major changes in the USA arose because of a combination of the emergence of television and the growth in smaller local stations. The US radio networks – NBC, ABC and CBS – abandoned the technology for television. Because of the coincidental growth of small stations serving local and ethnic minority interests, the total number of stations significantly increased in the USA in the period between the 1940s and 1960s. As commercial enterprises no longer tied to networks, stations were able to run a variety of experiments with making themselves profitable. This could be socially and politically creative, as when stations connected to neglected audiences. In particular, this includes, from the 1940s, the black audience with its different historical experiences and requirements, and, in the 1950s, the youth audience with its emerging musical and cultural tastes. These experiments also enabled the emergence of underground and progressive stations, responding to, and creating, the late 1960s 'politicised' youth movement and its concerns for questioning authority and imagining a more open society. Increasingly though, thereafter, the desire to make a profit encouraged stations to establish a format that would guarantee audiences in particular localities. Stations shifted quickly from, for example, being a rhythm and blues station to a country music station (or vice versa) in the search for profit. This is an increasingly uncreative form of radio, which is very well known in the USA: 'the tight play list combined with jingles, on-air promotions, ads, and the rapid-fire patter of a DJ' (Douglas 2004: 251).

In the UK in the 1960s, the new youth music and new radio formats were slow to appear on paternalistic BBC radio, which liked to prescribe education and proscribe some emergent entertainment forms to its listeners. What required change was the competition for the youth audience provided by 'pirate' stations (such as Radios London and Caroline), broadcasting pop music to the UK from ships moored outside UK territorial waters. In 1967, the BBC established its own youth popular music station, Radio 1, with the participation of some former pirate DJs, in order to compete in youth-orientated radio (Garfield 1998). This loosening-up of radio also allowed for the emergence of further BBC and commercial stations such as BBC Radio 2, 3 and 4, local BBC radio from 1967 and local commercial radio from 1973. The BBC had no national competition in radio until 1992 with the first UK national commercial station – Classic FM – and little or no competition in the realm of news and current affairs.

The dominance of national BBC news gathering and the promotion of a London-centred approach have kept BBC local radio in a state of comparative underdevelopment and, except in major cities, provide little sustained competition for BBC national radio stations. The dominance, also, has allowed the BBC to sustain high levels of commitment to radio news and current affairs services across its stations and, in particular, on Radio 4. Perhaps the most significant recent development in UK radio, from late 2005, is the recognition of the necessity for and the creation of, community radio stations in order to support groups that are under-served or unrepresented by the current media system. What the future holds in store for them and how they may transform the debate over the constitutive choice of public service as the basis for UK broadcasting is an open and intriguing question.

Perhaps the biggest development in radio in the USA since the early 1970s is National Public Radio (NPR). NPR emerged in 1971 as an expression of the liberal politics of the 1960s and the need for public interest media seen as neglected by the entrenched 'American System of Broadcasting'. Like other public interest broadcasters its funding, relation to listeners and programming made it different from commercial broadcasting. Though intended to have a participatory and inclusive relation to its listeners, NPR has tended to choose between that and becoming a more professional and dedicated news and current affairs provider, at least at the national level, favouring the latter (Engelmann 1996; Ledbetter 1997). NPR exists on a shoestring of funds compared to BBC radio and its audiences are smaller. However, NPR's professionalised style has made it an important supplement to US commercial radio even if it is, perhaps, unable to live up to its promise to 'see America whole in all its diversity'. This supplementation is especially important in the regulatory contexts of radio from the 1980s, which are leading to the neglect of news and current affairs. The consequent dominance of the right-wing talk radio show and its ability to serve partisan political perspectives and foster them in US politics arises directly out of those decisions since broadcasters are no longer required to provide a genuine range of views on controversial topics (Laufer 1995). Even the rise and minor success of a left-wing talk network, Air America, does more to demonstrate that the form of intolerant talk radio may have negative consequences for informing the public than it does to even up the contest between partisan viewpoints (Drobny 2004). UK broadcasters, by contrast, both BBC and commercial, continue to remain under obligations to explore a range of views pertinent to public life.

## Television in the UK and USA and India

The constitutive choices in radio in the three countries provided the framework for the creation of their television systems, and the forms of programming they pioneered on radio became part of television. Although both the UK and USA had television before the start of the Second World War, their histories are really, and overwhelmingly, post-war phenomena. In India, television arrived in 1959 but played a very small role until the 1980s.

Television in the USA became the dominant political medium at the time of the 1956 presidential election by which time the great majority of the population had access, and the NBC, ABC and CBS networks were in control

(Jamieson 1988). Television's political dominance in the UK came a little later, by which time, from 1955 onwards, the BBC had competition from commercial television: Independent Television (ITV), whose regional channels were created to increase the opportunity for advertisers to reach consumers. Competition spurred the BBC not only to compete in entertainment programming but also to increase its investment in, and update the presentation style of, its news and current affairs output. By the 1960s political parties' control over elections and political discussion was in decline, and politicians had to start to learn to use television as the main medium to engage the national audience (Cockerell 1989). The television election had started to become a key media event and regular element of the mediated public sphere. By the 1980s and 1990s, parties had to accept that they did not control this main public arena for political debate. However, in both the UK and USA, adaptation of news broadcasting from its radio incarnation to television was quite slow. It took the assassination of President Kennedy in 1963 to commit US broadcasters to regular, lengthy national news telecasts morning and evening (Greenberg and Parker 1965; Barkin 2003: 35–7). The public had shown an appetite for news over the weekend after Kennedy's death, when the average American watched television news coverage and updates for nearly 32 hours, and the three networks gave total coverage of nearly 187 hours; the networks subsequently invested as much as 500 per cent greater financial resources in news gathering (Greenberg and Parker 1965: 76). The big networks reorganised themselves to satisfy this appetite for news and current affairs with news functioning as a prestige product that won awards rather than being required to be a centre of profit. In the UK, the 1960s also saw the wider and more extensive coverage of news and current affairs, in which the ITV channels, which were required by the broadcasting legislation to cover current affairs, also extensively played their part, systematically breaking the domination of politics by the parties (Holland 2006: xiii). That television coverage inaugurated television's critical coverage of party policies and leaders, in particular, during elections. Once these regular network telecasts were established there was only one major development in US television: the rise of the Public Broadcasting System (PBS).

PBS has been an important supplement to US media. Like NPR, it is under-funded and has been politically destabilised by right-wing political attacks based on the idea that it is a bastion of liberal values. PBS, though, has been able to maintain that 1960s commitment to sustained current affairs and documentary production through *Frontline*, which established a repertory company of film makers and journalists to produce a range of investigative documentaries, thought pieces and topical programmes on fast-breaking stories (Engelmann 1996: 201). It has also been able to maintain responsible news journalism through programmes such as its *MacNeil/Lehrer News Hour* (Engelmann 1996: 204–5), the first hour-long network news show in the USA.

The BBC's public service commitment led in the 1960s and 1970s to investigative news and documentary making in a producer-led BBC, which allowed innovative programme makers full reign and control over their programmes. In 1982, the advertising-funded broadcaster, Channel 4, emerged with a remit to create innovative programmes, with more diverse representations and high levels of public service requirements to fulfil, thereby enhancing UK television news and current affairs rather than degrading it (Malik 2002). Even in the UK, however, some have claimed to find evidence of a decline in commitment to serious documentary programming and, in order to facilitate sales of programming abroad, the avoidance of some contentious programme issues (Kilborn and Izod 1997: 184, 186–8; Holland 2006: 219).

## Media commercialisation and public life

Since the 1980s, with the election of market-friendly governments in the UK and USA, policy has encouraged commercial interests in media (Feintuck and Varney 2006; Freedman 2008). Freedman (2008: 1) notes that this neo-liberal policy bears the following characteristics: audiences are conceptualised as consumers; knowledge is commodified; commercial space is expanded; trade is prioritised; ownership is concentrated and common resources are siphoned off into private enclosures. The major legislation of governments in the UK renegotiated upwards the acceptable levels of broadcast concentrated ownership allowable, encouraged a market of independent production companies through requirements that the BBC's productions should be 25 per cent outsourced, and reduced the levels of public service responsibilities that terrestrial broadcasters had to satisfy in the programming they aired. In the USA, the 1996 Telecommunications Act provided conditions enormously favourable to the corporations dominating US broadcasting, including free access to digital spectrum, easier renewal and extended periods of broadcasting licences, and relaxed regulation of charges in the cable sector. The consequence of the act was massive consolidation of media company ownership and frenetic trading. In India, liberalisation of the economy occurred in 1991 as an immediate response to a financial crisis that required the Indian government to swiftly access inward investment. However, liberalisation of media and entertainment, such as the sale of direct-to-home broadcast licences and radio liberalisation, began in earnest only in 2003 (Kohli-Khandekar 2006: 17). The Indian government generally freed restrictive state practices in media such as their control over the availability of newsprint and satellite uplinks, and subsequently encouraged direct inward investment of foreign companies, in small shares, in Indian media. We explore below the implications for media content and access of this commercialisation.

## Press commercialisation

Press systems in UK, USA and India, created historically because of different constitutive choices, have been undergoing intensive commercialisation and renewed competition since the 1980s, putting news values, democratic values and commercial values potentially in great tension with each other. This redefinition of newspapers' activity needs to be seen in relation to political reworking of prior 'constitutive choices'.

Since the 1980s, several national governments – the USA and the UK among them – transformed their philosophy of governing by a massively increased emphasis on the role of markets in all areas of government policy as a criticism of the perceived failures and rising costs of welfare state and new deal policies. This rise of neo-liberalism, as it has been labelled, has led to the promotion of the market as a major part of the solution to policy choices. It has led to rewriting media policy in order to encourage concentrated media ownership (owning a large proportion of audiences' access to a particular medium) and cross-media ownership (owning significant aspects of a variety of different media) (Freedman 2008). Some commentators have argued that this is making press across these countries more similar – a convergence of the press. Here I argue that press in the USA, UK and India have had to meet similar challenges but remain significantly different.

In the UK and USA, commercialisation has led to further consolidation in the newspaper industry whereby top newspaper companies control increasing proportions of press circulation. Monopolisation has gone further in the former since 12 national daily papers, with readerships of half the adult population, control much more of the news flow than is the case in the USA with its greater dispersal of the press in localities and regions (McNair 2003, 2007; Allan 2004; Graber 2006). Even in the case of local press in the USA, however, newspaper groups control more than they did and very few cities – only one in fifty – have the advantage of competing daily newspapers, increasing the potential for a decline in the diversity of news sources. In both countries slow decline in newspaper readership, which in the UK goes back to the 1950s, means that papers chase smaller readerships. This has created hyper-competition, with the consequence that the UK's tabloid press uses television marketing, prize competitions and free DVDs to sell papers and compete rather than supplying better news. The 'news' structures that actually do allow differentiation among the tabloid press are that of candid photographs of sporting, popular music, television and film celebrities and salacious stories. The 'quality' press, though having much higher levels of national and international news coverage than the tabloids, compete among themselves in similar ways, with supplements, commentary and, of late, gifts.

The US press, with its constitutional defence and its belief in its role as people's tribune, has also cut back on the gathering of 'hard news', and pays more attention to commentary and star columnists and, thereby, *interpretation* of the news. US city dailies, which in 98 per cent of areas have a monopoly, possess, to an extent, a captive audience, which privilege the UK national press lacks – therefore are under less pressure for readers than the UK press. Allied to this, some decline in the investment in investigative journalism appears to be occurring (Bernt and Greenwald 2000; Graber 2006). These developments raise serious concerns, noted in Chapter 1, about whether news serves citizens' needs in democracies.

In contrast, India, with its rising literacy rate, is experiencing great rises in newspaper reading (Kasbekar 2006: 113–14). It is also experiencing steep rises in regional press readership – evidence that regions are increasingly able to support the advertising base necessary for a commercial press. India's regions are also massively linguistically different and readerships require papers in a variety of non-English languages. The dominant-language, Hindi-language press has grown greatly, with a few titles overtaking the sales and readership of the best-selling English-language paper. Sales of newspapers in Tamil, Telugu and a variety of India's 20 or so languages that are each understood by over ten million of the population, are also on the increase (Vilanilam 2005: 85–7; Kasbekar 2006: 116–17). The encouragement to commercial, rather than 'political', press in India is not simply some natural development of commerce but is supported by government policy of the liberalising of the Indian economy. For example, in 2002, to encourage a controlled if substantial flow of inward investment and technical and journalistic expertise, the government allowed foreign investors to own up to 20 per cent of any Indian newspaper. Concerns have arisen that the advertising that pays for most of the emergent commercial press, which Indians consume, is having effects on the editorial stances of the press. This is seen as a particular problem in India where the commercially orientated press is a new phenomenon, constitutional guarantees are of questionable effect and conceptions of the press as able to represent the people are less highly developed and institutionalised than in the USA or UK.

## Radio commercialisation

Changes in media ownership regulation have made them more market friendly in both countries and, to a lesser extent in India, allowing media corporations to grow and monopolise media provision. The consequences of these changes vary in the national systems of media. Concentrated ownership has gone furthest in the USA where defence of 'the public interest' from within the FCC is now so tepid it can barely intervene to limit concentration of media ownership. A piece of neo-liberal media legislation, the Telecommunication Act of 1996, removed all ceilings on national radio station ownership and has led to a massive concentration of ownership with, for example, the Clear Channel Company owning in excess of 1,200 stations nationally, and also often is dominant in local radio markets (Jamieson and Campbell 2006: 158). By the late 1990s, the top four radio group owners controlled 90 per cent of the radio advertising revenue in the USA (Douglas 2004: 325). This has led to a decline in investment in radio news (Klinenberg 2007). In the UK, in spite of the increase in numbers of commercial radio stations from 40 to 300 in the quarter of a century from 1982, and the expansion of concentrated ownership, which gave the top three companies 73, 38 and 26 stations, BBC radio remained dominant since the BBC maintains a very well-resourced and responsive national system of stations supported by 40 local stations (Starkey and Crisell 2009: 33, 38). A revival of 'public interest' in media in the USA, however, has occurred from outside the regulatory system. The continued FCC friendliness to commercial media interests became expressed in new policies, further allowing local concentration of media and cross-media ownership. However, a wide-ranging public mobilisation against these changes in the name of public interest in media became aroused in 2003 and also led to court cases opposing the proposed changes, and gave an opportunity to revisit what a public interest in media might comprise (McChesney 2004; Klinenberg 2007).

Indian radio, however, is not dominated by commercial stations, in part because AIR has been part-funded by advertising from 1967 and sponsored programmes since 1993. AIR had become much more widely accessible between 1950 and 1970 as radio ownership increased twenty-fold (Kohli 2003; Kohli-Khandekar 2006), often with people listening communally, in both urban and rural areas. Radio has remained much more affordable than television. State taxation revenues have funded AIR and, until 1985, there was a specific tax on sales of radio sets. To supplement its income – especially since Indian tax revenue is low and Indians are reluctant to pay taxes – it allowed commercial advertising and a relaxation of music broadcasting policy to offer its listeners a choice of film songs and light music in order that it could success-fully compete with Radio Ceylon. Commercial income was further developed from 1993 as AIR allowed the sale of timeslots to commercial companies on AIR FM as liberalisation of the Indian economy was seen to require the expan-sion of advertising. In 2002, the Indian government allowed 38 commercial FM stations to be established in metropolitan areas to take this expansion of advertising opportunities further. These commercial stations were established to create competition for AIR in the provision of news and current affairs, however, and are not allowed to broadcast news. Therefore, they do not com-pete for news space with AIR's bulletins in 23 languages (Vilanilam 2005: 145). Further, only 22 FM stations in 14 cities were actually established since bidding for licences went so high that expansion was restricted. Furthermore, the cost of the licences gave great incentives for those FM stations actually established to gravitate towards output based on the most popular Hindi film and pop music. The stations broadcast to middle-class urban listenerships and 'most channels have ended up providing almost identical fare, delivered in the same breezy "Hinglish" (Hindi-English) patter' (Kasbekar 2006: 136). In radio, state influence is preserved against commercial developments. This occurs because of the massive reach of AIR to well over 90 per cent of the population. It is also a product of the fact that AIR broadcasts news in 64 regional languages and dialects, and has no commercial opposition in news and competition only in entertainment radio in a few large cities (Kasbekar 2006: 137). State dominance of radio through AIR has led to a lack of enthusiasm by governing parties to allow the development of a community radio to aid marginalised groups, issues and languages (Subiamaniam 2006: 212–15). This is different, as we shall see, to India's recent experience with television.

### The commercialisation of television

The rise of the cable and satellite channels is both the result, in the USA, UK and India since the 1980s, of shifts in regulatory philosophies and part of the reason for their further development. In legislation in India in 1991, in 1996 in the USA and 2003 in the UK, policy concerning media, and cross-media, ownership has favoured the concentration of ownership – though very much more so in the USA than the UK or India – and thereby the financial interests of media corporations. The BBC responded to these general commercial pressures in the 1980s by the development of an internal market with each 'division' of the organisation as a self-sufficient cost centre, to the detriment, some argue, of the creative programming that had underpinned its historic commitment to current affairs and documentary programming (Born 2005). The law- and policy-driven unleashing of cable television has enhanced commercial pressures. The expansion of cable has greatly transformed the US television scene and has begun to do the same, in combination with satellite television, in the UK and India.

Cable and satellite (C and S) bypasses much of the prior regulation and cultural assumptions embedded in television in all three countries. C and S broadcasters do not have to offer the mixed provision of television programming such as news, current affairs, science programmes and documentaries, and well-funded children's programmes that UK public service broadcasting required, and that was to be found, even if to a lesser extent, on US networks and Doordarshan. C and S, however, has channels devoted entirely to sport or comedy or cartoons, with no news or broader current affairs whatsoever – a form of narrowcasting to a specific audience not available for broadcasters to do – and an arrangement enabling audiences to entirely avoid news and serious discussion of public issues. Although such C and S stations have sometimes made a wider 'choice' of programmes available to many in the population – including television coverage of parliaments and senates – they have also focused in their advertising on an ideological conception of 'choice' whereas they control choice through selling bundles of channels. Further, even where they offer choice, such choice does not necessarily offer diversity or pluralism of media content if we consider that diversity might require: 'The presence of a number of *different and independent voices*, and of *different political opinions* and *representations of culture* within the media' (Doyle 2002: 11, my italics).

The variety of channels available and the increased likelihood that they address their audiences as consumers has eroded national and public service audience sizes, has had ambiguous effects on the quality of news and current affairs coverage, and probably made less of a contribution to public life. Election news has been downplayed relative to entertainment news. These changes in audience sizes can be seen from the fact that, in 1980, the big three US networks had 90 per cent of the news audience, which by the turn of the century was well below 50 per cent because of the rise of cable alternatives such as C-SPAN, CNBC, Fox News, MSNBC and CNN.

The resultant transformations of news have not, however, been simply negative in their effects since in India they required DD, the state broadcaster, to think more carefully about news provision and meeting the needs of a wider range of Indian citizens. Likewise, in the UK they have encouraged terrestrial broadcasters to think beyond conservative formats for news. Indian and foreign satellite television has offered a challenge to DD. Rupert Murdoch's Star TV brought in programming that had not been seen in India before; CNN taught news and news presentation techniques that were greatly more informative and innovative than staid state broadcaster approaches; Eenadu TV brought in different Indian approaches in Indian-language formats. It became clear in the latter 1990s that the programming that was most 'Indian' or, in relation to the wide variety of widely spoken languages of India one might say indigenised, was greatly more watched than straight 'international' programming (Thomas 2005; Kasbekar 2006: 157–63; Tunstall 2008: 180–3). This pattern of regionalisation and indigenisation rather than globalisation has been seen in other parts of the non-English-speaking world (Hafez 2007; Straubhaar 2007). DD has responded to the challenge by copying C and S providers in creating the specialist news and sports channels that gave commercial broadcasters success as well as a range of additional DD channels in Indian 'regional' languages. DD is still the most watched broadcaster, in part because of the success of these changes and mostly because of its enormous reach to 90 per cent of the population.

## The trivialisation of media content in the UK, USA and India?

The new competition for audiences promoted by commercialisation has produced forms of popularised news programming, reality television programming and sensationalised media in press and on radio. The next sections will analyse these formats in terms of their consequences for mediated public life and democratic ideals.

## Popularised news and current affairs formats

The media programming of broadcasters is being made in a context of increasing competition and declining audiences. Programme makers, therefore, have had to think about interesting a wide range of viewers in news and current affairs. One of the first ways found to keep the audiences interested was redesigning the presentation of news away from the conservative format that had dominated since the 1950s. In the 1990s many broadcasters has experimented with 'Ken and Barbie' journalism, in which attractive male and female newsreaders co-present. Through increased focus on the telegenic features of the newscasters, they hoped to create audience attachment to the presenters and maintain audiences that way (van Zoonen 1998). In the 1980s, the existence of a larger pool of female television journalists from which to select coincided with pressures to change broadcast journalism to emphasise human-interest stories and lifestyle news. This is the 'prime timing' of news rather than news as it had been in the 1960s and early 1970s as the prestige product of the networks (or the BBC).

The prime timing of news arose in the context of the rise of cable stations in the USA and with the FCC's decision to revoke the fairness doctrine. This gave an extra impetus and regulatory permission for news magazine programmes to become prime-time programming and, many fear, less distinct from entertainment programming. These programmes are structured differently than earlier documentary and current affairs programmes that featured the sustained and 'serious' analysis of a particular topic, typically for an hour (Holland 2006). Instead, they now feature (Barkin 2003: 9):

- shorter (but a greater number of) narratives
- an enhanced role for the reporter, who often becomes part of the story
- stories that are provided with a good-versus-evil orientation so viewers become caught up in the duplicity of the 'wrongdoer'
- profiles of famous people (celebrities) as key ingredients of the programmes.

This combination of news and entertainment was criticised as 'Hollywoodation' by network anchor Dan Rather, and has become an important television format in the UK and India too. The consequences of this programming for audience knowledge of the world are disputed. One argument is that if the programming engages a greater proportion of the audience then it contributes to a broad engagement with mediated public life. Another argument is that the lack of detail in the programming corresponds to a lesser investment of the broadcaster in the research base of news magazine programming, thus to a less well-developed investigation of public life.

The transformation of current affairs and news through entertainment structures has led to news lampoon shows. In the USA these include *The Daily Show with Jon Stewart* and *Politically Incorrect with Bill Maher* (Jones, J.P. 2005, 2007; Stewart *et al.* 2005). There are also distinctly UK variations such as *The Day Today, Bremner, Bird and Fortune* and *The Mark Thomas Comedy Project*. This mix of news and entertainment also exists across European television and in India (van Zoonen 2005). The existence of such news lampoons has led to both pessimistic and optimistic conclusions. Some argue that the comedy shows are also among the best news shows on US television and are particularly likely to be watched by, and politically inform, young people (Jones 2005). Further, others argue more specifically that the links these shows make between entertainment and politics have the potential to rejuvenate citizenship, endorse civic values and sustain civic commitment rather than 'dumb down' political understanding (van Zoonen 2005). More typically, they have been understood as the product of the dominance of market values against civic values (Barkin 2003: 12–14). This is perhaps best seen in Rupert Murdoch's, non-comedy, Fox News channel, whose output is slanted towards right-wing views via populist programming, with no attempt to display a balance of views (Kitty 2005). However, the comedy or lampoon news shows do contribute, as part of the broader media diet, to substantial political understanding and engagement of their audiences (Jones, J.P. 2007: 143; Pew 2007).

### Reality television programming

This is a type of programming that has been developed and become a dominant form of television and prevalent in public debate since the early 2000s In reality television (TV), ordinary real people come together in a contrived setting – a flat, a house, an island – usually for a sustained period in order that the programme can explore the developing unscripted relationships between the people concerned. Typically, the genre also offers opportunities to the audience for judging those relationships and voting for 'contestants' to win any prize on offer. Reality TV programming has its origins in documentary, soaps and game shows, and a key pleasure it offers is for audiences to assess the 'self-performance' of the contestants.

Reality TV has spread around the world as formats developed in one country have become licensed – or simply used – in many others. Programmes such as *Big Brother* (*Big Boss* in India), *Pop Idol* (*American Idol* in the USA, *Indian Idol* and *Super Singer* in India) and *Survivor* have been developed and localised in dozens of countries (Mathijs and Jones 2004).

The pleasure derived from the shows and the interest created in them appear to have something to do with the relation of television to 'real life', and the changing contents and contentious parameters of mediated public life. Reality TV has proven contentious because it disturbs the relation between public and private, which plays an important role in contemporary culture (van Zoonen 2004: 23; Humphrys 2005: 268).

Reality TV plays with the boundaries of public and private by exposing and amplifying talk and interactions between contestants, which, in everyday life, usually or typically remain private and unspoken. These assumptions include notions of appropriate modes of discourse, the speed of the creation and destruction of friendships and dealing with people with assumptions greatly divergent from one's own. Both the domestic (home television) and more extended (online, mobile, voting) audience activity in relation to these new forms of *visibility* highlight both issues hidden in everyday life – how to treat present strangers when systems of appropriate public manners are no longer universally shared – and also that television itself, and our experiences of it, are also ambiguous. As Lewis (2004: 294) argues, television:

> as an object ... is both external and internal to our world. Its characters live in two dimensions; they enter our lives from another place, beamed from distant worlds to take a routine and everyday part in the ordinariness of our own.

We are expected, even required, by reality TV to deploy such expertise, as we believe ourselves to possess about 'ordinary people', to comprehend the mediascape that it offers us, and the options it makes available for us within that mediascape.

Reality TV is defended for its democratic credentials – that it has proved successful in a variety of formats in creating passionately engaged audiences eager to 'test their notions of what is authentic, what is ordinary, what is public and private, [and] what constitutes participation and citizenship' (Reigert 2007: 4). Audiences for *Big Brother* in the UK, for example, proved to be entertained viewers, discriminating judges, interactive participants and empowered voters (Coleman 2007: 170).

Coleman (2007: 167) further argues that the success of *Big Brother* highlights how unengaging contemporary societies have made politics. We should learn from reality TV, he argues, how to make public discussion concerning to audiences.

### Sensationalised media coverage

Sensationalised coverage is the *raison d'être* of UK tabloid newspapers as well as making up a considerable element of the content of discussion of 'talk radio', television audiences' participation talk shows and the representational, melodramatic style of soap operas. In this section, we aim to assess the contribution to mediated public life of 'sensational content'.

Tabloid newspapers in the UK, such as the *Sun*, the *Daily Mail* and the *Daily Mirror*, unlike the US supermarket tabloids, are dominant national newspaper forms selling over 8 million copies each day and with a readership probably two or three times that number. They are believed by politicians to have the potential to influence greatly the public and therefore are taken seriously by them. Owners and editors of tabloid newspapers often gain access to powerful political leaders hoping to benefit from friendly press coverage.

Tabloids often bear sensational headlines articulating hyped concerns – for example, over crime, immigration and child abuse. Tabloids are typically nation-centred in their news focus and nationalistic in their identification with their readership. They reinforce the nation as a national community, quite often articulating a rhetorical construction of the 'normal' nation versus mad 'others' (McGuigan 1992; Conboy 2006). Tabloids are often replete with reactionary content – sexualised images of women, opposition to asylum seekers as unworthy 'invaders' of the nation, a constant focus on the Second World War as symbolic space in which the nation was forged – and rarely have a significant element of narrowly political content. Tabloids prefer, instead, to cover popular television, celebrities and sport. Tabloids may thereby contribute to 'cultures of ignorance' concerning public life (Lacey and Longman 1997; Anderson and Weymouth 1999).

Tabloids also, however, can articulate important political issues, such as the *Daily Mirror* raising sustained opposition to government policy in the rush towards the Iraq War in 2003. Mostly, however, they are sources of 'entertainment' for their readership – to be read on the journey to work or to be scanned at tea break (Frith 2000).

Sensationalism is also present in talk radio. Talk radio is a common form in the USA and Australia (where it is known as talkback) and less well developed in the UK (Laufer 1995; Drobny 2004; Flew 2004). Talk radio is a form of (often celebrity) presenter-led political discussion where well-known presenters, such as Rush Limbaugh and Al Franken in the USA, John Laws and Alan Jones in Australia, and Jon Grant in the UK, lead discussions based on current news contents (Craig 2004: 104, 105; Flew 2004). Presenters have power in selecting topics, filtering discussion and cutting listeners off (Craig 2004: 105). Talk radio has often been dominated, in the USA and Australia, by (sometimes extreme) conservative views – and has significant crossover with the contents of some tabloid newspapers. Talkback seems to appeal to listeners who feel alienated from political life (Craig 2004: 107).

Audience participation talk on television garners a broader audience than talk radio. Some forms of talk on television are especially sensationalist – *The Jerry Springer Show* – made in the USA but known across the world – is perhaps the most famous example, but such shows built on contention in human social relationships are common. Presenters of such US shows as Oprah Winfrey, Ricki Lake and Phil Donahue are well known across the world, and UK television has produced its own variants on the genre: *Kilroy*, *Trisha Goddard* and *The Jeremy Kyle Show*. Such shows have both informed the audience actively engaging with them (Livingstone and Lunt 1994; Lunt and Stenner 2005), and highlighted and given a voice to individuals and groups formerly excluded from the public (Gamson 1999). Gamson's (1999: 225) research into 'sexual nonconformists' (bisexuals, transgender, gays and lesbians) argues that:

> Becoming media-visible, especially if your social identity is routed in a status previously understood to belong to the realm of 'private' life, calls the question on who owns the public space . . . [and] the issue of what can and cannot be spoken about and seen in public, which the televised coming out of the last twenty years evokes, is really the issue of who is and is not considered a legitimate member of the 'public'.

Soap operas have also, in an often sensational, melodramatic manner, given attention to issues that mainstream media either did not wish to consider or considered through frames that made the issues invisible (Ruddock 2007). Lesley Henderson (2007) argues that soaps in the UK brought sexual violence, mental health issues and breast cancer to the forefront of the mainstream agenda. Since soaps are largely considered the province of female viewers they have not been given the attention they deserve as places for public discussion, but rather have been considered the site of a problem concerning the contemporary blurring of 'hard' and 'soft' news (Henderson 2007: 11).

The so-called sensational media coverage has been shown often to have great value for public life in connecting broader audiences to public discussion. Further, often it provides spaces for voiceless and under-represented groups, and supplements and transforms the mainstream news agenda.

The so-called trivialised media content proves to be neither as trivial as it might seem nor is it treated as trivial by its audiences. It is likely that popularised news formats maintain levels of audiences for 'prime timed' news that they otherwise would not enjoy. Reality TV provides a more approachable, extended space of engagement for its enthusiastic audiences, and provides us with an opportunity for reconsidering the already shifting boundary of public and private that plays such an important role in thinking and public life generally. Sensationalised media provide a competing array of possibilities. Tabloid newspapers and talk radio often promote conservative discourses on national belonging. Audience-participation television talk expands the range of voices heard, and faces seen, on television. Soap operas in the UK context have led to a wider and deeper public understanding of the health concerns, particularly of women, formerly hidden from the public space.

In short, these often despised media forms provide a wide range of media content and a chance to engage richly with contemporary mediated public life. What they do not do so well, however, is to influence the organisation of politics of communal life or systematically hold the institutions of politics accountable to voters (Jones 2005; van Zoonen 2005; Higgins 2008: 144) – perhaps the prime-timed news magazine programmes do this best. Further, what they all rely upon is that a significant level of high-quality news gathering is carried out somewhere else within the media system. It is this sustained news gathering that is particularly in danger in the commercialised world of news in thrall to demands of conglomerates that own the news operations, that they make very significant profits on the capital invested in them.

Davies (2009) argues that the commercialised media spaces outlined above have led precisely to such a decline in investment in news. News operations have cut staff in order to lower costs and raise potential profits for conglomerates. Simultaneously, journalists have been required to provide more rather than fewer stories in order to fill thicker newspaper editions, provide for the news content of the broadcast 24-hour news cycle, and produce stories for constantly updated mainstream news organisation websites. Increased production of stories with decreased staffing levels has overshot any possible increase in the productivity of journalists. Journalists have coped, Davies argues, by cutting out the journalism (2009: 56–9). Instead of doing real journalism, which requires talking to sources and finding out something 'new', journalists instead rely upon press releases from public relations firms and government propaganda (Davies 2009: 157–204, 205–56). Sources previously relied upon by journalists, such as the Press Association or Reuters, are in the same commercialised boat as journalists themselves – and are required to combine profitability with increased news output from fewer personnel. This decline in commitment to 'investigative' (i.e. 'proper') journalism can also be seen in India, especially in relation to the coverage of foreign policy and international relations (Subrahnsanyam 2006: 99).

However, the democratic ideal of media depends upon two things: connecting audiences to public life and the provision of diverse and well-researched information about public life somewhere within the media system. If well-researched information is no longer being provided but rather mainstream journalism – what Davies calls 'churnalism' – too much depends on PR (private power) and government propaganda (state power) then the connection of audiences to public life will suffer.

In the UK, the continuing existence of an important public service philosophy and institutions provides a significant counterweight to private commercial values. The future of television's relation to democracy and perhaps, too, print journalism, depends upon the articulation and protection of a public service or public interest notion. Perhaps even in the USA, after the media reform movement of 2003, which resisted further deregulation of media in the demand for media to serve the 'public interest', the idea that broadcast media are a public possession that, at the most merely loaned out to commercial enterprises, can be firmly articulated. This public interest has clearly been privately abused (Brown and Jacobs 2008). As Ed Murrow, the much admired broadcaster and journalist, argued as early as 1958 in a speech to a convention of radio and television news directors (which provided the 'book ends' to the 2005 feature film *Good Night, and Good Luck*, co-starring and directed by George Clooney):

> This instrument [television] can teach, it can illuminate . . . it can inspire . . . but it can do so only to the extent *that humans are determined to use it to those ends* . . . I find nothing in the Bill of Rights which says that [radio and television stations] must increase their net profits each year lest the Republic collapse . . . I am frightened by the imbalance, the constant striving to reach the largest possible audience for everything, by the absence of a *sustained study* [by television] *of the state of the nation.*
>
> (cited in Barkin 2003: 32–3, my italics)

What we require in the complex democracies (Baker 2007) in which we live today is even more than what Ed Murrow argued the nation required half-a-century ago. We need a sustained study of the state of the *world*. In Chapter 6, we analyse whether mass media are being usefully supplemented in achieving this 'sustained study' by the Internet.

## Conclusion

Though we have seen a degree of convergence and ongoing commercial pressures to convergence of the media systems of the UK, USA and India, still they are shaped by prior constitutive choices. The UK press is national and partisan, commercial and distinctively different in its reporting and newspaper styles than the US local 'objective' commercial press. The UK press is more directly involved than the US papers in affirming or disconfirming the political power of parties. The Indian press is undergoing a profound shift from partisan to commercial models, and literacy rates and newspaper readership levels are on the increase. Where this takes the Indian press in the future we do not know and cannot read off from the liberal media model we use to understand the US and, to a lesser extent, the UK experience. With regard to broadcasting, the commercial shift is also important. The UK only slowly created commercial broadcasting to supplement the BBC in 1955, 1982 and

1997 in television, and from 1973 and 1992 in radio. Access to commercial satellite broadcasting has greatly multiplied the number of channels people in the UK can receive, has caused a fall in the level of audiences for terrestrial channels and concerns about the future of public service media. However, in the UK they remain powerful providers of radio and television. In the USA, broadcasting in the public interest is largely left to PBS and NPR, with some support from the national networks. This demonstrates that, even in an under-funded, politically manipulated public interest media institution, distinctive and valuable provision is possible.

Therefore, the near future is not bleak as public interest media provide valuable resources for public life and the activity of there media sets a stand-ard, which much of the commercial media has to match. Further, the often despised and misunderstood trivial media contents often prove to be much less 'trivial' than first thought. Instead, they provide much information of value to their audiences and, furthermore, provide great opportunities for participation in a variety of demotic modes to mediated public life. What they lack and what does need to be provided from somewhere else in the media system is a commitment to sustained and critical investigation of contempor-ary public life. In India, we have the issue of creating a public service system out of the commercialising remains of a state broadcasting system (Tully 2006). How, or if, this is possible in a country where the government revenues are too small to be able to provide welfare, and therefore there is less of a history of providing for the welfare of your fellow citizen, is a tougher ques-tion. There are some intellectual resources in the Gandhian tradition, which tried to balance freedom of the press and social responsibility (Vilanilam 2005: 85). Furthermore, Indian governments have created an autonomous organisation – Prasar Bharati (PB) or the Indian Broadcasting Corporation – to run AIR and DD autonomously from government. This fits in with Indian High Court judgements asserting the independence from government control of media and the implication that its key role is public service not the security of India as interpreted by governmental officials. Despite the fact that PB's autonomy is only partial so far, it establishes an important principle on which a public system might be built. Finding practical answers to turning DD and AIR into media that serve public interest rather than sectional or state interests has large consequences for the future of Indian mediated democracy and, if India prospers and grows in importance economically and culturally as many think it shall, also that of the world.

## Further reading

Barkin, S.M. (2003) *American Television News: The Media Marketplace and the Public Interest*. Armonk, NY and London: M.E. Sharp.

Freedman, D. (2008) *The Politics of Media Policy*. Cambridge: Polity.

Jones, J.P. (2005) *Entertaining Politics: New Political Television and Civic Culture.* Lanham: Rowman and Littlefield.

Kasbekar, A. (2006) *Pop Culture India! Media, Arts, and Lifestyle*. Santa Barbara, CA and Oxford: ABC CLIO.

# 4 Democratic representation in the complex nation

> In modern times almost everyone *wants to be governed by representatives*
> ... every political group or cause *wants representation*; every govern-
> ment *claims to represent.*
>
> (Pitkin 1967: 2, my italics)

> America ... has become an *unrepresentative* democracy ... its leaders
> pass laws and implement policies contrary to the *views* of the American
> people.
>
> (Huntingdon 2005: 329, my italics)

## Introduction

This chapter is concerned with challenges to democratic representative politics arising out of the increased organisational and cultural complexity of the
nation. There exists a widespread concern that such challenges may be leading
to severe democratic deficits (Stoker 2006; Ginsborg 2008). Democratic deficits
exist when elected representation is either absent or systematically inadequate
in order to offer an acceptable level of popular accountability of political
institutions. Procedures and practices of national representation are being
modified at two levels. First, processes of political globalisation are affecting
how practices of representation have worked at the national level. For instance,
national membership of the European Union and a variety of other supranational or intergovernmental bodies causes a shift from central government
to *governance* in which the single national authority is supplemented by a
variety of other decision-making arenas. Second, modifications to practices
and procedures of national representation are also evident *within* the nation,
with the consequence, some argue, that the nation is fragmenting as social
movements challenge the democratic credentials of the national representative system, and small nations and ethnic minority identity groups seek

improved or alternative forms of representation and recognition (Lloyd 2001; Huntingdon 2005).

This chapter analyses and assesses these challenges by exploring the established system of national political representation, whose dominance was largely unquestioned until the 1960s (Brown 1945; Birch 1964). That system of political representation, built around the governments of nationally elected assemblies, was erected upon stable assumptions about who represented the nation, that interests were the main things being represented, and that the electoral system was built on territorial representation. For example, MPs in the UK and Members of Congress in the United States are formally representatives of designated geographical constituencies or districts (Judge 1999: 149–77; Hill 2002). The core principles of consent, legitimation and authorisation of decision making are built upon territorial foundations (Judge 1999: 149). In the course of this chapter, we will examine challenges to the territorial focus of representation. First, we consider challenges produced by the rise in demand for *microcosmic representation* in which the resemblance between the representative and the people represented is primary to practices of political representation. Further, microcosmic representation is necessarily built on cultural representation in that the idea that one person resembles another requires a structure of cultural meanings. Second, we also note and explore the phenomenon of the supplementation of territorial representation by party representation. Party representation is a form of political representation in which party success in general elections contested between parties with competing manifesto promises leads to the victorious party's claim that it possesses an 'electoral mandate' – a grant from the represented to bring into effect the policies and legislation so publicised. Party representation modifies both territorial and emerging microcosmic representational demands by allowing the ruling party to claim justification both for pursuing policies and its claim to know the needs and interests of the represented.

A range of *cultural* representations centred on the nation and the political representational system supported the established system of representation, until the 1960s. First, for example, until then media coverage of politics unproblematically foregrounded the nation. It did so explicitly, in national ceremonial occasions. It also did so implicitly, in taken-for-granted everyday assumptions whereby the nation was referred to in weather maps and pictures of national assemblies on the news, to mean 'national authority', and uses of indexical terms such as 'our' to suggest and invoke shared national membership (Anderson 1991; Billig 1995). Second, media played a subordinate role to politics. Media allowed political representatives to communicate with the nation, making few demands of their own to challenge that communicative representation of the nation. These relationships of political and cultural representation have come adrift due to the increased complexity of cultural representations of the nation, its members, more diffuse representative politics, and dynamic and challenging media.

This chapter explores how relationships of political representation have been modified and stretched in the shift from government to governance. National representation has been qualified in relation to less democratic and accountable forms of political representation developed in supranational and intergovernmental organisations. Further, within the nation demands of organisational complexity have led to the creation of non-representative, non-democratic and unaccountable public bodies. Both developments leave important areas of the political world without adequate representation and manifest a democratic deficit.

The chapter also analyses how demands are being made by a variety of groups and movements, and political representation is periodically being modified within the nation in order more adequately to represent the complex nation. This section explores how small nations challenge the dominant system of territorial representation through alternative cultural representations, denying the glorious history and simple models of national belonging expressed in national film and television, and variously raise demands for political fairness and recognition of particular claims. Further, the section investigates the demands for equality and inclusion within nations especially of black political movements in the USA and UK as challenges to the dominant national narrative of progress and the impediments to formal equality of citizens as they are represented *politically* in liberal democracies. The demands for inclusion, at the same time, have also led to broader demands for *cultural* recognition such as in multicultural policies. The future viability of multicultural policies as practices for the cultural reconciliation of minorities is, presently, under scrutiny as contemporary politics of terror and islamophobic cultural representations may undermine the recognition of the complex nation heretofore contained in multiculturalism.

Social movements challenge established political representation following on from the civil rights movement. At first social movements demanded radical change from the system of political representation to direct and participatory democracy. The movements distrusted mainstream media coverage, outlets and their domination of cultural representation. More recently, these movements have made demands for improved forms of representational democracy rather than alternatives to them. Feminists demand microcosmic representation – where women representatives are considered more likely to be knowledgeable and sympathetic to women's political interests and views – although the substantive policies supportive of women are not always delivered by women representatives. The anti-globalisation movement moves out beyond the national frame to organise a form of popular *global* politics tracking the expansion, and articulating pressures for the democratisation, of intergovernmental politics.

## Organisational complexity and representative deficit

In liberal democracies in the twentieth century, until the 1960s, there existed a dominant model of national political representation. That system of political representation was built upon territorial representation. The gathering in the representative assembly of all the constituency representatives across the country formed a framework for the assumption that *all* the interests of the nation were gathered together (Judge 1999: 25). The relations underpinning political and cultural representation in and of the nation since the 1960s have come adrift in the rise of a more complex nation. In this section, we investigate the key changes that have affected this dominant model of political representation, and explore how these changes are linked to changes in cultural and media representations.

### Supranational/intergovernmental complexity

National politics is increasingly affected by supranational and intergovernmental organisations. The European Union – established in the 1950s by the governments of France, Germany, Belgium, Luxembourg and the Netherlands – has since developed into a 27-nation organisation enabling European nations to co-operate on areas formerly reserved for national governmental responsibility, such as central banking, environmental protection, immigration and competition policy and a growing commitment to shared military protection. European law made in the EU is sometimes binding on states. Because of the autonomy of the EU from any particular member state, we call it a 'supranational organisation' since it can act 'above' particular states, requiring them to bring their governmental policy in line with EU regulations and directives (Pinder and Usherwood 2007: 59). The United Nations is also an important organisation above states, but it is not supranational in the same way as the EU. Set up in the aftermath of the Second World War, the UN is an intergovernmental organisation that now has 191 member nations and forms a world talking shop and very important intergovernmental organisation for activity on culture, environment, poverty reduction and peacekeeping. The UN is just one of 70 intergovernmental organisations of intercontinental membership in the contemporary world; others include NATO and the World Trade Organization. The EU is one of 180 regional intergovernmental organisations, of which other examples include ASEAN and the African Union (Vibert 2007: 145, 145 n. 3).

As we saw in Chapter 2, supranational and intergovernmental bodies contribute to the complexity of democratic political representation and the production of democratic deficits within the nation. Further, those 'representatives' of national polities in the intergovernmental bodies are only intermittently held to account – by other elected politicians, voters or the media – for their action or policy choices there. Furthermore, democratic deficits arise because the supranational and intergovernmental bodies, themselves, are hardly politically representative.

Among intergovernmental organisations, the EU is widely recognised as the most democratic as it has the most developed forms of political representation. For example, the EU has a parliament to which representatives are voted from the member nations. Members of the European Parliament (MEPs) contribute to making law and to holding the EU, as a whole, to account. Its powers include scrutiny of, and co-decision over most, legislation; the capacity to question EU Commissioners; approval of the EU budget; and prerogatives of appointment to the European Commission (Pinder and Usherwood 2007: 47, 49). Since the European Commission has the sole right of legislative initiative within the EU and is the executive of the EU the parliament's appointment powers enable it to influence the general policy direction of the Commission. Through the nationally elected MEPs, therefore, the European Parliament offers a supplementary form of representation to that available in national assemblies.

However, there are drawbacks to the representative relations so far created in the European Parliament that mean it has significant problems of transparency and accountability (Judge and Earnshaw 2008). First, MEPs are territorial members of constituencies that are larger and do not match up with the constituencies in national parliaments. Voters are significantly less likely to know who their MEP is than their MP, and correspondingly even less likely to communicate with them (Judge 1999: 169). Second, in all EU countries the electoral turnout for EU elections is much lower than the turnout for national general elections, thereby lessening the legitimacy of MEPs as representatives. Third, national publics are poorly served in their knowledge of what goes on in the EU parliament by national media. Media coverage of the EU parliament is intermittent. National media are largely indifferent and sometimes hostile to the EU project, in particular UK newspapers. Attempts to create Europe-wide media, such as *The European* newspaper, have failed for want of a readership or audience. Fourth, although the European Parliament is the most democratic, it is not the most powerful body within the EU. This limits the legitimacy of MEPs to those they seek to represent.

No other intergovernmental body in the world has a *popularly elected assembly* with *real powers* like those of the European Parliament. The form of representation that is present in most intergovernmental institutions is a form of 'indirect' or 'extended' representation. Extended representation exists when a body makes rules and decisions that influence national politics but where the elected representatives are not directly elected to that body but, instead, are elected representatives of *national* assemblies (or delegates selected by those elected representatives.)

The argument supporting extended representation as legitimate is that since national votes elected those representatives to national assemblies then they can legitimately represent (or select others to represent) their citizens in other arenas. The argument against extended representation is that in intergovernmental settings the system of accountability of representatives to those they represent is *too* extended for their actions and decisions to be held to account. Accountability may be limited for a variety of reasons. First, the intergovernmental procedures and issues may be too complex for ordinary citizens to understand. Second, media coverage of the intergovernmental arena is intermittent and too slight to benefit the electorate's awareness of the issues, let alone their understanding. Third, nationally elected representatives in the intergovernmental organisations rarely expend effort in making the issues in intergovernmental organisations clear, relevant and of interest to their national electorates. In short, extended forms of representation are less likely to represent the interests and views of the people.

The General Assembly of the UN does include extended representation of 191 of the world's nations. However, it is more of a talking shop than a decision-making institution. The most powerful institution of the UN is the Security Council, yet the Security Council is *deeply* unrepresentative of the world's nations. Only 15 nations out of the 191 are at any time privy to decision making. Five of those nations are vastly overprivileged in being permanent members. Further, each of those five members can veto the decisions of the Security Council however much the opinion of the other 14 is shared and however important the issue on which they are seeking agreement. The Security Council thus features the structure of power politics at the end of the Second World War not the demands of world politics in a vastly expanded world (Taylor and Curtis 2005; Kennedy 2007). In today's world whole areas of the globe are unrepresented (Africa, Middle East), under-represented (Asia, apart from China) and over-represented (Europe – with the UK and France as members).

## Sub-national organisational complexity: quangos

Unelected public bodies created by national governments can also contribute to democratic deficits. There has been an increase in the number and importance of such bodies since the Second World War, with increasing pace since the 1980s, to manage the size and complexity of the provision of public services (Judge 2005). In the UK, these bodies are called quangos (quasi-autonomous non-governmental organisations) but elsewhere they are known as parastatals, agencies, bureaus, institutes or tribunals. Their influence extends into most areas of daily life since they affect '[t]he air we breathe, the water we drink, the food we eat, the electricity we use, the phone calls we make, the value of the coins and banknotes in our pockets, our access to media, [and] the disputes we get involved in' (Vibert 2007: 7). There are great numbers of these organisations, which can usefully be grouped by distinguishing service providers (e.g. statistical agencies, research funding bodies), risk assessors (e.g. disease control agencies, food safety authorities), boundary watchers (e.g. equal opportunities bodies, water quality authorities, human rights commissions), inquisitors (e.g. audit agencies, social welfare inspection) and umpires or whistle blowers (e.g. election commissions, appeals tribunals) (Vibert 2007: 20). In the UK, in 2004, there were over 650 of them outside central government departments, and in the USA, there were over 1,000 federal agencies (2007: 18).

These bodies are not served by elected representatives and fall short of democratic legitimacy in a number of other ways. Quangos are constituted of technical experts, senior bureaucrats, senior ex-politicians and their appointed staffs. They may even escape oversight as part of the remit of a particular elected minister. These public bodies, therefore, often entirely escape the main forms of accountability built into representative politics.

The existence of these myriad public bodies puts a great deal of the activity of contemporary politics out of reach of elected political representatives. Furthermore, the *aim* of some of these public bodies is precisely to take the activity for which they have responsibility out of the realm of electoral politics, to depoliticise those aspects of public life. This may result in both positive and negative consequences. Depoliticisation need not be negative. For example, perhaps the most important and (accepted as) necessary form of depoliticised practice in liberal representative democracies is of the judiciary. It is crucial that the judiciary is widely accepted as a non-political body in order that its judgements have legitimate binding force. However, such is the range of activities and influence of other public bodies that they may be intended to depoliticise aspects of contemporary politics that actually need to be addressed politically. Politics involves choices among *competing* ends. Instead, quangos may attempt to turn their province of responsibility into technical problems that may be capable of being resolved into *optimal* solutions. Further, the unelected nature of quangos makes it more difficult to justify their existence if they come to the attention of a wide public through specific contentious cases. It seems likely that the depoliticisation of areas of potential public debate implicit in the existence of non-accountable public bodies hides areas of debate that need to be made public.

The massive growth of quangos has increased the complexity of national politics while taking much of the activity of decision making out of the reach of the representative system. Further, media coverage is necessary in order that voters know about the bodies and the expert services provided by them and have the chance to agree that they benefit public life. However, the complexity of the organisation of public life that is magnified by the role of these public bodies makes sustained, informative media coverage that accountability and legitimacy requires extremely unlikely. Quangos, therefore, create representational and democratic deficits, and contribute to the complexity of public life to which media give inadequate attention.

In the cases of intergovernmental/supranational organisations and quangos, both extended forms of political representation and the absence of political representation ensure that important political relations are unaccountable to the public. Further, in both cases, the new organisations created since the 1980s increase the complexity of public life and make it unlikely that media coverage will aid the development of appropriate levels of awareness of these developments congruent with their political importance.

## Representing complex nations

At the same time that nations have become much more organisationally complex they have also become more *culturally* complex. Groups that consider themselves culturally different may consequently organise themselves in order raise claims for political representation. The following sections consider two groups that make demands that increase the complexity of the nation. First, they investigate the demands of small nations for improved political representation and support, considering the example of Scotland as a small nation within the UK, and recognition of Native Americans as First Nations in the USA. Scotland was chosen since it has been successful since the early 2000s in gaining a greatly increased range of political powers and responsibilities vis-à-vis the UK; Native Americans in the USA form an example that demonstrates both the importance of the particular treaty status of indigenous peoples and how crucial cultural self-representation is to 'under-represented' groups in contemporary society. Second, they analyse the political activity of black people in the USA and UK and their organising from the 1960s for the removal of discriminatory laws and practices that have functioned as impediments to their voting and representation. Further, the second section explores multicultural policy arising from the 1970s and 1980s as a subsequent attempt in Western liberal democracies to include minority groups in the culture of contemporary nations. It explores islamophobic media representations as a recent challenge to multicultural recognition of Muslim minorities in the context of debates over terrorism and the demands of security.

### Small nations

The national unity of a single, central representative assembly to which representatives are elected from across the nation is challenged by the demands and successes of small nations. Small nations have asserted their cultural difference, and stated their demands for recognition and political representation for that difference. Their existence and organisation make the nation more complex. This section explores the example of Scotland desiring its own form of territorial representation within the UK, and its success demonstrates that the political organisation of the UK is not sacrosanct but a mutable political arrangement. It also explores the 'First Nations' in the USA, who sought fulfilment of their distinctive treaty rights and did so after the Second World War by creating a pan-Indian identity ('First Nations', 'Native American') and challenging racist stereotypes of the 'ignoble savage', which had underpinned their limited role in US representative politics and public life. The examples of Scotland and the First Nations of the USA also illuminate that similar small-nation activity that has arisen in other countries: Catalonia within Spain, Quebec within the Canadian Federation, and 'indigenous people' in Canada, Australia and New Zealand.

The successes of the demands for better representation for Scotland were the result of organising in Scottish society and its institutions in relation to Scotland's cultural and historical distinctiveness. Distinctive senses of identity had been maintained after Scotland united with England (and Wales) in 1707. Those differences include the system of Scottish law, the predominance of public housing in Scotland, the support for the national football team and its rivalry with England from the late nineteenth century, the greater importance of religion to Scottish society, and the existence of a Scottish press (Pittock 2008: 42). Scottish media – in particular from the 1970s – formed sites for the circulation of cultural representations in which a distinctive Scottish cultural and political agenda could be presented (2008: 46). What was not so prominent in Scotland but is crucial in the demands of other small nations – such as those of Catalonia and Quebec – is support for a widely used language different from the dominant national language.

Political demands were made from the 1930s by the Scottish Nationalist Party (SNP) for independence. However, what Scotland has achieved since falls short of independence. The SNP gained territorial representational success in the Westminster (national) parliament in London only from 1967. From that date, the SNP benefited from a broad disillusion with two-party politics in the UK. Success in the Westminster parliament through the 1970s and 1980s, and shifts in Scottish public opinion favouring greater autonomy put pressure on UK governments to consider constitutional change. These shifts also gave the SNP greater access to media, including support for some autonomy for Scotland in the UK of the Scottish *Sun* newspaper in 1992 and other papers thereafter (Higgins 2006; Pittock 2008: 48). The referendum in 1997 offered to the people of Scotland a Scottish Parliament with some tax-raising powers rather than independence. Scotland's press continues to provide a major forum for representing Scottish politics and culture, and demands for increased autonomy (Higgins 2006). In the 2007 election the SNP became the largest, and ruling, party, with 47 MSPs (Pittock 2008: 82, 173).

In the UK Parliament, MPs are elected in a first-past-the-post (or majoritarian) system, whereby whoever gains the most votes in a constituency gains the seat. Multiplied across hundreds of constituency elections in a general election this often leads to over-representation of some parties and under-representation of others as a relatively small proportion of votes cast can lead to parties gaining a very much larger proportion of seats. However, the Scottish Parliament was designed to provide *fairer* forms of political representation within Scotland than the first-past-the-post system does for the UK. This was intended to ensure a closer correspondence between numbers of seats and numbers of votes and therefore required a form of *proportional representation*, in particular one that would select men and women 'broadly proportionate to their shares of the population' (Judge 1999: 182). The system established to enable such outcomes combined territorial representation – using the 72 UK parliamentary constituencies in Scotland – with an additional 56 members, seven from each of the eight Euro-constituencies in Scotland. The latter members were to be drawn from 'party lists' in which parties nominate candidates in their order of preference and party electoral success decides how far down the list candidates become elected.

In the hybrid form of its representation, therefore, the Scottish Parliament forms a challenge to the dominant UK system of representation. It combines two forms of *territorial representation* (UK and EU parliamentary constituencies) in addition to voting arrangements allowing for more *proportional representation*. Such arrangements also offer an opening for *party representation* since parties control the list members and gain list MSPs proportionally to their vote.

In the view of some people, the new system of representation in Scotland is unfair to England. Certainly, in the UK, representational anomalies have arisen because of the existence of the Scottish Parliament and its devolved powers. Those anomalies and perceived unfairness, some argue, threaten the future existence of the UK. The anomaly is that laws may be imposed in England without the consent of a majority of MPs of *English* constituencies. This arises because Scottish MPs (i.e. who are the elected representatives of UK parliamentary constituencies in Scotland) are free to vote on policies that will be imposed only in England, Wales and Northern Ireland. It involves a *representational* anomaly since the declared votes of territorial representatives of the constituencies within which the law or policy is implemented will not suffice to make the decision. This has stoked concerns for the future viability of the UK and fears that virulent forms of English nationalism may be provoked by perceived unfairness of the anomaly. Three answers have been provided to the question, of which actions have been taken only on the first: to reduce the number of Scottish constituencies in the UK Parliament, to create an English Parliament and to restrict the issues on which MPs from Scottish constituencies in the UK Parliament may vote (Pittock 2008: 86).

The case of the Scottish Parliament is interesting since it has been highly successful in creating more democratic and responsive representation within Scotland, showing that the small nation can be accommodated in the complex nation by redesign of the representative system. However, it continues to lead to representative anomalies that might in the future undermine the broader political entity – the UK. Further, the Scottish Parliament may be a staging point to the full independence of Scotland, which forms the main policy of the ruling party in Scotland – the SNP.

Indigenous nations such as those considered the 'First Nations' of the USA have had different routes to recognition than the forms of territorial representation made possible in Scotland and other similar cases. Instead they are 'nations' whose way of life and traditions were all but destroyed by the expansion of the nation, the imposition on First Nations of 'the nation's' 'civilising' values, and the violent and systematic suppression of their own ways of organising (Guibernau 1999: 69, 74). Therefore, instead of seeking representation within 'the nation' they have focused on the return of their stolen resources (e.g. land, water and fishing rights) and their right to live their lives according to their own cultural patterns. That way of life and the story it articulates forms a cautionary tale for the power of the nation to suppress alternative life-ways and its attempt to write a monological narrative of national progress.

First Nations – the name itself is the result of a long cultural-political struggle – called themselves 'First Nations' since they preceded, historically, the nation-states in whose name national representative politics is organised. Such First Nations signed treaties with emerging nation-states from the eighteenth century in order to guarantee their existence and the land necessary to their way of life (Wilmer 1997). It has been quite common for those treaties to be torn up by national politicians whenever dominant interests saw another and more profitable use for Native Americans' land. New treaties parcelled out smaller and less fertile portions of land to Native Americans until the land became reservations to which native people were allotted. Consequently, the federal government has had the responsibility for administering the land, lives and welfare of Native Americans. However, in response to the subsequent legal and political struggles of indigenous groups after the Second World War, some land rights and public recognition of First Nations have been granted, for example, in the USA, Canada, Australia and New Zealand.

The special status of Native Americans often worked against their interests and needs. For example, the special status was recognised in the US Constitution's denial to 'Indians' of US citizenship since they were separate nations. Subsequently, in a long attempt to renege on the special status as it proved inconvenient, Native Americans were made US citizens between 1901 and 1924. That citizenship rarely included the right to vote, however, which was denied in state law to those who were wards of the federal state. The special status of Native Americans was also denied by successive US governments finding reasons for abrogating treaty obligations such as land rights, and educational and healthcare provision incumbent on them as guardians of native people through the Bureau of Indian Affairs (BIA). In a concerted effort from 1946 in the Indian Claims Commission Act the US government attempted to pay off Native Americans in order to 'quiet Aboriginal title' to the land and territories recognised in US treaties and also be rid of future welfare obligations. That Act was the last great attempt to *assimilate* Native Americans to US public life (Wilmer 1997: 197).

Sustained *pan-Indian* political and cultural identities were created for the first time in the cultural and political mobilisation fostered by the attempt to remove native title to land. Native Americans subsequently won legal and political battles against this 'termination' policy (Nagel 1997: 198). Native Americans in the post-Second World War period organised through the National Congress of American Indians, the South Western Regional Youth Conference and the activist American Indian Movement (AIM). Practices of political self-representation developed by them subsequently have been used in both national and international settings including the political and adminis-trative struggle to gain official and NGO recognition for Native American organisations within the UN system.

Such self-representation has created pan-Indian identities – such as 'Native American', 'First Americans', 'First People' and 'indigenous people' – and has been symbolised by 'Native Americans' wearing a 'uniform' of ribbon shirts, braids and eagle feathers. Such self-representation also functioned as an effect-ive response to the dominant racist *cultural representations* of 'Indians' as dis-organised savages. Such negative cultural representations were prevalent, for example, in the Western genre of films and television programmes that so dominated the USA throughout the twentieth century. Those negative repre-sentations focused predominantly on 'Indians' as savage peoples who had no viable place in the future of 'civilised' societies. Such contending self-representations sought both improved cultural representation in media and adequate recognition from the federal state, such as legislation for educational expenditure, consultation over adoption of Native American children, Native American religious freedom, and consultation over Native American archae-ology. The political and cultural self-representation – especially in the form of Red Power and the direct action of AIM – also contributed to the success in the early 1970s, in restoration of the status of 'terminated' tribes and proper fulfilment of the treaty obligations of the USA (Nagel 1997: 200).

The cultural or symbolic importance of First Nations to national politics, rather than their electoral importance in territorial representation, continues. It is manifest in newly dominant images of Native Americans as emblems of environmental consciousness and spiritual wisdom. It is also manifest, for example, in the recognition of Native Americans on the websites of key Democratic presidential hopefuls in 2008, in their efforts to create political coalitions with 'First Americans'. For instance, Barack Obama's website showed recognition of the identities and needs of 'First Americans'; he had meetings with the First American Caucus, which led to the establishment of a working party of First American tribal representatives to act as advisers on 'First American' issues. Native American votes hardly made a difference to elections but their symbolic importance may have.

In the cases both of Scotland in the UK and Native Americans in the USA, the recognition of small nations makes political representation of the nation more complex. With the creation of Scotland's parliament, real political power has been transferred from Westminster (the London site of the UK Parliament) to Holyrood (the Edinburgh site of the Scottish Parliament) and territorial representation within the UK has become more complex and contentious. The cultural-political self-representation and organisation of Native Americans makes it much more difficult to narrate simplistic stories about, for example, the Pilgrim Fathers as 'First Americans' and the only origin of the American Creed (cf. Huntingdon 2005). The existence of small nations also opens up the question of whether members of the 'big' nations have enough in common, or whether enough central control exists over practical politics to justify the label 'national'.

### Whose nation?

The demands for equality and inclusion within nations made, for example, by black political movements in the USA, also form a challenge to the dominant national narrative of progress that finds its ideal expression in the equality of citizens represented in national assemblies. That narrative of progress is the founding text of the USA, built as it is upon equality and the removal of impediments to people's life, liberty and pursuit of happiness. That US narrative finds its popular, cultural counterpart in the idea of the 'American dream' and anxieties about the impossibility of its realisation in notions of the 'American nightmare' (Hansen 2003: 172, 201–2). As President Johnson said, concerning the tardiness in granting equal rights to 'negroes' in a speech on the Voting Rights Bill in 1965, it is a challenge 'to the values and the purposes and the meaning of our beloved nation' (Sanders 2006: 184).

'Black' is a political rather than a descriptive label. Black political movements have had to deploy categories of political and cultural identity through which to assert solidarity, shared interests and concerns. For example, in self-help groups in the nineteenth and early twentieth century, notions of 'coloured persons' and 'negroes' were counterposed to the racist and administrative labels used by white people. Negro became the preferred word for 'black' cultural and political movements until the mid-1960s. In relation both to the politics of 'black power' and the cultural politics of black pride, *black* became the more credible title by the end of the 1960s.

Black Americans, in particular in southern states, were second-class citizens because of their illegal exclusion from their political rights through racist voter registration practices and intimidation at the polls. That exclusion meant that white politicians did not have to court the black vote and black politicians were at a very distinct disadvantage in any attempts at becoming representatives. Therefore, the mainstream political system was not at all open to black people.

The organisations through which black Americans were mobilised, such as the National Association for the Advancement of Colored Persons (NAACP), the Southern Christian Leaders Conference (SCLC) and the Student Non-violent Coordinating Committee (SNCC), used varied tactics in order to challenge that second-class status. Respectively they used court cases against individuals or public authorities who denied black Americans the right to vote or to an (equal) education; non-violent action to put pressure on vote registrars and police forces that defended illegal denial of the vote in southern states; and direct action tactics in order to challenge racist practices and the flouting of the law. All were part of the US civil rights movement.

Martin Luther King's role in the movement was distinctive and crucial (Sanders 2006). He articulated a belief that the American system could change and accommodate black people, and that the best route to such change would be non-violent protest. King had argued the former point in his view that 'the great glory of American democracy is the right to protest for right' (Frady 2006: 35). Voting, in King's view, had the status of both a *means* and a *symbol*. As a means, it implied some control of black people over their own lives. As a symbol, it implied equality of citizenship, dignity and personal worth. For King, non-violence was not merely a tactic but rather a key part of a moral crusade whereby 'negroes' could demonstrate that they were greatly superior to the racist caricatures of black people. Black people had been culturally represented in minstrel shows and radio and film as 'loud, slovenly, childishly emotional, witless of discipline and dignity', and such views were also present in the everyday assumptions of many white people (Frady 2006: 16). King believed that the moral dignity of non-violence might be able to touch people in ways that law never could and thereby challenge those racist stereotypes. Within the movement, King's role was as a charismatic orator who was able to express the moral case for 'negro' political rights, rather than as an organiser.

Martin Luther King Jr's 'I have a dream' speech, given on 28 August 1963 at the meeting after the March on Washington, was attended by over 200,000 civil rights marchers, and forms the first example of civil rights organisations co-ordinating their political action nationally. The speech articulated both the hopes and the real achievements of the movement. Today historians and commentators often symbolise the movement as a whole through reference to King's speech (Hansen 2003). The speech articulated the progress of the movement in ensuring the political rights of black people and the hope for future progress towards an equal society in which all people would be judged on the basis on the 'content of their character' rather than the 'colour of their skin'. The march provides an example of the fusion of political representation and cultural representation in the activity of the movement. The march formed both a political demonstration organised for 'freedom and jobs' and a cultural event consisting of speeches and the music of both black and white singers, such as gospel queen Mahalia Jackson and voice of protest Joan Baez. The music was central rather than peripheral to the march since some well-known black singers had become 'mandated to speak on behalf of the community in elaborate, celebratory, ritual performances' (Gilroy 1987: 177). The march was also organised in order to demonstrate the moral status of the movement to a broad public watching television (Hansen 2003). The march contributed to the creation of federal support for the movement's aims since it, for example, convinced President Kennedy of the genuineness of King and the movement.

The focus of the movement on the issue of black Americans' access to voting led to measurable change in the years immediately after the march. The Civil Rights Act of 1964 and the Voting Rights Act of 1965, respectively, banned the exclusion of black people from public places, abolished literacy tests in voter registration and made illegal the kinds of manoeuvres that had prevented black people from voting in large numbers (Paterson *et al.* 2001: 147, 152). The impact of that legislation – in tandem with further civil rights activism and federal support to ensure the enforcement of the legislation in the south – led to dramatic change. In southern states, voter registration increased three- or four-fold, and voter turnout likewise (Paterson *et al.* 2001: 182). In the later 1960s, this required white politicians to give attention to the concerns of black voters. Into the 1970s and thereafter black people's votes – in particular – led to a great array of black elected officials – councillors, alder-men, mayors, representatives, senators (Paterson *et al.* 2001: 298–9) and, in November 2008, a black President – Barack Obama – who was inaugurated in January 2009. The US Congressional Black Caucus – established in 1971, and now made up of 43 House Representatives and three Senators – and its black representatives are held, in polls of black people, to represent black Americans more adequately than do white representatives (Whitby 2007: 203). That 'representation' and the 'home styles' through which it is communicated and expressed are constantly being developed in politics (Friedman 2007).

The continued struggle for full inclusion demonstrates that 'black solidar-ity', which was achieved clearly, however precariously, in the civil rights movement, has been transformed (and has declined) in the 1980s and since. Black middle classes increasingly accept integration, with the maintenance of some aspects of a distinctively black culture and attendant cultural pride, into the majority culture. That acceptance can be seen in media representa-tions such as *The Cosby Show* (1984–92), which was an extremely popular US television sitcom concerning the family life of a well-off black professional family. Urban poor blacks, however, seem to have 'accepted' their permanent marginalisation in the USA. The marginalisation of the black urban poor finds some expression in the cultural representations that make up the culture of gangs and hip-hop (Gilroy 1987; Castells 1998). Therefore, black people as a minority group, in spite of their many successes in voting and political representation, 'continue to struggle for full inclusion in mainstream American society' (Whitby 2007: 207). This fact raises fundamental questions about the efficacy of structures of mainstream (American) society in promoting inclusion.

There are parallels to the US experience in the UK. However, 'black' as a cultural-political category arose in different struggles in which African, African-Caribbean and Asian people collectively organised to counter the common experience of racism in UK society. 'Black' therefore is a political and cultural identity created in the 1970s, which drew on the US experience in, however, a different context. Although all three groups have been a significant part of the UK's history from the eighteenth century, it was only in the post-Second World War period that the UK became the home to very significant numbers of people from the West Indies, Africa, India, Pakistan and Bangladesh. The movement of people followed recruitment by the British state of migrants to work in low-paid jobs. Since the migrants had formerly been citizens of the British Empire, they had rights to come to the UK even if those rights were subsequently severely restricted. In the UK, too, 'black' people organised in order to challenge discrimination and their apparent lack of full inclusion in the nation.

In the UK, similarly to the USA, black people sought some say in their lives through self-organisation and attempts to influence mainstream representative politics. In the UK, however, voting was legally and institutionally accessible to black people, unlike in the southern states of America. Black people in the UK from the 1960s successfully organised nationally and locally, particularly in the Labour party, finding its policies more relevant and the informal routes to involvement more open than those proffered by the Conservative party. The solidarity among black people produced through the notion of black pride and black power aided that organising. In the 1970s, that organising pressured the Labour party to allow for the development of black sections as interest groups within the party in order to influence policy (Shukra 1998: 97). Black people in the 1980s also managed to influence local councils in urban areas with significant black populations. Opportunities opened up both for jobs in 'race relations' for black professionals and as black local politicians. The broader influence over territorial representatives was much more difficult to achieve, however, in large part because of the small proportion of black people, who constitute less than 6 per cent of the UK population. Much effort was put into 'get out the vote' campaigns since the relative poverty of black people in the UK tended to lead to low voting turnouts. Only in the 1980s, in the UK, were black people able to have a significant impact on the election of territorial representatives in the shape of black MPs. Those MPs have remained so few in the UK Parliament, however, that there is pressure for each MP not only to represent their constituents but also to become a broader national (microcosmic) representative for various black issues and concerns (Shukra 1998). As is the case in the USA, some black British people seem to have done well and found the representative political system responsive to their needs and interests. However, there do seem to be limits to the full inclusion of black people in British society, as if they were 'different' and did not fully belong (Gilroy 1987).

More recently, however, the issue of exclusion from the nation has centred on Muslims. This focus has arisen most powerfully in relation to the growth in islamophobic media coverage. Muslims have been targets of negative media representations in most Western liberal democracies since at least the late 1980s in relation to reactions to Muslim protest and subsequent *fatwas* issued against Salman Rushdie because some Muslims considered that his novel, *The Satanic Verses*, salaciously mocked the prophet Mohammed. Such islamophobic media coverage has multiplied both in intensity and level since the terrorist attacks of 9/11 in the USA, 7/7 in the UK and elsewhere. The negative representations of Muslims focus on religious fanaticism and the perceived lack of civilised (Western) values of Islam; in short, the idea that Muslims do not really belong in Western societies.

The issue of inclusion in the nation has been addressed most closely and persistently by those developing and demanding multicultural policies (Modood 2007: 84). Multiculturalism refers to a set of policies variously developed in liberal democracies – for instance Canada, the USA, Australia, the UK and the Netherlands – at national and local levels as recognition of the multi-ethnic and multicultural reality of nations dawned from the 1960s in the context of anti-colonial struggles and civil rights protests. Those policies have mostly emerged *piecemeal*, often in relation to demands from various minority groups to allow for various divergences in practices from (former) national norms. These divergences include multiple citizenship; government support for media in minority languages; support for minority festivals and holidays; the acceptance of traditional dress or religious dress in schools, the military and society; support for music and art from minority cultures; and programmes to encourage minority representation in politics, education and the workplace. The multi-ethnic and multicultural reality of nations poses challenges for which new political and cultural agendas appear necessary (Modood 2007: 3). Multiculturalism assumes that diversity needs to be recognised and supported rather than ignored or challenged (Parekh 2008: 94). However, recognition of diversity poses all sorts of challenges for national narratives and national identity in both politics and media since it affects both political and cultural representation:

> The story that a country tells itself about itself, the discourses, symbols and images in which national identity resides and through which people acquire and renew their sense of national belonging . . . [has] to be recast . . . in order to reflect the current and future . . . ethnic composition of the country.
>
> (Modood 2007: 18)

Such policies typically recognise differences among individuals as members of groups, rather than merely asserting the universalistic ideals of national citizenship for all or narrow notions of the responsibility of minorities to assimilate to national society and culture. Multicultural policy has led to encouragement of those demands for cultural recognition and changes in policy, but not so much for political representation.

## Challenging democratic representation

In this section we explore two social movement demands in the 1980s and since for improved forms of representative democracy. They are the demands for microcosmic and substantive representation for women by the feminist movement, and the global organisation of civil society politics and opposition to neo-liberal globalisation by the World Social Forum as part of the anti-globalisation movement.

Many of the social movements of the 1960s and 1970s at first were quite hostile to representative democracy, seeing it as part of a system that had degraded democracy rather than realised it. From the student movement to feminists organising their own direct democratic relationships, the demand was for *direct* rather than *mediated* relationships. Accompanying suspicion of political representation was a distrust of media and their circulation of dominant cultural representations. Distrust of media was especially prevalent among feminists, who attempted to avoid distortion of their movement and its activities by either banning or carefully vetting journalists attending their meetings. In the 1980s and after, social movements became more engaged with mainstream politics as the radical changes to society and politics that some desired remained unfulfilled. Instead, movements made demands for improved forms of representative democracy.

### Microcosmic representation of women

Microcosmic representation involves representation by people who resemble those they are to represent. Feminists have made demands for microcosmic representation of women since the existing forms of territorial representation elected so few women and this appeared unlikely to change. For example, in the UK Parliament in 1929 only 2.3 per cent of MPs were female and this proportion had risen to only 3 per cent as late as 1979 (Judge 1999: 36). In the UK Parliament, the figure rose to 18 per cent after sustained efforts to increase the number of women candidates in the 1997 election, but it is still a very much lower figure than that in Scandinavian countries (Judge 1999; Squires 2005: 141). Because of this under-representation, it is fair to say that 'women have not been recognized as civic and political equals' (Phillips 1998: 22, 1991: 63).

The argument for microcosmic representation is two-fold. First, the argument is that territorial political representatives are selected from such an *unrepresentative sample* of the population as to profoundly flaw democracy (Phillips 1998: 5). Second, the argument states that different experiences, such as those typical of men and women, do create different values, priorities and interests therefore it is important to encourage or enforce the wider representation of women (Phillips 1991: 65). Recognition of these arguments and pressure from the movement has led, across the world in liberal democracies, to the development by parties of policies favouring finding and foregrounding qualified women candidates. These policies have resulted in an increased number of candidates and elected representatives. Scandinavian countries have made the most headway with the election of female representatives by establishing policies *requiring* such representation. In Sweden, as a result, 45 per cent of representatives in the national assembly are female (Squires 2005: 121). The 'affirmative action' quota policies developed in Scandinavian societies have been unpopular in the USA and UK since they are seen in liberal political thought to negate equal opportunities for equally qualified candidates.

However, microcosmic political representation has also been greatly criticised among feminist scholars. The criticism questions the assumption that an increase in the microcosmic representation of women in parliaments will automatically, or even generally, translate into an increase in substantive representation of women's policy concerns (Celis *et al.* 2008). The criticism raises a range of other considerations concerning how women's substantive concerns should be identified if we accept, as feminist typically do, that women's experience is diverse (Celis *et al.* 2008). Further, it has been argued that a focus on the elected arena may not be the most promising for increasing the substantive representation of women. Rather, some argue, women's policy agencies and their interaction with the women's movement where that provides access to resources and authority might provide better outcomes (Celis *et al.* 2008). Other arguments suggest that microcosmic representation has benefits and costs that vary greatly by context and therefore ought to be valued situationally according to a calculus of costs and benefits. These contexts include the quality of communication in a representative relationship, the level of crystallisation of interests of a group, and the level of legitimacy within the 'group' (Mansbridge 1999: 40). If these contexts undercut microcosmic representational relationships then it would seem good to keep the institutionalisation of microcosmic representation fluid. In that case organising for permanent quotas might be undesirable since they are static and essentialising (i.e. assume that the group is fixed and has a clearly shared set of interests and identity) (Mansbridge 1999: 40).

The demand for microcosmic representation of women in parliaments has its counterpart in debates concerning the media. Most mainstream broadcasting organisations in the 1960s, for example, employed entirely or overwhelmingly a workforce of male newsreaders (Douglas 1994: 157). The inbuilt assumptions enforcing the choice of men as newsreaders included the notion that men are more authoritative than women and that women's voices are too shrill for them to be given such an important role (Karpf 2006). Feminist challenges to these paternalistic or patriarchal assumptions directly and indirectly affected the choices broadcasters made, and have led to increasing numbers of female newsreaders in most Western media outlets in the 1980s and thereafter (van Zoonen 1998). The media have also been crucial in structuring women's access to feminist politics in part because it is through media coverage that most women learn about the movement in the first place (Douglas 1994: 165). The media have also been crucial since media played an enormous role in sidelining radical feminists and partially validating liberal, equal rights, feminism by promoting coverage that reinforced the distinction between 'legitimate' and 'illegitimate' feminism (Dow 1996: 28). Such a distinction validates representative politics and downgrades unmediated forms. In short, media have played a central role in reflecting, selecting and deflecting the reality of the feminist movement.

### Democratising global politics

Social movements outside as well as inside the nation have articulated demands for better forms of representative democracy – for example, members of the anti-globalisation and other movements set up the World Social Forum (WSF) in 2001 in Porto Alegre in Brazil. Subsequently it has been held in different cities around the world; meeting in 2004 in Mumbai, and in 2006 jointly in Venezuela, Mali and Pakistan. In 2009, the WSF meeting was held in Brazil again, this time in Belem. The WSF is an attempt to organise a global civil society forum for discussing issues of common concern that have impacts both within and across national boundaries. Its organisation indicates and creates a 'scale shift' in the contention over key issues in global politics, economy and society, which consequently aids the formation of transnational coalitions (Tarrow 2005: 32, 132–3). Such an organisation challenges monopolisation of the relations between nations that the activity of national political leaders and undemocratic supranational and international organisations might otherwise allow. In that sense, it is organised in opposition to the World Economic

Forum (WEF), which meets in Davos, Switzerland, every January. The WEF is a non-profit forum funded by large corporations, which brings global elites in business, politics and intellectual life together with 'communities'. The WEF proved, however, to be closed to discussion of the social issues surrounding globalisation, which the later founders of the WSF had desired to raise there (Tarrow 2005: 131). They, therefore, founded the WSF specifically in order to remind national political leaders that there were populations to whom they were responsible and whose interests they were supposed to represent. National leaders gathering at large-scale international conferences appeared to be a world away from the needs and concerns of the public and, in particular, the world's poor. The popularity of the WSF idea has led to the development of a set of supplementary forums: thematic, regional, sub-regional, national, municipal and local, making its organisation adequate to the emerging scales of contemporary politics (de Sousa Santos 2006: 35).

The charter of the WSF articulates its main values as organising a democratic debate of ideas in which the international dimension of contemporary politics and society is central (de Sousa Santos 2006: 1–8). In that sense the WSF contributes a large collective process for deepening democracy (2006: 129). The key frames for the discussions are ideas that are in opposition to those aspects of processes of globalisation commanded by large multinational corporations. Neither political party representatives nor members of military organisations can attend. The WSF is intended to be a permanent world process seeking and building alternatives to neo-liberal policies.

Such WSF face-to-face meetings have also been supported and enabled by emerging media technologies such as the Internet. Such complex cross-country meetings of many tens of thousands of people would be very difficult to arrange without new technologies and the complex circulation of relevant information made possible by websites and blogs. The anti-globalisation movement and the WSF, therefore, find their counterparts in forms of e-democracy by which discussion, debate and information are enabled by computer technology. However, e-democracy can be individualising, which the WSF does not wish to encourage. Rather it focuses on face-to-face meetings supported by information and communication resources made available online. In the plan for the WSF meeting in Belem, Brazil, in 2009 there was a development to allow for decentralised participation in the Belem activities, intended to multiply initiatives of participation in the forum process. This was not merely an online activity, however, but rather a rich, communal participatory exercise. Chapter 6 explores debates over how Internet use might aid challenging national representative politics, and how it might function as a tool to make representative politics more convivial.

Both social movement challenges to representative democracy keep representative democracy under surveillance. They each aim to contribute to the sharpening and improvement of representation. Each therefore takes representative democracy's own self-declared status seriously and seeks its greater fulfilment.

## Conclusion

The national representative system has been modified since the 1970s by increasing organisational and cultural complexity. What has arisen is a new, plural and unstable model of political representation to replace the one dominant until the 1960s. In the new model leaders represent (supplemented by alternative national assemblies), what is being represented is the complex nation itself involved in intergovernmental relations, the something that is being represented is the interests, opinions, values and identities of the represented, and media are the main resource for representing, and the main place where the activity of representing takes place. Supplementary territorial representation of the small nation and the increasingly important microcosmic and party forms of representation modify the dominant national territorial form of representation.

There are good reasons to suspect that the increasing organisational complexity brought to the fore in supranational and international organisations and the rise of quangos limit accountability of these important areas of governance and lead to democratic deficits. There is likewise reason to think that the increased cultural complexity of the nation evident in the increased importance and recognition of small nations with their demands for modified territorial representation and recognition may contribute to – for some people – a too complex idea or reality of the nation. The challenge to the national narrative of progress brought to the fore by the continuing problem of the inclusion of black people demonstrates the need to realise fully the promise of equality built into the ideals of the political and cultural membership of the nation. Further, though multicultural policy can aid inclusion, it is under severe challenge in contemporary politics and media, and that challenge especially implicates Muslims in Western societies as a 'problem'.

The wide criticisms of – and demands for improvement in – representative democracy made by social movements likewise are calls for fulfilment, and reconsideration of the meaning of, those ideals. Feminist demands for microcosmic representation demonstrate that some degree of felt similarity between represented and representative may be necessary in order to ensure that the interests and concerns of women are included. Environmental movements' desire for a more deliberative politics requires proper openness and transparency on the part of governments in their dealings, and requires them to publish and discuss the evidence base for their policy choices and decisions. The global political activity of the anti-globalisation movement demonstrates that the democratic deficit present in supranational and international political institutions will not remain unchallenged.

As we have seen in this chapter, each element of the governance and transformation of politics from the 1960s, and the challenge of cultural complexity, has its own counterpart in media coverage, which can contribute to our awareness of issues and concerns or contribute to our neglect of them. We explore and evaluate the contemporary political audience and their role in contemporary public life in the next chapter.

## Further reading

Alia, V. (2004) *Media Ethics and Social Change*. Edinburgh: Edinburgh University Press.

Judge, D. and Earnshaw, D. (2008) *The European Parliament* (2nd edn). Basingstoke: Palgrave Macmillan.

Kennedy, P. (2007) *The Parliament of Man: The United Nations and the Quest for World Government*. London: Penguin.

Pitkin, H.F. (1967) *The Concept of Representation*. Berkeley, CA: University of California Press.

Vibert, F. (2007) *The Rise of the Unelected: Democracy and the New Separation of Powers*. Cambridge: Cambridge University Press.

# 5 Exploring the contemporary audience of mediated politics

Politics, like popular culture, is about creating an *'audience,'* a 'people' who will laugh at their (politicians') jokes, understand their fears and share their hopes.

(Street 1997: 60, my italics)

Throughout the world ... people routinely spend *a huge amount of time* with *different forms of media*, often more time than they spend at work or school or in face-to-face communication.

(Livingstone, Van Couvering and Thumim 2005: 10, my italics)

Children once looked to national heroes as their models and today they admire Hollywood celebrities ... [the former is no] automatic sign of their greater civic virtue ... [the latter] are not necessarily indices of some sort of degeneration .... [it depends upon] the *meaning* of the choice to the child.

(Greenstein 1965: 149, 151, my italics)

## Introduction

We are interested in audience activity because of the important role audiences play in society generally, not merely because audiences are intrinsically interesting. As Ang (1996: 4) asserts, studying the audience is of concern because 'it points to a broader critical understanding of the peculiarities of contemporary culture'. This chapter explores the audiences of politics in order to challenge claims that audiences, especially youth audiences, are politically apathetic and therefore all future citizens are likely to become *merely* docile consumers rather than engaged publics. The audience brought together via media has a structure – as discussed in Chapter 1 – that resembles that of mediated quasi-interaction rather than the ideal face-to-face publics of 'direct' democracy.

The notion of a media audience is in tension with the notion of a media public: to a degree, they mirror the relation between individual and collective even though they are composed of the same people (Livingstone 2005). We might define the audience by its common access *to the same text* and the public by the active relationship *to other people* through media texts. They may have a lot in common, too. The latter, for example, may be greatly dependent upon 'exploration of experience, tentative trying out of viewpoints' among audience members (Livingstone 2005: 21). Drawing upon the discussion of Craig's (2004) work in Chapter 1, we might distinguish audiences from publics by noting that the notion of public is, in part, defined in relation to certain values such that a public 'fosters a particular ethico-political orientation towards others' (2004: 47). Publics are also more associated with a sense of agency than are audiences. The proper role of publics involves doing something, making things happen and making decisions. Craig gives as examples of the sense of agency of publics things such as 'which governments to elect, which values inform our identity, and how we should punish wrongdoers' (2004: 61). In this chapter, we will be concerned with media audiences and their study. We shall, however, note where and when we find examples of a fairly common event – where and when the relatively individualised 'audience' of a media text constitutes itself as a public through the creation of an active, ethico-political relation to other audience members through the media text where that is used as a basis for action.

The chapter investigates the active audience model that has been used by audience researchers since the 1970s. Further, it explores claims that audiences have been so changed by their transformed access to multiple television channels and new media that a new type of audience is emerging: the extended audience. The chapter goes on to focus on youth as exemplars of the extended audience and of the 'crisis', and therefore of the future, of politics, public life and democracy. It does so through two case studies: it explores youth involvement in political protest against the UK government's role in the Iraq War and in the campaign (and expanded voter turnout) that elected Barack Obama as the 44th President of the United States.

## How do political audiences make sense of politics?

### The active audience: making sense of mediated politics

This chapter rejects traditions of media research which assume that media have direct and powerful causal effects on people (hypodermic model) or who reduce the complex mediating role of media to the mere gratifications that people might derive from the consumption of media (uses and gratifications research) (Brooker and Jermyn 2003; Ruddock 2007). Both of those traditions of research fail to understand the cultural and social settings and meanings of media consumption. Contemporary studies of audiences, however, *do* pay a great deal of attention to the detailed social and cultural understandings that audiences necessarily bring to make sense of the complex cultural representations embedded in media. They explore audience sense making, the complex activities, and the everyday settings of listening, viewing or reading media (cf. Morley 1980; Ang 1991, 1996; Gamson 1995; Gillespie 1996, 2005; Abercrombie and Longhurst 1998; Buckingham 2000; Ruddock 2007).

Media scholars have called the ongoing audience use of social and cultural understanding in order to make sense of media an 'active audience' conception. This position has been articulated thus by Abercrombie and Longhurst (1998: 140): 'audiences are not blank sheets of paper on which media messages can be written; members of an audience will have prior attitudes and beliefs which will determine how effective media messages are'. This notion has been incorporated into studies of audiences of television news, current affairs and political cartoons (Gamson 1995), and confirmed by broader studies of how, for example, children make sense of political institutions, policies and the roles of leaders via a combination of media and social experience (e.g. Greenstein 1965; Cullingford 1992; Buckingham 2000, 2005).

'Active audience' theory arose out of the cultural studies tradition of media research in the UK (Ang 1996: 4; Corner 1999: 82). This distinguished itself from prior audience research which suggested over-simple models of influence (Brooker and Jermyn 2003: 6). The important theoretical development informing this tradition is Stuart Hall's (1980) 'encoding/decoding' essay, which is concerned with the 'systematically distorted communication' between production elites in broadcasting and audiences (Gurevitch and Scannell 2003: 236). Hall's model forms the theoretical basis for the most famous and detailed study in the beginning of this tradition of research: David Morley's (1980) 'The *Nationwide* audience'. Once we have outlined Hall's model we will explore Morley's empirical study of audience understanding of a media text.

Hall's (1980) encoding/decoding model is a sophisticated Marxist analysis of the role of media in class-divided societies where media content is encoded with dominant (class-based) meanings. Hall's (1980) model attempts to make sense of the whole circuit of meaning making in media. This circuit goes from the complex making of the cultural representations embedded within programmes, the distribution of the programme to audiences, and the various ways audience members use their understandings of encoded cultural representations to perform the complex, individual and group 'work' of decoding the 'messages'. In Hall's theory, the assumption is that any society's dominant ideas will be encoded into its media messages. For example, strikes typically will be reported on television news or in the newspapers as the disruption of the ordinary, legitimate daily activity of the businesses by which striking workers are employed. The news stories, therefore, usually will incorporate this preferred meaning of strikes into the story, will treat the business managers and owners as legitimate sources of news, and typically will offer broad support to their perspective. Strikers will be given less opportunity to name their grievances and typically will be asked to justify their actions in terms of the disruption their strike is causing to 'ordinary people' deprived of the good or service they produce (Ericson, Baranek and Chan 1987).

Hall's model assumes three typical forms of response to, or 'readings' of, dominant encoded messages:

1   *the preferred reading* – one that accepts the encoded media message
2   *the negotiated reading* – one that accepts the main aspects of the encoded message but contests the meanings or applications of some of the ideas
3   *the oppositional reading* – one that disagrees with main aspects of the encoding of messages embedded in the media text.

Hall's model was utilised in a sustained study of audiences for a BBC television programme. *Nationwide* was a popular BBC news magazine programme watched by about six million people each weekday late afternoon when broadcast from 1969 to 1983 (Morley 1980: 38). Morley used Hall's (1980) theory as the basis of his study. Morley showed two editions of this programme to nearly 30 focus groups, each made up of similar people such that the focus groups 'represented' different social locations in UK society. Morley assumed that members of UK society from different social locations would have a different relationship to the dominant meanings encoded in mainstream media texts (Morley 1980: 134). The focus groups included professionals, trades unionists, teenage students, those training to become teachers, technical workers, and included all-white, mixed and all-black groups (1980: 37–8). The first edition of the programme that Morley showed to his focus groups covered a variety of items, such as industrial disputes, human interest stories and consumer issues. These stories cover a variety of themes and examples from both narrower and broader conceptions of 'politics'. The second edition was a 'budget special', concerned with annual changes in government taxation, and addressed 'what the budget will mean to you ... looking at how three typical families across the country will be affected. We'll be asking ... union leader Hugh Scanlon and industrialist Ian Fraser about what the budget will mean for the economy' (Morley 1980: 39–40, 96–7).

Morley's original initial intention was to use Hall's (1980) encoding/ decoding model to make sense of the whole circuit of meaning making in media. As mentioned above, this circuit goes from the complex making of the cultural representations embedded within the media programmes, the way programmes are distributed and the various ways audiences members use their understandings of encoded cultural representations to perform the complex, individual and group 'work' of decoding the 'messages'. Through practical circumstances the Morley study is *only* of the audience decoding phase and does not include a similarly detailed media producers' encoding of the *Nationwide* television programme.

The central problem of the *Nationwide* study – what Morley it is really trying to understand – is:

> whether audience members are incorporated into *the dominant ideology* [assumed to structure preferred meanings in the media text] by their participation in media activity . . . [or their resistance] to that incorporation.
>
> (Abercrombie and Longhurst 1998: 15, my italics; cf. Morley 1980: 145–7)

Morley, further, is exploring *how* and *to what extent* audience members are incorporated into the dominant ideology – the culture or meanings 'that receives the widest circulation in society' (Abercrombie and Longhurst 2007: 110) such as the notion that audiences of the programme belonged unequivocally to the unified 'nation' (*Nationwide*) in which all were equal members.

Morley found quite a deal of evidence to confirm Hall's model: 'non-political' engineering students offering *preferred* readings in their criticism of strikers, trades unionists defending workers' rights, and young African-Caribbean students rejecting the mode of address and concerns of the programmes. The engineering students, therefore, were confirming the dominant coding of the programme. Both union officials and African-Caribbean students were thereby reading the texts in *opposition to* preferred meanings. Morley also found photography students *negotiating* the programme by means of technical analysis of its representations rather than substantive concern with its content.

Two aspects of the news were understood differently. First, there was a focus on the *content* of the programme in its portrayal of striking workers as 'self-interested groups working against national shared interests'. Second, there was a concern with the extent to which the different groups welcomed or accepted the *mode of address* (its vocabulary and the way it addressed the viewer) of the populist *Nationwide* show. It was too lacking in the seriousness of current affairs or news programmes for some and, for others, far too serious and alien in its approach to compete with similar programming on commercial television.

Morley's research produced two main findings, which influenced subsequent audience research. First, he confirmed the very complex work of decoding that viewers undertake in order even to make sense of the cultural representations encoded into the *Nationwide* programme, and therefore all media content. This gave encouragement to later audience researchers to give greater weight to audiences' cultural knowledge and the specific social settings (domestic, school, workplace, institutions) of consumption, and has led to detailed, qualitative (ethnographic) studies of television viewing (Gurevitch and Scannell 2003). Second, he explored, in detail, the complex and contradictory way individuals and groups made sense of the preferred or dominant meanings. He found not just preferred, negotiated and oppositional readings but differences *within* these forms of interpretation of the media texts. Morley understood these differences within types of interpretations to relate to two features of his focus groups and their members. First, there were subtle differences within and among the groups of interviewees in their precise socio-cultural location in society. Second, focus group members also had different discursive resources (ideas and narratives) available to them in order to make meanings from the programme. The second point was particularly noted by Morley in differences in trades union groups, where the most coherent oppositional readings to the dominant codes were produced by trades union 'shop stewards' (grassroots labour union officials) who are both less incorporated than full-time trades union officials and have a workplace experience that aids 'the development of such a coherent and articulate oppositional reading' (Morley 1980: 141).

The Hall/Morley model thus commenced with a powerful appreciation of the complex meaningful activity of audiences *even to be able to* decode dominant encoded meanings even as it assumed a dominant, preferred, message in the programme itself. The Morley/Hall model as a more generic 'active audience' model has been developed in the disciplines of cultural and media studies by researchers tending to give emphasis either to the *dominant text* or the *dominant audience*. These two emphases proclaim either the likelihood that dominant coded meanings will tend to be confirmed or the likelihood that audiences will read the text in an unconstrained way. The latter approach has been more fruitful. No audience researchers, however, deploy pure models that therefore interpret all power as inhering in *either* the text *or* the audience to the exclusion of the other (Abercrombie and Longhurst 1998: 18–28).

Perhaps the main emphasis of the majority of audience researchers since has been the *creative cultural activity* of audiences as a point of investigation *in itself*. For example, some key studies of the cross-national consumption of the US drama series *Dallas* – feared to produce 'Americanisation' in its overseas audiences – confirm this. They do so by demonstrating the complexity of interpretation of the meanings offered by the television text when read in the light of an array of nationally and regionally different cultural assumptions (Ang 1985; Liebes and Katz 1990; Gillespie 1996; Ruddock 2007: 70–4). The findings of the Liebes and Katz (1990) study of *Dallas* audiences in their own homes, audiences located across the world, are usefully summarised by Rogers, Singhal and Thombre (2004: 440) as follows.

> Arabs in Israel saw *Dallas* as a parable of the moral degeneracy of modernism; Russian immigrants in Israel saw the television program as an exercise in the politics of capitalism; Moroccans interpreted *Dallas* as showing that wealth is itself evil; and Israeli Kibbitzniks concluded that all Americans are unhappy. . . . Israeli viewers were particularly impressed by the tremendous wealth of the Ewing family, and by this family's disruptive interpersonal relationships, qualities that many Israeli viewers of *Dallas* attributed to *all* American families.

Audiences did not even necessarily understand the programme as American – the Ghagyi people of Nigeria, for example, understood the J.R. Ewing oil multimillionaire character as a trickster from Ghaygi mythology (Rogers *et al.* 2004). Study of the complex, cross-national understanding of media output, then, produces knowledge of the complex differentiated interpretive activity and contexts of audiences, and highlights the political as well as cultural and societal differences between the place (the country) of production of the programming and its places of reception (typically, the home).

The focus is on the audience's meaning-making activity rather than referring that activity back to the dominant ideological views of society supposedly contained in media texts that have become popular (Turner 1992: 135, 136). The consequence has been that a full emphasis on active audiences tends to destroy the ideological concerns of the Hall/Morley model altogether since it makes it difficult to combine such close and situated audience study with an even approximately strong theory of ideological hegemony (i.e. how dominant ideological views become taken-for-granted 'commonsense') (Abercrombie and Longhurst 1998: 31). Further, it is not clear that a 'preferred' reading of a text can be established to exist independently of readings actually given by researchers or the 'audiences' they research (Livingstone 2008: 8). This means that full appreciation of the effect of social and cultural contexts of audiences on their understanding of media texts tends to draw analysis away from any confirmation of the existence of dominant preferred meanings (let alone their regular reproduction and confirmation by audiences).

As audiences 'play' with media texts 'trying out' characters in popular dramas and controlling fan versions of these texts – extended versions of what in Chapter 1 we analysed Thompson (1995) calling 'discursive elaboration' and 'responsive action' – then constraints of the text on what audiences can do with it start to disappear. Recognition of this lack of audience constraint has led to the perception of a need for a new form of audience study of the diffused audience of spectacle and resultant narcissism rather than the domination of preferred meanings in media texts (Abercrombie and Longhurst 1998).

### Framing and the limits of active audience control

In spite of the relative lack of constraints of media over audience interpretation found in active audience research, media do seem to impose some restrictions since, even if media do not tell us what to think, 'they do tell us what to think about' (Ruddock 2007: 41). As audiences we are, virtually all of the time, geographically separated from the locus of the stories media tell and therefore highly dependent upon media for knowledge of those remote events and actions. Framing concerns the way that media stories work as stories with protagonists, and the assignment of causation and responsibility (Street 2001b: 37). Unlike with Hall's ideological model of media, however, frames do not assume a single ideological position or preferred reading.

Media, through news values, tend to prefer particular broad ways of framing issues. For example, media have been criticised for favouring episodic frames that focus on individual actions over thematic frames that focus on systemic concerns (Franklin *et al.* 2005: 85) and for preferring the simple over the complex and emotions over facts (Street 2001b: 38; Graber 2006: 99, 101). Such preferred framing of issues can lead, for example, to coverage of crime that massively over-represents the levels of serious and personally damaging crime such as murder or sexual assault over robbery and burglary (Graber 2006: 100).

Such framing may cultivate beliefs about the world, 'which are just plain wrong' (Ruddock 2007: 34). Ruddock cites the example of the dominant framing of sexual abuse as 'stranger danger' rather than as a systemic problem of families and abuse by those who know the abused. In the UK, it has been the soap operas rather than the news media that in the 1990s challenged this dominant framing of sexual abuse. We will refer to the limits imposed upon audiences by media framing when we analyse youth protest versus the Iraq War that took place in 2002–3.

## Do we need a new paradigm in audience research?

Abercrombie and Longhurst (1998) have argued for a shift from Hall and Morley's work, which they label the incorporation resistance paradigm (IRP), to a spectacle performance paradigm (SPP) in audience research. The shift they argue for is still a version of active audience theory. What it seeks to reject from the IRP model is three-fold. First, they seek to reject the narrow focus on class. Second, they do not believe that complex media texts contain singular dominant meanings that audiences can merely confirm, negotiate or oppose. Third, they emphasise that audiences are not merely constituted by watching a particular television programme. Rejecting the focus of the IRP model, Abercrombie and Longhurst argue that changes in society since the 1990s require a theory shift to explore what audiences are actually doing with media and how audiences relate to media culture.

The changes Abercrombie and Longhurst foreground include the expansion of the role of consumption in individual lives and the economy, shifts in the forms and 'choices' of media available, and the shift from a class-based conception of society to a post-class one (cf. Chapter 2). In short, they argue, we have moved from an era of mass-media audiences to one of *diffused audiences*. It is arguments for this new form of audience theory I wish to explore now, giving particular emphasis to the way that concern for mediated politics gives a very particular perspective on claims for the new paradigm of audience research. In short, I will be arguing two key points against the diffused audience conception. First, that the shift towards a spectacle/performance paradigm for audience research suggested by Abercrombie and Longhurst works better to understand fan audiences of fictional dramas than audiences for news of either the more serious or more popular kind. Both the latter rely upon an attitude towards truth and truthfulness that the fan media can, and often do, completely bypass in fantasy little constrained by a sense of the realisable or need for sincerity of performance (Williams 2004). Second, I will be questioning the analysis of media change and its likely consequences offered by Abercrombie and Longhurst, which underpins their argument for the need for a specific new paradigm – of a shift towards a media-drenched environment.

### The extended audience versus the diffused audience: what's in a name?

Abercrombie and Longhurst's (1998: 68) argument for a new paradigm for audience study is underpinned by a claim that changes in media and culture lead to changed audience experience – to what they term a 'diffused audience'. They assert that, '[t]he *essential* feature of this audience-experience is that, in contemporary society, *everyone* becomes an audience *all the time*. Being a member of an audience . . . is *constitutive* of everyday life' (1998: 68–9, my italics). The notion of the 'diffused audience', they explain, refers to multiple processes working at different levels. These processes include the increased amount of time people spend consuming mass media; the way that media and everyday life have become closely interwoven into life's routines; and the creation of a performative society. The performative society, for Abercrombie and Longhurst, is one where audiences are aware of performance modes and frames both in viewing or listening to media and in a variety of other areas of life.

The diffused audience, they argue, arises out of the combination of

> the construction of the world as spectacle and . . . the construction of individuals as narcissistic . . . Spectacle and narcissism [consequently]

feed off each other in a virtuous cycle, a cycle fuelled largely by the
media and mediated by the critical role of performance.

(Abercrombie and Longhurst 1998: 75)

They further argue that audiences in these new realms of spectacle, narcissism
and performance have a tendency to resemble fan and enthusiast audiences.
Fan and enthusiast audiences are particularly associated with combining
intense and widespread media consumption with varying levels of fan media
production such as the writing and distribution of fanzines and 'slash' fiction.
In slash fiction, characters in a television series are written into sexually
subversive encounters (such as *Star Trek*'s Captain Kirk and Mr Spock as lovers).
The diffused audience has become dominant, Abercrombie and Longhurst
argue, not because the diffused audience replaces simple (face to face) or mass
audiences but because the spectacle – narcissism interaction within a changing
media sphere transforms the relations between different audience types,
and their access to media content, within the everyday lives of audience
members. Abercrombie and Longhurst have gained broad support for their
view that a new form of audience has arisen (Huggins 2001: 127, 135; Laughey
2007: 182–3).

However, it is crucial that we closely consider claims about new forms of
audience. First, we must explore difficulties with the conception of diffused
audience where expanded *audience* experience is conflated with wider audience access to media *production*. They are not the same thing. I could regularly
consume dozens of television channels, listen to many radio stations, scan
many newspapers and magazines, and use the Internet daily – all examples of
expanded audience experience – without any necessary widening of access to
media production. Couldry (2005) argues this point against Abercrombie and
Longhurst. He says that the media changes such that most people in wealthy
societies have access to multiple television channels and multiple forms of
other media content within their everyday lives relate to the *expansion of the
audience experience*. However, the diffused audience notion also, crucially,
implies easier and more sustained access to *media production* as does occur in
fan communities (Ruddock 2007: 77–98). Couldry argues, rather convincingly,
however, that the experience of being a media performer or producer is still
rare. Further, he notes that the distinction between being a 'member of the
audience' and being a 'media person' is very closely policed by media themselves (for example, those chosen to appear on reality television shows form an
exceptionally small minority). Since media are such important 'centres' of
symbolic power it is crucial to that power that the boundary between media
and non-media be closely policed. In fact, that boundary is more strictly
policed and valued *even more highly* as audience-hood has become more
common. We need, Couldry argues, to make sense of how the experience of
being in a media audience is *both* very widely shared *and* highly differentiated.

Couldry further suggests that we recognise the expanded use of media in contemporary society by use of the concept of 'extended audience' (rather than 'diffused audience') to explore the whole spectrum of talk, action and thought that draws on media or is orientated to media. This involves, for audiences, the complex activity of how to interpret texts as a story and compare that story to their own lives. The extended audience exists, as we have seen Thompson (1995) already demonstrate in Chapter 1, far beyond the original viewing of the text as people use their own experience to understand and, thereafter, question or validate television programmes (Couldry 2005: 200, 204). This activity typically involves two main features. First, there are multiple, interactive and multidimensional audience experiences. Second, there is the requirement for audiences to keep up with changes in the technical interfaces used to access media. These shifting social and spatial forms of 'audience-hood' are profound enough changes to take into account, without overestimating, as he argues Abercrombie and Longhurst have done, the speed and breadth of change (Couldry 2005: 219). In the light of this criticism of Abercrombie and Longhurst, we will use Couldry's notion of 'extended audiences' to make sense of youth political audiences.

## Youth as a problem

In exploring changes in society and media consumption that have led to demands for a new version of active audience theory, I will focus on the youth political audience. There are several reasons for this. First, young people are the future of societies around the world. Therefore, changes in their everyday life activities of media consumption and of their relationship to mediated politics may be indicative of likely futures of these activities for all people in the future. Second, that 'youth' are associated with the lack of adult qualities and therefore are an important element of society through which to explore difficult questions of the political meanings and consequences of media (and social) change.

Youth is a problematic category – one that emerged as a crucially import-ant stage of life only in the last half-century or so of human societies, with the 'teenager' and the rise of the rock 'n' roll culture in the 1950s and youth subcultures since. 'Youth' has since become associated with differentiated forms of consumption of music and clothing, and the use of distinctive forms of slang and, sometimes, expression of a jaundiced or cynical attitude towards many institutions of the 'adult' world. The social category of youth is associated either with threat, uncontrolled freedom, rebellion, vulgarity and dangerousness on the one hand, or deficiency, vulnerability, neglect, depriv-ation or immaturity on the other (Munice 2001: 5). In both cases, the focus is on *a lack* with regard to taking up adult responsibilities: through rebellious choice or insufficiency of character or development. Further, youth is very socially protracted in contemporary society where education often extends the dependency of people into their early twenties, and the structure of the job and housing markets can lead to a delay in full economic independence until people are nearly 30 (Wyn and Harris 2004: 272; Laughey 2006). The socially protracted nature of youth in contemporary society has especially become associated through the notion of youth as 'lacking' with regard to taking an interest in politics and current affairs. We will explore youth's relation to politics in a time of extended audience-hood, below.

Young people's relationship with changes in media consumption is crucial, then, not only to an account of their everyday lives and to how they construct meanings for those lives but also for theories of media audiences developed to comprehend those consumption practices. We explore contemporary youth audiences in a section on youth protest against the Iraq War in 2003 and youth mobilisation for, and voting in, the 2008 US presidential election.

### Youth and concern for their interest in politics

Concerns that young people lack an interest in politics (and news) have been expressed in many countries across the world. Remedial action has been taken up in mainstream forms of political and media activity. For example, after the low voter turnout for the 2001 UK general election, broadcasters tried to see if they could make their politics, news and current affairs programming more engaging to the youth audience, with very mixed results (Citizenship Foundation 2004). Further, mainstream political parties and related main-stream political organisations have developed youth sections in order to provide spaces for debate. For example, during the 2006 Liberal Democrat party conference, young people from the YMCA (2006) movement took part in debates about the role of youth in society (*Teenagers: Saints or Sinners*) includ-ing discussion of lowering the voting age from 18 to 16 and whether this would increase the likelihood of young people engaging with mainstream electoral politics. In the USA, the non-partisan Declare Yourself movement has encouraged young people to vote after poor voting turnout figures for youth in the 2000 election. A further example of this attempt to connect young people to politics can also be seen in the education system. In many contemporary countries, citizenship education has either begun for the first time or been greatly enhanced in order to address perceptions of youth apathy or lack of understanding of politics. In the UK, citizenship studies became part of the national curriculum in 2003, and existing courses in Australia and New Zealand have been revamped (Crick 2003; Wyn and Harris 2004). These changes, so far, have had some, but only limited, impacts on young people.

What is required is a more fundamental understanding of young people's relation to mainstream mediated politics. This understanding needs to take into account two things. First, that *alienation from* politics is very different, and implies different responses, to *apathy about* politics (Buckingham 2000; Henn, Weinstein and Forrest 2005). Young people are not typically apathetic about politics, and research has suggested that they suffer, rather, an alienation from the mainstream mediated political arena, in some measure produced by the institutions of media and politics themselves. Second, it needs to take into account the fact that complex changes have occurred in the lives of young people since the 1980s, which need to be properly considered in making sense of their media consumption (and other) activity.

Even though it is the case that young people live lives outside many of the daily interests of mainstream mediated politics they are engaged with politics in the narrower sense of mainstream party politics even though they often do not (feel they) understand them very well. At the same time, the majority of young people typically say they are 'bored' by politics. One thing is certain. Young people typically mean by 'politics' a very narrow range of public affairs associated with governments and parties (Buckingham 2000, 2005). What young people are interested in, care about and know something about differs significantly from the adult political agenda (Stanyer 2007: 163, 172). This can be seen, especially, in young people's involvement in the broader arena of politics that includes community and voluntary associations.

## The extended youth political audience engaged

However, in 2003, perhaps the dominant story in global politics and global news became a key concern to young people in a variety of countries – for example, from Malaysia to Ukraine, Germany, the USA, Australia and the UK (Lemish and Gotz 2007). In what follows, my focus is on young people in the UK, though the lessons have application that is more general.

The object of the concern of young protestors was the impending, and then actuated, decision of the USA and its close allies, which included the UK and Australia, to commence a pre-emptive war with Iraq in contravention of international law. Many young people took a concern with 'the need to feel connected to events in the news and public life' into co-ordinated forms of responsive action: marches, demonstrations, the creation of campaigning organisations and the organisation of school strikes. The action of young people – especially those of school age – did not flow out of any renewed understanding of citizenship as provided by the school curriculum but rather was actively created by themselves as extended audiences of media coverage.

These youth political activities in relation to media coverage of the Iraq policy are best considered extended audiences in Couldry's sense rather than diffused audiences in Abercrombie and Longhurst's understanding. This is for three reasons. First, Iraq policy was the dominant story across press, radio, television and the Internet for months; it was virtually unavoidable because of its mediated ubiquity. Second, it is precisely because they had no significant access to media production that young people felt so acutely disempowered in relation to a government policy (and its initial domination of the news agenda) that appeared both morally wrong and misinformed. Third, the question of truth did seem paramount in the attitudes of protestors. In part this is because in the UK the government tried, through a specially written 50-page dossier, to explain and justify its policy, in particular that the Iraq regime possessed, and was likely to use, weapons of mass destruction (WMD). In part, it was because young protestors were aware that no such WMDs had been found and that UN weapons inspectors were prepared to continue their search for them and confirm their (non-)existence. The truth of competing claims was a crucial part of what was in dispute.

### UK youth political protests against the invasion of Iraq

By organising their own political actions, as well as taking part in others organised by adults, some young people demonstrated not only an interest in a key issue of mainstream politics but also that they are politically alienated from mainstream party politics rather than politically apathetic (Henn *et al.* 2005). Young people do desire to contribute to public life, but the organisation of public (media, political) life can make that difficult.

So where and what were these youth protests, and what implications do they bear for our understanding of (youth) extended political audiences? Young people's response to a possible, then an actual, war versus Iraq involves an opposition to military conflict and its associated suffering in a setting that allowed them to draw upon a wide range of media content and feel able to create and maintain their own political activity in an environment often hostile to that activity. The involvement of young people in demonstrations and co-ordinated responsive actions gave them methods by which to make sense of the political world around them and communicate their conclusions to their youth peers and the wider society in a virtuous cycle of activity. Such demonstrations also operated as a way of handling negative feelings associated with death and suffering present in news coverage (Buckingham 2005: 18). Since protests involved actually organising activity, they helped young people to express their political idealisms, and collectively organise and deal with their anxieties and powerlessness. The youth political protests constituted (some) young people as publics, not merely audiences of media.

National cases differ in the extent to which media fostered concern with Iraq. In the UK – unlike in the USA – media were important resources for questioning the push for an invasion of Iraq. Many young people in the UK drew widely on media – broadcasting (radio and television), press (newspapers and magazines) – in order to comprehend and then to articulate views concerning the appropriateness of an invasion of Iraq.

For example, broadcasters in the UK – especially with the existence of their institutional requirement to provide balanced coverage of news and current affairs – raised important questions about the government stance. They did this in spite of the fact that the dominant framing of Iraq supported the existence of weapons of mass destruction and the potential danger of Iraq to the UK's security. For example, fewer than one in seven of the broadcast news reports in the build-up to the invasion of Iraq registered any doubt about the existence of weapons of mass destruction (Davies 2009: 35). Children's television news – which provides much more contextual information than adult news (Buckingham 2000) – focused young people's worries and concerns on the likely consequences, in terms of loss of lives and suffering, of any invasion. That young people, very generally, were concerned about the Iraq War can be confirmed by the result of a poll conducted by the BBC children's news programme *Newsround*, which found 82 per cent of 10- to 14-year-olds opposed the war (and 45 per cent thought that politicians didn't care about their views). Broadcast material was viewed in family settings as well as by children alone in their bedrooms. The media coverage formed an important part of the knowledge of young people, informing their discussion of the situation with their schoolmates. Broadcast stories were also widely available via extremely portable transistor radios, which might even be taken into schools and listened to in groups, and the Internet and mobile devices provided both information sources and resources for organisation.

In the UK, newspapers in particular gave enormous amounts of coverage of the build-up to the invasion. Some newspapers broadly supported the government case for the invasion and framed the story in terms of the security danger of the Iraqi regime. However, newspapers that were less secure in their support emphasised doubts and the likelihood that the invasion might be prolonged and, therefore, would be costly in (UK) lives. Further, two UK national newspapers – the *Independent* and the *Daily Mirror* – explicitly opposed the war on Iraq and campaigned against it, and a third newspaper, the *Guardian*, severely questioned both the reasons for the proposed war and the likelihood of positive consequences arising from it. As we saw in Chapter 3, campaigning rather than merely 'objectively' reporting the news is a feature of the UK national newspaper market. The *Daily Mirror* is a tabloid newspaper selling, then, over two million copies daily, and the *Independent* a quality broadsheet newspaper selling around 250,000 copies. The readers of those newspapers and the broader national media mix in the UK benefited from media outlets seeking to scrutinise closely the grounds for government policy. The *Independent* was particularly interesting for, in addition to its sustained opposition to the Iraq invasion, it provided space for the dissenting 'alternative' voices of journalists such as Robert Fisk and George Monbiot, whose regular analyses in (at least) weekly columns suggested broader geo-political contexts and explanations of UK and US policy. Young people, though unlikely newspaper readers, greatly benefited from the stocking of school common rooms with newspapers following 11 September 2001 and in relation to citizenship classes, as both a measure of, and resource for the satisfaction of, the increased desire to know what was going on in the world. In relation both to the newspaper reading and engaging with broadcast news, the potential invasion of Iraq became the *'only thing* kids [had] been *talking about* in [the] playground' (Brooks 2003).

National media contexts varied in terms of media support for criticism of pro-Iraq War government policy. The UK media context of campaigning news-papers and well-resourced public service radio and television, in this case, gave very much greater resources for criticism of government policy than did the US media. In the USA, its 'objective' press, its Fox news-dominated US television system and right-wing talk radio 'tradition' made it more difficult for audi-ences to keenly question US foreign policy (cf. Chapter 3; Arsenault and Castells 2006). A by-product of news coverage – the news media assumption that demonstrations might be violent or unsafe – may have influenced young people's desire to demonstrate, or their parents' encouragement or permission (Cushion, forthcoming). Differences in both broader political culture and political institutions also make a difference to potential political mobilisation (Oates 2008).

Some of the young extended UK audiences of this news about an impend-ing invasion of Iraq didn't merely remain audiences of news, but constituted themselves as ethico-political publics and became involved in mainstream protests against the war led by adults. In spite of the barriers to protest of young people perhaps, more than one in five protested in some form (Cushion, forthcoming). Distinctively, however, their ethico-political concern and extended discussion of the situation also led young people to organise *their own* protests. This included 'school strikes' – where, for example, 5,000 children from Birmingham, 3,000 each in Manchester and Edinburgh, 1,000 from Sheffield and 300 in Swansea abandoned school and took part in marches and demonstrations in their locality (Brooks 2003).

The difficulty of young people organising political protest was exacer-bated by the school context. Such youth political concerns, for example, found little address in citizenship classes since those classes focused mostly on individual aspects of responsibility and moral education, and very little on engaged co-operative citizenship and politics (Cunningham and Lavalette 2004). Rather, school authorities functioned as forms of resistance to young people's protests. Teachers did not see schoolchildren's protests as part of a valuable, if difficult, learning experience about contemporary media and politics but, rather, as a challenge to their authority. Thus, young people's political protests were reduced to a form of truancy. Consequently, teachers put a great deal of energy and ingenuity into curtailing future attempts at protest (Collins and Kennedy 2003; Cushion 2009). Further, news coverage of children's protests, in spite of the media support for criticism of government policy, either belittled them, and treated them as truants 'bunking off' for the day, or viewed them as examples of youth manipulated by sinister adult influences. Furthermore, the idea that the right to protest might also be applied to children seemed to be used conditionally – *only* if responsible adults approved of the *object* of that protest (Such, Walker and Walker 2005).

The conditions for youth political activity to thrive and bypass active resistance from schools in addition to extended and engaged media access included prior political involvement, membership of voluntary groups and parental support. For example, one group of teenage political organisers of Hands up for Peace had drawn upon support from 'non-political' voluntary organisations aimed at giving the child a voice. Among the more influential student organisers were those who had already been members of groups such as the Woodcraft Folk or the Young People's Parliament, and had parents with experience of campaigning (Brooks 2003). They also drew in many children with no prior interest in politics or protest.

Youth protests versus the war against Iraq demonstrate young people's interest in mediated mainstream politics when it involves large-scale issues about which they care and towards which they can take an attitude. The protests make particular sense from within the 'extended audience' model. That model emphasises the complex activity of making sense of media, which might take place across the spaces of children's lives: from the home, to the school and on the street – and how this complex sense making helped them challenge government authority – since only some of the media outlets operated as powerful resources for their protest. Wide access to mainstream media opposed to the war and mainstream media fully reporting the war and access to alternative strands of media gave students a chance to inform themselves more fully and, importantly, to debate anti-war perspectives (Atton 2004; Atton and Hamilton 2008). That some young people were already involved in 'non-political' groups gave them access to perspectives antithetical towards pre-emptive violence as a solution to political concerns. Some young people became activists based on their prior commitments and knowledge, and were able to encourage the mobilisation of others lacking prior commitments. The political organising as a 'co-ordinated responsive response' to media coverage and the rich discursive elaboration ('the only thing talked about in the playground') that underpinned taking an interest in it provided resources for that mobilisation (Thompson 1995).

Since the anti-war protests did not stop the invasion it might be worth asking what has happened to those youth political protesters since. We might speculate that some have been turned off from political activism, feeling more alienated than before because their voice went unheard. Perhaps this is the largest of the groups of those involved. Some may have stayed part of the politics of Iraq occupation – going on marches and calling for the troops currently deployed to be recalled. Some may have joined other political groups, and we find some examples of that in relation again to single-issue politics in recent development in green activism. Some young members of Plane Stupid – one of a 'new wave of militant environmental groups that are determined to force the pace of the climate-change debate' – learned their direct action political skills in the campaign against the war in Iraq, in addition learning that 'marching is not enough' (O'Keefe 2006: 1). Their understanding of the nature of contemporary extended audiences demonstrates to them the need to make and take part in creative political demonstrations. Such demonstrations not only create news in a whole variety of media forms but also require the use of direct action skills at airports, delaying planes and thereby, by the inconvenience caused as well as the media interest sparked, give greater attention to the effects of airplane carbon dioxide emissions on global warming. Thus, the understanding of their own extended audience-hood, their enthusiasm, skills, networking and organising have not gone to waste. Some young people politicised by the Iraq War protests continue to demonstrate a keen concern with mediated-political issues. The experience of the anti-war campaign may well have alienated some, but has politicised, skilled up and enthused others who will bring their single-issue politics to bear in the mediated politics of the future.

### Obamania: the engaged youth audience of mainstream politics

We find another example of youth interest and involvement in mainstream politics – as a challenge to claims of youth political apathy – in the election of Barack Obama to the presidency of the United States of America. That election is historic and important in all manner of ways (Thomas 2009). I will focus on the mobilisation of the youth vote in support of Obama's campaign. Further, I will explore what the mobilisation of youth reveals about the extended youth audience for mainstream politics. Obama's success generally, and specifically with regard to younger voters, can be understood as the product of four main features of his campaign. These features of his campaign are his political message as present in his speeches, policy positions and his published books (cf. Obama 2008); his attempts to increase the level of political registration of the American people; his mobilisation of ordinary Americans to raise money and consciousness in localities across America; and his distinctive use of new media (cf. Castells 2009: 364–93).

Barack Obama's key political and campaign message focused on change as necessary for America. What he argued in speeches and his books is that America has created a 'dead zone' of political factionalism, which simply works against Americans addressing systematic flaws in their political institutions and correctly balancing self-interest and community, or markets and democracy, in their political arrangements (Obama 2008: 8–9, 193). Obama's calmly expressed 'audacious' vision that America could be changed and improved, making the American dream more fully available for a greater number of Americans, rang true in the ears of many. That audacious vision rang more true, in particular, from the moment that economic recession seemed unavoidable and Obama's opponent, Senator John McCain, appeared to have little appreciation of either the problem or the knowledge base with which to tackle it.

Obama's focus on political registration of the American people – since registration depends upon Americans asserting their right to registration to the appropriate local political authorities – also encouraged and depended upon political mobilisation. Obama here was building upon prior efforts by organ-isations such as Get out the Vote (Get out the Vote 2008). Get out the Vote, which describes itself as 'a voter *empowerment* and *information* source' (original emphasis) was established in response to significant decline in electoral turnout in previous presidential elections. It provides information concerning poll locations, places to report voting issues and non-partisan political infor-mation, and the space for interactive involvement in political discussion in order to encourage higher voter turnouts.

The mobilisation of ordinary people was essential to Obama's strategy since it gave him access to funding that didn't tie his campaign into powerful 'special interests', a large potential volunteer force to further aid registration and turnout on the day, and an email list for mail-out and to encourage ongoing involvement in the campaign issues and debates.

Social networking sites were of particular importance to involving young voters in the registration and mobilisation processes mentioned above. Obama's use of new technology not only distinguished him greatly from McCain but also significantly contributed to his earlier victory, in the Democratic nomination process, over Hillary Clinton (Evans 2008). Obama's use of social networking sites didn't merely focus on those well known through press discussion (MySpace, Facebook, Twitter, Flickr) but also included those used by smaller, more niche, audiences. This meant that Obama opened a dialogue with youth in, for example, African-American, Asian, Latino and faith-based communities (such as BlackPlanet, Faithbase, MyBatanga and AsianAve) (Evans 2008: 2). Obama also showed a higher level of understanding of social network sites and their audiences, invested more time and energy in them by creating entirely new blog posts for their different profile areas and personalised tweets on Twitter, rather than, as Hillary Clinton did, merely posting already existing blog posts from her own website across all the sites. Obama certainly has more experience of, and trust in, Internet-based communications such as blogs and Twitter (Obama 2008: 41; Castells 2009: 389). This trust and experience is apparent in that Obama circulated much larger numbers of videos, including candid as well as controlled and professional video, of his campaign on YouTube, whereas Clinton circulated smaller numbers of controlled, professional videos. Obama's trust in blogs and social networking sites is a form of trust in their extended audiences.

Obama attracted and connected to the youth political audience, two-thirds of which voted for him (Keeter, Horowitz and Tyson 2008: 2, 6; Castells 2009: 368–9). He connected to youth, first by offering them a compelling and hopeful political message (Obama 2008); this was crucial since the younger voters are more 'liberal' in their political assumptions (they expect the government to do more to solve problems) and more anti-Iraq War in the political conclusions they draw from the issue dominating the Presidency of George W. Bush (Keeter *et al*. 2008: 5). His campaign also created spaces for the activity of young people and their mobilisation within his campaign – both online and offline – and communicated to them in sincere, engaged and sustained ways in the variety of social network spaces that they had, as extended audiences, built into their mixes of media use. He also gave the youth audience access to less controlled media materials that they could enjoy exploring and forwarding to friends and relatives. In short, Obama's connection to the youth political audience in the United States drew not only on their nascent and developing political idealism and opinions but also on them as distinctive extended audiences of media.

## Conclusion

Among (youth) political audiences, we have seen evidence of complex understandings of political activity and events. Even for the young people who are so often accused of political apathy we see, rather, engagements with the political world – more narrowly (the US presidential election of 2008) and less narrowly conceived (the anti-Iraq War protests of 2003). When events make news more relevant and a larger feature of their lives, young people are often able and willing to take up not mere 'play' with media texts – important as that might be in other contexts – but sustained and engaged action. That action is, in part, in response to media discussion and debate and their extended access to it. Eventually, it arises from the judgements they and others they connect with make about the relevance of such debates for their lives. They often take this action even with no encouragement from teachers and adults, and even in active opposition to them.

Those lives, as we have seen, have to be seen as changing. The structure of young people's lives is more taken up with education than for previous generations. Their lives are changing, also, because mediated experience is a more extended experience, which is at the heart of their lives more than those of previous generations are. However, as we have seen, this does authorise us to accept the notion of a diffused audience of performance and spectacle. Couldry (2005) instead convincingly suggests an idea of the active extended audience – spatially and socially organised in new forms and accessing media via a variety of new technical 'platforms'. Moreover, we have seen, too, that the precise sense made by that audience of the contemporary world and ongoing events is crucially affected by the exact nature of the media mix in particular places.

## Further reading

Buckingham, D. (2000) *The Making of Citizens: Young People, News and Politics.* London and New York: Routledge.

Couldry, N. (2005) The extended audience: scanning the horizon', pp. 185–219 in *Audiences*, edited by Marie Gillespie. Maidenhead: Open University Press.

Ruddock, A. (2007) *Investigating Audiences*. Los Angeles and London: Sage.

Van Zoonen, L. (2005) *Entertaining the Citizen: When Politics and Popular Culture Converge*. Lanham: Rowman & Littlefield.

# 6  The Internet, public life and political change

Rather than becoming a post-industrial totalitarian menace or the means for a utopian transformation of society, the Internet has become *integrated* into our *existing reality*.

(Margolis and Resnick 2000: 117, my italics)

The Internet is having a *profound impact* [on] ... forms of human association, modern forms of organization, the self and experience, publicness ... [and] globalization.

(Slevin 2000: 234)

Technological systems are *socially produced*. Social production is *culturally* informed ... the *culture* of the producers of the Internet *shaped* the medium.

(Castells 2001: 36, my italics)

## Introduction

In earlier chapters we analysed the ideal and realised role of media in contemporary public life – in particular the extent to which they aid in fulfilling the democratic requirements of public life by involving publics in debate and making available to the public the diverse and grounded information necessary to the accountability of public life. We continue this exploration in the present chapter with regard to the Internet, in order to assess its uses and their consequences for democratic politics.

The Internet – or should we say Internets since the actual software and hardware involved here have multiple historical, organisational and cultural origins, and thereby purposes, from email, to ftp, newsgroups, the World Wide Web, social networking sites, podcasts and weblogs (blogs) – is a distinctive medium. The Internet offers many ways of connecting cultural-political content in a variety of forms and styles to audiences (Collins 2006: 353). Whereas media developed earlier in human history offered one-to-one (letters, telephone calls) or one-to-many communications, the latter often referred to as mass communications, or mass media (print, broadcasting), the Internet affords other relations between communication pairs. These include many-to-many (Usenet, discussion boards, mailing lists, weblogs and peer-to-peer networks) and many-to-one communications (email, feedback forms and online polls). Of course, the reality is even more complex than that since email, for example, is increasingly used for promotional purposes such as political advertising as a many-to-one medium. It has also been argued that:

> A web page may appear at first glance to be a simple one-to-many device, but often web pages are composed of information, such as news feeds, from many different sources that have been brought together by automated scripts that dynamically update content without human intervention. Web pages may also contain discussion forums alongside more traditional forms of content. Understood in this way, they start to resemble many-to-many communication.
>
> (Chadwick 2006: 5)

What Internet-empowered computer communication offers is the capacity to 'automate, search and mediate' all the forms of communications – one to many, many to one, many to many, and one to one – that have previously been developed in human history as separate and specifically organised media (Deuze 2006). This has led Leadbeater (2009) to describe the cooperative possibilities of the net as 'We-Think' and Castells to call the form of communication it provides 'mass self-communication' (Castells 2009). Because of the dual capacity to use both the *affordances* (the particular functions or capacities offered to users by particular software) of these different forms of communication, and the capacity they allow for automating, searching and mediating communications, the Internet offers increased possibilities for 'consumers' to become producers (Burnett and Marshall 2003; Foot and Schneider 2006: 12, 67). In short, the Internet allows the heavily policed boundary between producer and consumer, and the inequalities between communicants that the boundary reinforces in the media of print and, in particular, broadcasting, to be challenged and bypassed (Thompson 1995; Couldry 2000, 2005; Slevin 2000; Tapscott and Williams 2008; Castells 2009; Leadbetter 2009). Burnett and Marshall (2003: 74) draw upon these affordances of the digital technology of the net in combination with an understanding of active, skilled audiences, as discussed in Chapter 5, to develop their *cultural production thesis*, which argues that users *can* create a 'form of literacy that is simultaneously about reception and production'.

As such, the Internet has functioned in public debate as a tool or sphere of concern about the complex phenomena of Internet use, but, more broadly as a trope for thinking of the future of human societies in dystopian and utopian scenarios (Bauman 1999: 130, 145; Calcutt 1999: 93–4; Margolis and Resnick 2000: 2; Wilhelm 2000: 20). Because of this, the most widespread anxieties and the most common yearnings have become imposed on the Internet phenomenon since it became widely discussed in the early to middle 1990s. According to *Time* magazine, 1994 was the 'Year of the Internet'. In 2007, *Time* magazine declared the Person of the Year to be 'You', 'Yes, you. You control the Information Age. Welcome to your world.' Moreover, on the cover the computer screen pictured had a mirrored surface in order that any readers looking at the magazine would have an image of their own face reflected back.

## The Internet as 'the fabric of our lives'

Instead of accepting the imposition of the views of dystopian and utopian visions of the Internet, we should explore its uses in particular political and societal contexts through examples and cases. The metaphor of fabric, which comes from Castells' (2001) book, *The Internet Galaxy*, may guide us here. Fabric is made of cross-woven patters of fibres, which intersect each other at a 90-degree angle. Each of the parallel strands of fibres, called the warp, is then threaded between the other strands of fibres, called the weft. The metaphor, then, is of Internet use being threaded, in dense and complex ways, through the social, cultural, economic and political activities of contemporary societies. As Slevin (2000: 4) asserts, the Internet is 'enmeshed with [the] cultural transformations of modern societies' (cf. Lally 2002 and Haddon 2006 for the insertion of the Internet in domestic settings). This includes the way that Internet use is threaded into use of existing media by both media organisations and audiences (Freedman 2006). Such an approach to analysis of the Internet – which is our interest in this chapter in its use in relation to politics in all it guises – recognises that the Internet was created in the context of (some) existing structures and projected futures (Abbate 1999). Its subsequent uses *modify* existing structures and practices of politics and the social relationships in which they are carried, and are in turn *modified by* them depending upon the precise development of uses (Albrow and Washbourne 1997; Miller and Slater 2001). It is to the exploration of the complex uses that we now turn in exploring key themes that have emerged in literature attempting to summarise the Internet's impact on politics. These are commercialisation of the net, whether the Internet fragments society, whether the net can contribute positively to global public life, the role of the net in 'freeing' information, and the net's challenge to the political mainstream.

## Commercialisation and the Internet

Commercialisation is the making of goods or services into items for sale. Claims that the net has become commercialised look back to a time when the net was a product of 'pure research' into communications at the end of the 1960s, answering to the need of scientists to send large datasets to geographically separated colleagues in order to carry out co-operative research activity (Abbate 1999). In its second phase, the Internet's use expanded the network of researchers to a variety of higher educational institutions up to the late 1980s and early 1990s (Abbate 1999; Bell 1999). At that stage the World Wide Web (WWW) graphical software developed by Tim Berners-Lee – to set up websites and spaces in order to aid particle physicists at CERN in Geneva to share their results across national and software and hardware boundaries – was seen to have the potential to open up the Internet to much wider use in society. The Internet up to that point was run predominantly based on a *gift economy* rather than a commercial economy. It worked because people gave away information and software for recognition, or status, within the Internet community.

Various authors have suggested that commercialisation of the net has destroyed that original ethos and that, further, this creates a commercial dynamic in Internet development and culture, which disables the Internet as a space with potential for politics and public discussion (Gutstein 1999; McChesney 2000; Chester 2007; Halavais 2009). So what are the claims being made about Internet and the world of consumption, and do they presage the decline that some (Bauman 1999; Gutstein 1999) hold out for it?

The commercialisation of the Internet can be seen in a variety of areas. First, in the funding structure of the Internet this has shifted from US government research and US educational funding to the dominance of commercial money. In part, this was a result of US government communications policy (McChesney 2004; Klinenberg 2007), and government policy elsewhere has played an important role in the development of e-commerce (Wong 2003; Mathiason 2009). Second, increasingly from the 1990s, individual access to the Internet has been made available via commercial Internet service providers, rather than government offices or universities, and this individualises and commercialises access. Third, the ability to use and research the growing space of the WWW depends upon the commercial search engines and portals provided by the likes of AOL, Yahoo! and Google (Chadwick 2006: 108; Halavais 2009). Each is funded by advertising revenue. Each also represents the diversity of the net unequally (Spink *et al.* 2006; Halavais 2009). In short, Google does not live up to its mission 'to organise the world's information . . . and make it universally accessible' but uses search algorithms that prioritise previously linked-to, established information (Chaffey *et al.* 2009: 565). Since Google handles over 53 per cent of the global searches online, this has consequences for the accessibility of information in public life wherever people live (Halavais 2009: 6). Fourth, a powerful dynamic in this commercialisation is in the use made of the Internet to streamline the organisation of established profit-making businesses. Such businesses use the Internet as a major tool, as a point of contact for consumers and suppliers with the digital information as an important structure of their whole business practice. Companies that use the Internet and digital technology to entirely transform their businesses and reconfigure their workforce and capacity to track supplies and orders have been called 'network enterprises' (Castells 1998–2004).

The successful commercialisation of the Internet in all the forms listed above has depended upon the exploitation of the distinctive use of the Internet in marketing (Chaffey *et al.* 2009). In recent times, this has developed in line with the great expansion of the use of social networks and the use of Web 2.0 features such as blogs, feeds, mashups, IPTV and widgets. Thus, the extensive and expansive user participation that is a feature of these aspects of the web also provides openings for viral marketing. The two main forms of viral marketing online are passalong emails and commencing or contributing to discussions within social networks (Chaffey *et al.* 2009: 556). Since discussion within social networks contributes to the perception of brands, products and suppliers, it presents a great marketing opportunity (Chester 2007: xi; Chaffey *et al.* 2009: 558). Commercial concerns can take this marketing emphasis even further. For example, in 2005, in an attempt to connect to difficult-to-advertise-to audiences and as a way of drawing upon the creativity of cultural production of members, News Corporation bought a range of website-based companies, including MySpace.com.

However, the attempt to commercialise access to and use of the Internet has also been resisted. Movements have been established that distribute software free of commercial motivations (Copyleft) or with code that is open to be developed by the open source online software community (Berry 2008). In Scandinavian countries – those where a public service tradition and collective political values are defended – they have explored how to use the Internet to foster public service values by providing explicitly public service – rather than commercial – web content and sites (Moe 2006). Likewise, the websites of public service broadcasters such has the BBC no doubt function in this fashion (Naylor, Driver and Cornford 2000; Tapscott and Williams 2008: 192–3). Further, access to the Internet has been subsidised by governments or provided through public libraries in order to allow public access to the net rather than private commercial access being the only option.

In spite of this evidence of resistance to net commercialisation, some argue that the institutions that might aid in resisting commercialisation of access to the net may have already been sidelined. The broader dominance in society of commercialised services has been understood as drawing some consumers away from formerly more important public institutions such as public libraries. Gutstein (1999) persuasively argues that this phenomenon also fits into a more general move towards defence of intellectual property, where companies exploit the copyright to films, music, books and software to make profit and hive off those intellectual goods that were themselves a product of communal, rather than purely individual, activity. The Copyleft and open source movements mentioned above are powerful exemplars of an alternative approach to the legal and cultural dominance of private intellectual property (Berry 2008).

Consumers, however, should not be treated merely as dupes of the powerful (whether corporations or advertisers), as we saw in Chapter 5 in relation to audiences. For example, one area of consumer activity is use of price comparison websites in sourcing everyday (gas, electricity) and more exotic purchases (designer clothing, holidays). People who set up price comparison sites have a sense that the corporate world often provides goods and services that pretend to a competitiveness they do not really manifest – so price-informed consumers put pressure on businesses to be somewhat more competitive or to offer better after-sales or other services to compensate. Further, rather than merely focusing on individual purchasing decisions, consumers both in the past and now have worked collectively to assert principled stances to forms of 'unethical' consumption (Sassatelli 2007: 182–90). The anti-slavery movement is one good historical example – the idea that you cannot (should not be able to) treat people as consumer items became an important ethical injunction and greatly contributed to the end of the slave trade. The anti-apartheid movement in the 1970s and 1980s put pressure on the 'apartness' (legally institutionalised racial segregation) of the racially divided South African society through bans on sporting activities and boycotts on the purchase of South African produce. Here purchasing decisions have broader ethical and political meanings. These days the growth in fair trade foodstuffs in supermarkets, especially in the UK, is a less activist form of consumer activity but still one with ethical (and possibly political) meanings (cf. Burn and Parker 2003: 29–44). Naomi Klein, author (most famously of *No Logo* (2000)), and consumer activist, is only one of many suggesting that the intertwined local–global production of goods can usefully be challenged by contemporary consumer politics.

Consideration of the relationship between politics and consumption raises the issue of the relationship between 'consumers' and 'publics', between more individual and more collective ways of conducting social and economic lives. Many ways of discussing consumption (and no doubt many examples of 'doing consumption') focus on individuals and their particular decisions and judgements. These discussions construct consumption as almost entirely antithetical to public and 'political' action (van Zoonen 2005: 148). While there may be dangers in pretending that there are no relevant distinctions to draw between the activities it seems to me to be foolish to assume that the public and collective activities of our societies will never and can never have fruitful interplay with consumption (Sassatelli 2007: 188).

## Fragmentation and the Internet

One of the concerns about commercialisation of the Internet is that it leads to the fragmentation of collective values. Others have argued that some fragmentation is also occurring with the use of multi-channel television (cf. Tewkesbury 2005; Webster 2005). That concern remains whether it is the product of commercialisation or has other origins, too. The concern about the contribution the Internet makes to fragmenting contemporary societies raises broader issues. Wachbroit (2004) usefully distinguishes for us between *associational* and *informational* fragmentation. The former relates to organisations people establish or join, the latter to variations in media contents people consume. The acclaimed multiplying effect of one upon the other is particularly seen to be leading to the decline of the public and politics. As we saw in Chapter 4, the idea is that the key *associations* of contemporary life are falling in membership or are being replaced by others less representative of people and too little known because of the apparent indifference of those providing media coverage to these shifting forms of governance. There we explored the idea that it might lead to a democratic deficit.

Associational fragmentation, at least as seen from the perspective of nation-state society (often an implicit assumption of analysis) was the prior common experience before nation-states came into existence. Small-scale village communities, clans and tribes were created, to a degree, out of such geographical features as mountains and rivers, which tend to sub-divide human relations. Even the great historical empires of China and India were based on myriads of smaller, often culturally different groups (Chang and Halliday 2007: 8). The fear in 'end of politics' notions is in part that the nation-state is no longer quite as important to people's lives as it was in some liberal democracies between, say, 1930 and 1970. It is too big for many issues in local lives and too small to master the storms of global economics and global politics (Albrow 1996). Thus the forms of devolution and the rise of governance structures to replace central government discussed in Chapter 4, which could be given positive readings – in that government in some cases moved 'closer to the people' – are understood as aspects of a negative phenomenon – *political fragmentation*. This emphasis on *national fragmentation* has received its US counterpart in Putnam's (2000) 'bowling alone' thesis. However, even though the Putnam thesis of associational decline has been quite influential, the extent to which it is true has been systematically disputed by Ladd (1999), who argues that the American associational life is so complex and dispersed that it is hard to reveal and measure. He further argues that Putnam has emphasised the declining membership of some associations but not the rise of others, such as membership growth in the environmental and conservation movements, the increase in church attendance, the expansion of the Boy Scout movement and more widely attended Parent Teacher Association meetings. What we find in US associational life is, he says, 'Churning, not decline' (Ladd 1999: 25). Likewise in other countries the decline of some forms of association, such as the membership of political parties, has been used to state simple decline in collective relationships when it more closely measures 'strong competition' (1999: 52) between different forms of associational activity rather than simply the replacement of association by 'de-sociation'.

Informational fragmentation refers to the acclaimed effect of people engaging with different, rather than shared, forms of media output. The concern is that people will engage with such different ideas that they will no longer desire to say anything to each other, or have anything to say, or even a common language in which to say it, as Norris (2001: 147) has put it: 'fragmenting any broader sense of the national interest into incoherent pieces'. However, we can see from the rise of the discussion of fragmentation more particular concerns being expressed. Press coverage of 'audience fragmentation', for example, starts in the UK in the early 1980s and is associated with the interests of marketers who were finding it difficult to connect to audiences. Audiences had previously been gathered around nationally broadcast television: in the US popular 1970s television shows such as *M\*A\*S\*H* could get audiences of over 50 million (Iyengar and McGrady 2007: 55) and, in the UK, over 27 million people watched the Christmas edition of the *Morecambe and Wise Show* in 1977. Such widely watched programmes opened up great possibilities for the advertising and marketing of goods and services to mass audiences in the 1960s and 1970s. So the decline in audience sizes for specific television programmes in the emerging multi-channel world were not fragmented in any real sense that affected *them* or audience members per se, rather the phrase was used by marketers and advertisers to name *their own* problem: getting to the audience. This was felt especially acutely by commercial broadcasters but was also a concern to public service ones. At the same time, some fragmentation of information or media use – to the extent that it was occurring – created a great opportunity for those who wished precisely to find 'niche' rather than 'mass' audiences.

One assumption that dominates the 'fragmentation' debate is the notion that 'fragmentation' of media and information access is a new phenomenon. Jones (2000: 179) asserts the opposite in that newspaper readership, in particular, has always been 'fragmented'. As we saw in Chapter 3, the UK newspaper market is made up of antagonistic relations negotiated across different broadsheet and tabloid papers. The US newspaper market, even though somewhat concentrated in ownership, is regional and local rather than national in coverage and distribution, and works less to bring the national together than regional and local identifications. Wachbroit (2004: 39) agrees that many 'traditional' services were customised and that therefore there was informational fragmentation without the Internet, well before the Internet. The debate on fragmentation, then, has predominantly been conducted with little or no appreciation of the history of media consumption nor, as we saw above, that of associations.

Further, if we either suggest replacement words or phrases for 'fragmentation' of associations or of information, we see that a value judgement is being imported into a situation rather than an analytical description. For example, if we instead called the assorted phenomena 'pluralism' or 'choice' or 'specialisation' (Webster 2005), we would be likely to understand the import of the changes differently even if we recognise that all the alternative words also carry value judgements. Wachbroit suggests 'accelerated pluralism' as an idea for making sense of the way Internet information is used by groups to articulate particular causes, and this might more accurately reflect the 'effects' Internet access can have on information use. Clearly, people are using the Internet – this is especially true in the US context – to customise their news services, and are therefore consuming different news items to others, so the potential exists for more plural informational consumption (Pew 2007). However, there exist limits to this pluralisation – the power that exists for some news voices to set news agendas regardless of the number of outlets for different commentaries on the 'news of the day' (Allan 2006). Thus, blogs rather than fragmenting debates typically depend upon and repeat the dominant content of mainstream news sources (Scott 2007: 45–6). However, worries exist, still, that the capacity to intelligently customise the news out of the variety of news sources available off- and online is unequally distributed in society according to educational levels, income, background and wealth, and therefore may build upon the 'digital divide' that some fear is affecting both richer and poorer societies.

## The Internet and global public life

### Who's not surfing the net? the implications of unequal access

The wide, high-quality accessibility of the Internet is a crucial necessary condition for even the possibility of the emergence of – anything resembling – global public life. So how does the current availability match up to these ideal requirements? Across the world, fewer than one in five of the population has Internet access (Chaffey *et al.* 2009: 622). In both the United States and the United Kingdom, as wealthy, highly educated countries, access to the Internet has grown dramatically since the late 1990s and thus stands at a much higher level than that of the world as a whole: 70 per cent and 62 per cent respectively (Chaffey *et al.* 2009: 622, 623). Young US adults below the age of 30 are even more likely – 84 per cent – to have access, as are the young elsewhere (Kaid and Postelnicu 2007: 151; Mesch and Coleman 2007; Xenos and Bennett 2007). Subsidies from the federal government for individual access and state funding of access through public libraries in the UK and USA, respectively, enable those too poor to afford computers or ISP charges some level of accessibility (Mossberger, Tolbert and McNeal 2008: 156–7). The Internet is widely available and used by the majority of the population. However, the figures demonstrate that a significant proportion of the adult population in the UK and USA – around a quarter – do not access the Internet and may even have no idea about how, or even if, such access will benefit their lives. Furthermore, differences persist in the exact level of access and quality of access defined either in technological terms (broadband access) or in social-educational terms (how well can people use Internet contents, how well can they rework Internet materials and become producers of content). There are some grounds for the belief that the gap is widening (Norris 2001; Livingstone *et al.* 2005; Chadwick 2006).

In both countries, age, education level, income and disability affect home access, as the resources needed for high-quality Internet access include features inequitably distributed across society, such as free time, available space, social resources (who fixes it) and cultural resources, of which literacy is highly important. Since general inequalities in access to these types of resources are high in the USA and UK this does not bode well for the excluded quarter (Wilkinson and Pickett 2009). In fact, access to political communication via the net tends to increase interest in voting and engagement in public life, further sidelining the excluded (Mossberger *et al.* 2008: 93).

Access to these resources likewise distinguishes mere inclusion and exclusion from high-quality Internet access across the regions where general access levels are very low – for example, most of Africa, some of Latin America, much of Asia and some parts of Eastern Europe (Madon 2005; Chadwick 2006). In the first three areas, access rates run at 5 per cent, 20 per cent and 12 per cent, respectively (Chaffey *et al.* 2009: 622). Some variations even within these generally poorer and excluded areas of the world can be explained as the results of particular efforts by governments funding Internet and communications access as a part of broader development goals. Furthermore, international institutions have commenced to prioritise raising Internet access levels and trying to ensure that the net is run with an eye to the benefit of the excluded (Mathiason 2009).

The implication of these various levels of unequal access – within rich societies, within poor societies, and between rich and poor societies – is that already existing inequalities may be reproduced and even magnified. Disturbing as these inequalities of access are, they do not always, and only, reinforce existing inequalities. Widespread Internet access may develop very quickly in poor, small-scale societies such as some islands of the West Indies (Miller and Slater 2001). Access to the net in many parts of the world will be created through mobile devices such as telephones rather than desktop and laptop computers, and thereby might increase the access of the less well-off across the world to some of the communication and information increasingly necessary to managing their lives.

### The Internet and the organisation of global public life

The sometimes massive inequality of access to the Internet within and between countries and regions does not, of itself, invalidate the possibility of the creation of global public life. It does so no more than low levels of literacy did for the nationally based 'public sphere' of the seventeenth and eighteenth centuries in Britain and France. Further, conceptions of public life other than Habermas's may more easily open the way to consideration of something like a global public life (Thompson 1995; Craig 2004).

This further extension of the geographical scale for public life and the way that a public may cross the boundaries of many established political communities, however, does add enormous complexity and runs up against more narrowly constituted notions of the public meaning *spaces for debate* and *civic identities* (Craig 2004). The role of the Internet in providing these spaces and encouraging broader larger civic identities is, as this chapter demonstrates, complex and fraught. However, what is clear is that the contemporary world is particularly interdependent in media, political, cultural and economic terms, and that interdependency – to the extent that it is recognised and acted upon – forms an ongoing ground for 'global public life'. The four key ways that the public is understood (cf. Craig 2004) – as relating to shared spaces, as created by visibility thus opening activities to scrutiny, by its association with the state, and in relation to values such as public spiritedness – feature differentially in this global public life. There are some shared public spaces on the net – from chat rooms to bulletin boards and social networking sites – though access to them (in terms of the complex factors that differentiate people's access to digital domains as outlined above) is very far from equal and, as spaces, they are not always established in such a way as to foster either broader access or shared values. In terms of visibility, the Internet can create new forms of visibility – literal and metaphorical – by allowing more people to create and circulate images and texts via new networks of activity and social relations. These may be disruptive and even anti-social, involving such activities as vituperative speech and incivility, but also include helpful voluntary action such as providing information to those missing relatives during the tsunami disaster in late 2005, where mass communications and even state activity had broken down (Allan 2006). The Internet was used in similar ways during, and in the aftermath of, Hurricane Katrina in New Orleans (Klinenberg 2007). In terms of state practices spanning the globe we saw in Chapter 4 that the shift from government to governance involves new forms of cross-border state practices – the UN, the EU, and global treaties and protocols in addition to many cross-border regional organisations. Our concern in that chapter was with the extent to which they were democratically accountable to their 'citizens'. Finally, in terms of public spiritedness and public values, the examples of the tsunami and Hurricane Katrina disasters give a sense that under some conditions both national and transnational solidarities and 'aid' can be encouraged by the Internet but so too can less savoury forms and activity (cf. Davis 1999: 157–60; Atton 2004; Brachman 2006; Brandenburg 2006; Conway 2006). The uses of the net that will be engaged in future may well contribute to the creation of a greater sense of a global public, and may provide information and tools to enable that, but such will be the case only to the extent that people choose to use it in that way and encourage others also to do so.

## The Internet, freedom of information and democracy

Much information is 'un-free' in being commercially owned or privileged, or inaccessible because of state control. In this section, we will explore commercial and state control of information and how the Internet allows means of bypassing and relativising that control.

As we saw in the section on commercialisation of the Internet, access is increasingly a commercially based affair. Even assuming people own a computer they need to connect it to the net, pay an ISP for access, and the bills for dial-up or broadband access. The resources of finance, education and motivation required are not equally distributed in society, tending to divide social groups. Differential access in the home is somewhat mitigated by access via school, university and libraries, though even here the greater educational and skills competence of some reinforce level of access. These inequalities can be seen in the light of the growth in regimes of intellectual property, which has privatised access to a whole range of formerly public information goods (Gutstein 1999; Drahos and Braithwaite 2002). These intellectual property regimes may have been dented in the world of popular music downloads with which Napster in its 'illegal' phase was associated and the sites since that allow high levels of such downloads to continue, such as Gnutella and Limewire. However, they have grown in the world of biotechnology especially in relation to the DNA mapping of the human genome and the creation of new spheres of intellectual property in human health, which may have dire consequences in the future. Since dominant transnational economic institutions such as NAFTA, the World Bank at and the World Intellectual Property Organization assume a corporate-interest-orientated intellectual property regime, this cannot merely be sloughed off by alternative practices but also requires addressing at the level of national and transnational policy and practice (Hafez 2007; Berry 2008; Freedman 2008; Mathiason 2009).

However, the net itself – if not its mere access – though commercialised, retains a great deal of information and resources that are *not* paid-access. Linux software as an alternative operating system to commercial ones such as Windows is part of the gift economy of the net, as are other forms of alternative access to informational goods: Copyleft versus the commercial control of copyright; shareware and freeware versus commercial software (Berry 2008). Wikipedia, an Internet 'people's encyclopedia', and Wikinews are produced entirely by volunteers as a public good to the rest of society and as an example of the more widespread cultural production created by people in contemporary society (Allan 2006: 135–8; Tapscott and Williams 2008).

Another feature of information in contemporary society affected by networked computers is information control. Most literature has focused on the state. This concerns data mining of people's purchases, credit card uses, library records, and so on. It may also occur in attempts to develop formal examples of online deliberation, though they may also be developed in such as way as to widen access to information and allow real space for deliberation (Albrecht 2006). In the post-September 11th world, states even have hastily drafted laws giving them a greater range of powers or more radically used laws previously passed concerning these matters. In the United States, the USA Patriot Act of 2001 (Uniting and Strengthening America by Providing Appropriate Tools Required to Intercept and Obstruct Terrorism) is an example of the former; in the UK, the Regulation of Investigatory Powers Act 2000 is an example of the latter. It has also led to a range of laws and the expansion of executive power in many other countries. However, though, there are alarming and sustained real-world examples of the use and abuse of these powers, our perception of them and the likelihood of their effectiveness in controlling citizen or consumer behaviour is as much the product of cinematic and televisual representations as reality. For example, representations of corporate and state informational control draw upon ambient anxieties about contemporary society in such films as *The Net* with Sandra Bullock, *Conspiracy Theory* with Mel Gibson and Julia Roberts, *Enemy of the State* with Will Smith and Gene Hackman, and the CIA espionage film series with the Jason Bourne character played by Matt Damon. In television, assumptions about the power of state-controlled databases and information techniques are routinely built into such programmes as *CSI*, *24* and *Without a Trace* (Allan 2007). Both the films and television shows, though from the USA, have been widely viewed around the world and shape anxieties about state (and corporate) power not only in America but more generally. It is crucial to recognise, however, that governmental power is crucial to control over the net (rather than control over people through the Internet) in the sense that the Internet is a less anarchic domain than is often represented (Goldsmith and Wu 2006: 65–86).

The perceived structuring power of information control is not only relativised by our recognition that it is at least as much due to visual representations of surveillance as its effects on our real world. Further, attempts to manage the 'visibility' of people, institutions and themes through information control must be seen in the context of the rise of widespread information leakage – leading to a limit to the ability of authorities to control information (Thompson 2000; Castells 2009). The example of the UK government's attempt to explain its Iraq War policy to its citizens before the invasion via a 50-page dossier backfired as the document was compared to others from around the world. It was subsequently seen to be a botched paraphrase and bricolage of an early 1990s doctoral thesis and 'sexed up' claims deriving from the secret intelligence community (Coates 2004).

In short, in some ways information control is less easy in the Internet world. This occurs in part because of information leaks from within government or the administration where the leaker has reason to distrust policy, and in part because of the multiple audiences who access the information whether or not they are the direct audience for it – and bring to bear upon it alternate information, perspectives and connections. A great example of information leaks encouraged by the Internet is the ability to track illegal 'extraordinary rendition' flights. Extraordinary rendition is the euphemistic term for the illegal airplane transportation, by the CIA, of 'terror suspects' to US prisons on foreign soil where the suspects can be tortured on the basis of CIA orders but where the CIA would be buffered both by secrecy and by the fact that foreign nationals actually conduct the torture. The most sustained exposé of the CIA's 'torture taxis' depended upon the existing fan activity of airplane spotters all around the world. Spotters logged flights into particular airports and listed such logged flights on spotters' websites and in chat rooms (Paglen and Thompson 2007: 99–112).

Information is also, in some ways, more widely available because of the attempt to practise, more generally, open and transparent forms of government and provide information about government services, or even the service themselves, online (Kumar and Best 2006). Parliamentary, congressional and government websites, even if rather gingerly, are treading the path to the ideal of open government, making masses of information about policy, law, politicians' voting patterns, and so on, much more widely available. This is accessed by knowledgeable minorities of people and is passed on by them where especially relevant to wider groups.

Freedom of information legislation, which has begun to transform access to public information, has been passed in the USA in the 1960s, and in Ireland, Scotland, Canada, Australia and the United Kingdom, among other countries, since (Brooke 2005: 11). Information leaks may or may not be supported specifically by practices of freedom of information through organisations such as the Campaign for Freedom of Information and via the informational resources provided, for example, by the UK Freedom of Information Act Blog (foia.blogspot.com) and Helen Brooke's Your Right to Know website (www.yrtk.org).

Freedom of information legislation is quite widespread and typically does widen the amount of information members of the public may access. In quite a few countries, such as India, debates are taking place about the possibility of introducing such an act (Chand 2001). The laws in different countries broadly provide rights to access public information concerning the activities of public bodies. In the UK this covers more than 100,000 agencies that were formerly able to escape high levels of public investigation because of the culture of secrecy in UK government, but they must now issue a 'publication' scheme outlining the role of the organisation, its publications, a description of what it does and a contact for information requests (Brooke 2005: 20–1). Most of these publication schemes, in the UK, are now online. The campaigning groups listed above encourage use and 'surveillance' of the uses and misuses of the Freedom of Information Act to support this 'freedom of information' movement. Some even provide education in freedom of information law to journalists during their training – especially in the UK – which training usually does not equip them very well to use the information that is already widely available from public sources (Negrine 1996).

'Freedom of information' as a general category, rather than practices associated with freedom of information laws, has been expanded by Internet activity – in part because it is so easy to blog or use social networking sites or in other ways to put people's own information out into the world. There are over 30 million blogs, many of which manifest and encourage participation in public life (Tremayne 2007: 5). People increasingly use online newspapers (Flavian and Gurrea 2006; Hall 2008). The Iraq Body Count website has continually, and credibly, updated loss of life in Iraq – both military and civilian – from the military invasion in 2003 and during the ongoing occupation. The site keeps the loss of life in the news and values civilian, Iraqi losses as much as those in the military (Sloboda and Dardagan 2005). Atton and Hamilton (2008: 80) report on the way that alternative media sites can monitor – they call it 'gatewatch' – a wide range of media output by drawing upon large numbers of willing volunteers in order to challenge the routines and formulae of professionalised mainstream journalism. Scott (2007: 50) likewise argues that journalism as a fourth estate is under surveillance from blogs in that 'Bloggers have taken the tools of the Fourth Estate and used them *on* the Fourth Estate.' Research conducted in 2005 demonstrated that a third of 14–21-year-olds in the UK have their own online content (Gibson *et al.* 2005) and other studies support this view (Buckingham 2005; Leadbetter 2009).

What overall impact this may have is hard to suggest. It may have led to more complex gatekeeping in arenas of news as institutional online providers both co-operate and compete with the rising forms of cultural production of people (Allan 2006). In relation to Islam, the very much wider availability of primary Koranic texts and different versions of the 'sayings of the prophet' (Hadith) will open up these religious materials to a range of interpretations and may involve challenges to the authority of currently constituted traditions (Bunt 2000, 2009). Therefore, we can see that we live in a new world where information is both closed off and spills out of control. Still, powerful authorities in media may control agendas (Baker 2007: 101, 112) but whether they will be able to do so so easily in future in part depends upon how we engage in the years ahead in consumption and production choices as individuals, members of associations and groups.

## The Internet and the expansion of the mainstream of politics

There is some evidence for the view that online participation may be able to expand the numbers of those politically active even in reaching groups who were formerly inactive or less active in mainstream offline politics (Gibson *et al.* 2005; Deuze 2006: 67–8; Ward and Vedel 2006: 213; Loader 2007: 11). The uses of the net in politics demonstrate a degree of widening of the mainstream of politics – including some genuine attempts of governments to consult in a deliberative manner with their citizens (Albrecht 2006; Wright 2006) – in part because it bears the potential to somewhat equalise the power for groups to circulate their messages and publish their ideas; this equalisation means both of the groups who are referred to as legitimate voices in debates and the themes and topics worthy of consideration and that have been made into political issues. With regard to the latter, for example, since the 1950s human rights has become a frame of reference for political debate across the planet; since the late 1960s the environment and humans' relations to it have done likewise, and so on for issues to do with women's lives, freedoms and rights. It can also give more access to mainstream social good and information to the disabled – allowing them to take a broader, more public role in public life (Cheta 2004; Guo, Bricout and Huang 2005). So even before the Internet the mainstream of politics had been shifting, as we saw in Chapter 4, in great part due to the rise of cultural social movements during the 1960s and since (Della Porta and Diani 2000; Nash 2000). In fact, we therefore have to understand any existing mainstream of politics as a product of past and present struggles. We might add, too, that the Internet itself – its forms and open structure – is in part the product of the social movement ideas of participation and information freedom (Castells 2001: 36). In particular, the Internet allows the spread of social movement perspectives around the world – via elites for the most part – questioning authorities, whether religious, political, patriarchal, cultural or economic (Spender 1995). The variety of uses of the Internet in public and political life have been tracked by informative guidebooks to this expanding sphere (White 1999; Dale 2001; Osler and Hollis 2001; Stein 2003; Buckler and Dolowitz 2005; Chaffey *et al.* 2009).

As we saw in Chapters 4 and 5, the activity of social movements and pressure groups has opened up the possibility for a wider range of themes in politics and a variety of ways of treating or discussing politics. Therefore it is not just discussed in 'serious' modes of masculine politics of the past but also in forms of popular cultural discussion integrating humour, commentary and analysis (cf. van Zoonen 1998, 2005; Corner and Pels 2003; Street 2003, 2004; Jones, J.P. 2005, 2007; Reigert 2007). These forms – including satirical comedy – have spread unevenly around the world (see the analysis of the talkingcock-.com website). These challenges to mainstream politics can be usefully explored under a variety of headings: challenges to what ideas or themes politics can engage with; challenges to the practices or styles of representation legitimately associated with politics; and challenges to the organisations and procedures currently at the heart of politics.

### The Internet and challenges to the ideas in politics

The Internet allows for challenges to the main ideas in politics in a variety of ways. It does so by allowing for some equalisation of political voice between very powerful and very much less powerful actors. This occurs, in particular, in countries that can be seen as in transition to democratic representative politics (Norris 2001: 239–40). Even so, the growing sophistication of, and need for investment in, influential websites makes this equalisation perhaps less effective than it was (Norris 2001; Ward and Gibson 2003). For example, the Internet can allow for a wide variety of voices to be heard, ranging from 'green and radical politics' to labour politics (Osler and Hollis 2001), though socialism or full social democracy does not seem to be making a political 'comeback' in the UK, Europe or USA in spite of the recession brought on by the credit crunch. The recession does, however, seem to allow for more consistent evocation of ideals of greater equality between citizens and the idea of regulating the provision of (commercially provided) goods and services on the basis of public needs rather than commercial profits, which before were found sidelined in contemporary market-orientated society. Engaging with blogs tends to lead to exposure to a wider variety of ideas and arguments than does access to traditional media (Meraz 2007: 59), though some have argued that they can function as self-referential 'echo-chambers' (Sunstein 2007). Minority ethnic groups can use the Internet to discuss their place in contemporary society as well as to address the broader public with issues and concerns they feel should be addressed. However, it is also fairly common for them to build boundaries between themselves, other minority groups and mainstream society, online (Siapera 2006: 12). The Internet can also be used to give greater public weight to right-wing and reactionary political groups, which gain from it more sophisticated tools for mobilising action (Atton 2004). It generally provides a resource for alternative political identity (Dahlgren and Olsson

2007). It can also allow for linkages between citizens in oppressive regimes to each other and to those in the international sphere (Oates and Gibson 2006: 5). Publicity for websites is not automatically generated, however, since usually people will see websites only if motivated to go to them. Further, alternative political sites are also less likely to be able to publicise themselves on the Internet since they are less recognised by search engines (Halavais 2009).

However, we can find many examples of groups who get their ideas across into public life, who mobilise action via the Internet and who may never have had such prominence without the Internet. These groups include:

- anti-corporate campaigners using websites for mobilisation and information provision, thereby 'holding big business democratically accountable' and thus highlighting the activities of companies such as Coca-Cola, Nike, Amazon and BP (Rosenkrands 2004: 59, 72)
- pro-hunting protestors as part of the rural political movement the Countryside Alliance in the UK (Lusoli and Ward 2006)
- Hezbollah, which provides alternative news perspectives to a broad global public and, in particular, some Israelis outside the information control of their own government and media, thus engaging in a 'battle over the cultural codes' of their societies (Conway 2006: 100)
- moveon.org as an attempt to change the media agenda from a focus on President Clinton's affair with Monica Lewinsky to contribute to the political web sphere in the elections of 2000, 2002, 2004 and 2008 (Foot and Schneider 2006: 33; Leadbeater 2009: 189)
- the Free/Libre Open Source Software (FLOSS) movement, which uses the net to create, modify and circulate open source software and the idea that the Internet should remain free of proprietary software control such as that of the Microsoft Corporation (Berry 2008: 98–146).

More broadly, the Internet may play a part in linking different groups in developing an idea and its broader role in politics. New social movement organisations seem to be especially able to benefit from use of the Internet (Negrine 2008: 190–2). In the period between the 1960s and 1980s, the environment became part of mainstream politics in the rise of Departments of the Environment in mainstream politics. This meant, at the same time, the incorporation of a body of concerns raised by environmental activists over nuclear weapons (Greenpeace) and resource use (Friends of the Earth), and their downplaying and expression in *administrative rationalism* – that the state could control the problems within the boundary assumptions of liberal market society (Dryzek 1997: 63–83). The battle since has been over new themes such as that of 'greenhouse gases' becoming the problem of 'global warming' and being managed, in part, via the concept of 'climate change' since that seems more benign than the former constructions. Thus, the environmental battle cannot clearly be distinguished from a 'battle over the cultural codes' of the societies in which we live (Melucci 1996; Castells 1998–2004). Even in the more 'benign' forms, this appeared to name a problem on which administrative rationalism could not 'deliver the goods' (Dryzek 1997: 79). The boxed example below uses methods of website analysis (Slevin 2000; Burn and Parker 2003) to make sense of the radical critique of the ecological injustices, built in to the structures of contemporary 'global society'.

---

### The Friends of the Earth International website

Friends of the Earth International (FOEI) is the largest transnational non-governmental (environmental) organisation. It is has the following distinctive feature: it has a democratic participatory structure. This has encouraged the selection of several directors from the global south of the planet. Further, it argues for a radical social justice model of environmentalism, which suggests that inequalities in wealth and life chances between people are a major reason for the way humans value and use the environment. It asserts, therefore, that environmental action needs also to be situated in the economic, political and cultural contexts of people's lives (Doherty 2006). It has been supported by the benefit NGOs and transnational advocacy networks, particularly, get from the use of interactive technologies (Norris 2001: 239; Bach and Stark 2004: 102–3) and the fact that new organisational forms can be supported via its use (Ward and Vedel 2006: 215–6). The website homepage is predominantly green in colour, expressing the environmental identity of the organisation. Although it allows for 'cyber activism', it is not a very interactive public site – more a space for press releases and publication of reports and, therefore, their very much wider distribution and readership. It does, however, have a blog that is largely used by the transnational activist members of FOEI to discuss and co-ordinate their transnational action (Friends of the Earth International 2009). The main interactive activities of the website are devoted to the use of members – activist-campaigners in the different national member organisations who use the website's intranet resources to engage in transnational research, mobilisation and campaigns: a new geography of political activity in the organisationally and culturally more complex contemporary world (cf. Chapter 4). It aims to co-ordinate these campaigns in order to raise environmental issues to a higher place on the political agenda all over the globe, link these agendas and promote the idea that environmental realities are tied up with the fundamental unequal structures of contemporary societies. As such, its website is serious – even if it provides photographs from campaigns involving playful ways of gaining attention – built around the research it conducts and the truths it wishes to highlight against the contemporary organisation of politics, economy and society. FOEI is *not* a large bureaucratic organisation dominating its members, but a hub to encourage the largely independent but interlinked translocal (cf. Washbourne 1999, 2001, 2005), transnational and transregional activity of national groups. (The annual expenditure of FOEI is less than one-third of that of a largish national member group: FoE England, Wales and Northern Ireland.)

## The Internet and the 'presentation' of politics

The Internet – drawing also as it does, as we saw earlier, on popular culture and consumption-based contents – opens up the possibility for politics to be presented, to be done, in a different way. For instance, it allows very local community groups to create news materials in blog form and with contents especially relevant for them (Bentley *et al.* 2007; Rutigliano 2007). The Internet, in supporting the activities of alternative politics, also allows for the different presentation styles, graphic histories and alternate hybrid organisational forms of alternative media (Atton 2002, 2004; Atton and Hamilton 2008). In doing so it can explore the wider conception of politics concerning the ways we organise collective public life – not just politics as state-related activity (Chapters 4 and 5). Those wider forms of politics are built around a more activist conception of citizenship in which citizens may not only vote but also protest, march or engage in other forms of direct action politics (cf. Chapter 5). Such action involves the amateur construction of political banners, posters and other materials that draw on the history of activism and manifest a tension in relation to mainstream 'serious' politics. The Internet contributes to the diffusion of a broader notion of the 'political', which particularly connects to young people's understandings and experience of alternative politics (Gerodimus and George 2007). Websites built on such grounds will explore a range of fonts and forms of political utterance, and may constantly move across 'boundaries' between public and private. They might also explore aspects of politics underdeveloped by mainstream politics but do it in a serious mode of their own. The boundary between 'serious' and 'non-serious' is one policed by groups themselves in relation to their intention and their assumptions about how others will make sense of the messages. In the example of the rural activism of the Countryside Alliance this builds upon calls for better representation of non-urban people (Lusoli and Ward 2006: 62), predominantly in serious mode though posters and banners for marches, whose designs were circulated via the Internet, allowing for the use of a mocking tone and of popular cultural slogans. In the example of the talkingcock.com website (discussed below), the popular cultural discussion of politics – an expanding feature of offline media in recent years (Jones 2005; van Zoonen 2005) – is particularly important in authoritarian political situations where being 'political' may get the website banned.

---

### Talkingcock.com

Talkingcock.com is a Singapore-based website opening a popular-cultural humorous space for discussion of what it means to be a Singaporean in contemporary politics, culture and society (Talkingcock 2009). Colin Goh, who set up the website, spent time away from Singapore in the 1990s and was able to take his distance from his homeland and see with clarity what was lacking. The problem he saw was the authoritarian political culture of Singapore, dominated since the 1960s by a single dominant political party: the People's Action Party (Ling and Shaw 2004: 65–80). It espouses a paternalistic conception of what Singaporeans should want from life, and a conception of the 'Singaporean dream' that is entirely devoted to material values and personal conformity. These broader social and political structures have shaped both the need for, but also the less developed use of, Internet technologies for politics in Singapore (George 2005). In such a setting, conceptions of active citizenship (Crick 2003) have not thrived. In negotiating these contexts of Singaporean life, Talkingcock.com goes out of its way to say it is 'not political' – it titles the website 'Singapore's most powderful [sic] satirical humour website' – which in a narrow party-political sense it may not be, but clearly being 'political' is reserved for the government, not citizens or members of Singaporean culture. In the authoritarian politics of state media-controlled Singapore the site could all too easily be closed down as clashing with national values or interests – thus it opens up and challenges attempts to manage 'who controls the imagining of the nation and minds and attitudes of Singaporeans' (Bokhorst-Heng 2002: 564). What the website does through its parodies of popular culture and government action is make visible – literally and metaphorically – the visibility management of the government and institutions, and open them up to ridicule, satire and challenge (Thompson 2000). It also articulates alternative, vibrant varieties of being Singaporean, including their expression in 'Singlish' (Singaporean English) with its distinctive rhythm, structures, slang, etc. The website has garnered enough interest to be able to publish dictionaries of Singlish and make films such as *Singapore Dreaming*, which, likewise, explore excluded or sidelined aspects of Singaporean life. One key example of this satire is the use of what is everyday knowledge for those with cable television – the television show *American Idol* – and a parody of Singaporean politics based on this – the idea that politicians should be judged on their ability to sing 'the party's tune', to dance the 'old dances', etc.

Changes in the meanings of politics and its presentational styles may be seen as either 'dumbing down' or appropriately translating politics into demotic terms (Street 1997, 2003, 2004; Jones, J.P. 2005, 2007; van Zoonen 2005). I think there is much to be said for the latter perspective since the current organisation of politics seems to alienate many people and, even in mainstream US electoral politics, such popularised presentational forms may actually benefit the political knowledge, either more narrowly or more widely conceived, and the mobilisation of people (Jones, J.P. 2005, 2007).

## Changing mainstream organisations

Mainstream political parties and political candidates have been widely using the Internet since the 1990s and more intensely during the period between 2001 and 2006 (Norris 2001; Foot and Schneider 2006). The levels of use and expansion of use from informational to communicational or interactive features seems to be strongly related both to the wider Internet availability within society, the nature of the political system – especially if it focuses on individual candidates – and any limits built into electoral spending or in electoral regulations. The widest and most dynamic use of the Internet seems to have occurred in the USA from 2003 onwards in individual-candidate-focused, high-spending (especially television spot advertising, cf. Jamieson 1988; Diamond and Bates 1992) elections, in which the use of websites to circulate political messages and create mobilisation is little hampered by electoral regulation (Foot and Schneider 2006). In the UK, where candidate elections are as much political party elections as about individual qualities of candidates, where constituency elections have very tightly controlled limits on overall electoral spending and where electoral rules mean that you cannot use incumbency as a major promotional tool, local use of websites in campaigns seems limited to very marginal seats (where previous election results were decided, in the previous election, by very few votes) (Ward and Gibson 2003). In Russia, likewise, the use of party websites is closely related to the structures of the party system (March 2006: 150). However, these websites could be changed to encourage youth trust in mainstream politics (Calenda and Mosca 2007: 83). Yet this seems unlikely since very few parties or candidates have very much content relevant, or made relevant, to young people (Xenos and Bennett 2007: 65). Such connecting of politicians to young people via web resources is certainly possible if properly funded and moderated (Ferguson 2007: 164). In the UK, national party sites are much more developed than local candidate ones, but still the electoral spend is much lower than in US politics and little or no money is raised via UK party websites. Major UK political parties have used websites to co-ordinate national political activity, engage in continuous campaigning and counter mainstream news stories in relation to the recently emerged 24-hour news cycle (Gibson and Ward 2000;

Painter and Wardle 2001; Gibson, Ward and Nixon 2003). We explore below the Liberal Democrat website as that of the third party in UK national politics (though it runs many local councils and is involved in the governing coalition in the devolved Scottish Parliament, cf. Chapter 4).

---

### The Liberal Democrat party federal website

The Liberal Democrat party is the 'third party' – is neither in government nor is the official opposition party – in the UK's Westminster Parliament (Walter 2003), though it has shared governmental power in the Scottish Parliament. The party has a federal structure granting large areas of autonomy to the various 'national' units of the party – especially Scotland and Wales, thereby recognising the devolutionary policies that have been developed in the UK political system since the late 1990s (Ingle 2008: 140–2; cf. Chapter 4). One consistent party policy is support for elections based on proportional representation – seen as much fairer, a much more adequate way to *represent* people's views and opinions (cf. Chapter 4). The unfairness of the existing first-past-the-post system can be seen most clearly from the results of the 1983 general election. In this election, the party (it was made up then of two parties in an alliance: Liberal and Social Democrat) garnered 26.4 per cent of the vote, compared to Labour's 26.9 per cent, but gained only 13 seats in parliament compared to the 148 of Labour (Kennedy 2001: 112, 117). In the 2005 election, it gained 62 seats in parliament (Ingle 2008: 138). The party stands for liberal values of freedom and the rule of law in both the domestic and international arena and in participative politics (Ingle 2008: 137), and its party emblem is the yellow bird of freedom. On that basis, the Liberal Democrats were the largest UK political party to oppose the UK's involvement in the 'War on Iraq' (cf. Chapter 5). The party also stands for social justice in the contemporary context, which requires public welfare spending to mitigate some inequalities of access to goods and services. Earlier research into Liberal Democrat websites showed they were more likely to use them and their interactive capacities than other political parties (Ward and Gibson 2003) were. Comparison of the national website with those of its main competitors – Labour and Conservatives – shows them much more likely to address, in particular in customised versions of their manifestos – a wide variety of 'audiences': youth, gender, lesbian and gay, and minority ethnic (Liberal Democrats 2009; cf. Kennedy 2001: 117) and also to use a wide variety of social networking web tools: MySpace, Flickr, weblogs, summary weblogs, etc. Three key reasons can be adduced for this. First, that they believe, and the party's activity is embedded, in a more democratic and dialogic conception of democracy and public life than other mainstream UK parties. Second, that they may feel they have more to gain from the use of these tools to connect to people in new ways and, eventually, increase their votes in elections. Third, that use of the new technologies gives the impression of a party that exists in the contemporary fast-changing world and looks 'go ahead' in its approach to that world.

Parties will no doubt use websites to co-ordinate their activities where they believe they have possibilities for political gain from the resources they put into web activities. There exists greater potential for gains in the UK as analysis of the support of young people organising online for Barack Obama's presidential campaign given in Chapter 5 demonstrates, though the political culture and organisation of elections makes a key difference. Party leaders may increasingly used personalised weblogs to create their own 'vehicles for communication' (Negrine 2008: 175). What would be a valuable development for public life is for those resources also to be used to support politics more generally. To a degree, they do so in making political information such as party manifestos, leaders' speeches, and reports and research much more widely available. However, it is primarily 'politicos' (Stoker 2006) who will use such benefits, rather than wider 'audiences'.

## Conclusion

This chapter has argued against the idea that the Internet and it uses in public life merely confirm the status quo in politics, media and society. It has suggested that the Internet is being woven into the activities of contemporary public life and is able to support mainstream media in making it understandable. It also adds new dynamics and encourages change. In spite of the great inequality of access to the Internet, there also exists the slight possibility of creating something resembling national public life but on a global scale – yet there are assuredly tremendous barriers to such an outcome – of wealth, language, interest and the politics of fear, which seems one of the predominant politics of our times.

The features of the Internet are being used to affect media and politics within countries – widening debates, making available access to a wider set of information and even perspectives – thus supporting and extending democratic mediated public life. Such use may build upon the electoral volatility that has arisen in many societies across the world since the 1970s – opening up the spaces for parties or movements to create representation for underrepresented groups by widening representational practice. The Internet *can* provide modes of discussing politics that are more apposite for the everyday language of people in our mediated publics, and therefore encourages participation (Coleman and Blumler 2009; Dahlgren 2009).

Between some nations, the Internet may offer ways of bypassing the dominance of national media and their limits – though those assuredly continue to exist with regard to news programming and the boundaries set by language (Hafez 2007). The wide availability of online forms of offline media gives opportunities for national audiences to draw systematically upon media created elsewhere to bypass limits on media structures in their own land. Klinenberg (2007) instances examples of Americans using British media for information concerning the Iraq War, which was not making it into mainstream US media. However, in addition to online versions of offline media, the net is mostly a space for the distribution of perspectives, and the health of the mainstream media is crucial to the Internet since it still forms the basis of investigation and fact-finding concerning contemporary public life. Some have argued that the health of increasingly commercialised mainstream media is very poor (Davies 2009). The position may be exaggerated but the underlying analysis is that media produced *only* for purposes of profit, without some commitment to public life, may become dominated by propaganda and public relations. Weblogs and related technologies often expand the range of perspectives brought to bear on contemporary issues. They may form the basis of new news services. Blogs may be especially apposite to aid people in times of disaster – such as the 2005 tsunami – when local media are likely to be 'down' and national media do not have access to their useful local 'feeds' (Allan 2006). Yet, at present, they are parasitic on mainstream media not an alternative to that news gathering. However there are increasing signs that they are being used in collaborative efforts to draw on the knowledge and spare time of active audiences in order to create something like a civic journalism. What the future of online self-produced content is no one can predict. It depends upon what we and people like us commit ourselves to as consumers and producers.

We need to recognise that we inhabit an 'open future' – that human society has unpredictable future potentialities, positive and negative – and that many of the activities in which we engage through the Internet – our consumption (in all of its guises), our democratic political organisation, our attempts at self-fulfilment, and so on – will help create that future. We, too, are responsible; we, too, are part of the interdependence of the world.

## Further reading

Allan, S. (2006) *Online News: Journalism and the Internet*. Maidenhead: Open University Press.

Chadwick, A. (2006) *Internet Politics: States, Citizens and New Communication Technologies*. New York and Oxford: Oxford University Press.

Halavais, A. (2009) *Search Engine Society*. Cambridge: Polity.

Loader, B.D. (ed.) (2007) *Young Citizens in the Digital Age: Political Engagement, Young People and New Media*. London and New York: Routledge.

Mathiason, J. (2009) *Internet Governance: The New Frontier of Global Institutions*. London and New York: Routledge.

Slevin, J. (2000) *The Internet and Society*. Cambridge: Polity.

# Conclusion

We inhabit a 'complex democracy' (Baker 2007) and a complex mediated public life. This complexity, however, is often confused with the end, altogether, of democratic politics and public life. Part of the challenge, then, is to avoid overly simplistic formulae about contemporary change. Politics is extensively mediated in contemporary society: through press, radio, television and news media. Politics is also mediated – structured and made – through specific political institutions. Difficulties with contemporary mediated politics arise in both areas. How the media cover politics creates or distributes public awareness and dominant frames for discussion. How party systems work and the way parliaments are organised structure outcomes, public involvement and understanding.

Contemporary societies are also caught up in other changes such as the regionalisation of media and economy, transnational and diasporic reworking of identities and culture and the supra-nationalisation and internationalisation of politics. Each change has implications for politics in national settings. Media regionalisation has affected the level of media provision that serves the national political community; transnational and diasporic reworking of identities creates challenges to myths of national belonging; the supranational supplementation of politics has contributed both to cross-border co-operation and to democratic deficits. Societies are more complex organisationally and culturally – the latter in relation to societies transformed by migration in the last half-century, and have increasingly had to respond creatively to that recognised fact in the last quarter of a century. Societies have also become more organisationally complex as public services have become more extensive and have been managed through the creation of hundreds of autonomous public bodies. Many escape democratic accountability. This has contributed to the creation of a complex democracy in contemporary societies, which leads to exacting demands for publics and media to fulfil their democratic roles in testing circumstances.

Each of these contexts of change also has to be negotiated by politicians and parties since they need to access audiences, citizens and potential voters. Parties have been changing to facilitate clear communication with uncommitted electorates. Politics is increasingly focused on political leaders who can expressively engage audiences. These changes, however, might also give leaders greater power to dominate political executives and international political gatherings. Further, leaders seem sometimes simply too narrow political entities on which to base much of the trust we have in contemporary public life, yet the leader who tries to represents 'us' is a major aspect of the functioning representative politics that we have. The competing 'leadership' of musicians and figures from our broader culture might positively benefit us in creating supplementary representation outside the mainstream political system and also validate a broad range of more active roles for citizens and the public.

Mainstream media provide us with vibrant mixes of information and debate, much of which relates to the central role of public policy and political debates and decisions. Yet it often does not seem to provide us with the full coverage of local or international structures of governance, which we increasingly require. It might also be falling short in providing us with information significantly grounded in investigation, and that might leave us open, from time to time, to (undeclared) government propaganda and manipulation by public relations practitioners. Mainstream media do, however, seem to be exploring a range of demotic content, which encourages our participation in many of the important contemporary mediated debates. Audiences, too, seem up to the challenge to take media content and convert it into a broad understanding of key issues in public life. Young people in particular, often claimed to be apathetic, seem potentially available for significant engagement with mainstream politics let alone broader affairs within public life.

The use of and access to the Internet allow access on the part of large proportions of contemporary dwellers in rich countries to a range of perspectives and information supportive of public life, and offer sophisticated tools for political engagement and mobilisation. Since mainstream media have moved online, they provide journalistic underpinnings for the broader 'culture of commentary', which, predominantly, the net supports. The net, of course, also offers space for self-created content. The use of the net in politics and public life appears to have expanded the mainstream: in the exploration of a wider range of ideas; the use of demotic approaches to public life discussion; and the experimentation by mainstream political institutions in order to connect to broad audiences. Without those journalistic underpinnings, however, the net would have a less impressive shared informational background. If mainstream media should become less reliable, as some suggest it already has begun to be, then mediated public life might be less understandable and a less coherent sense of it be able to be created.

A greater commitment to public uses of media may need to be developed

# References

Abbate, J. (1999) *Inventing the Internet*. Cambridge, MA and London: MIT Press.

Abercrombie, N. and Longhurst, B. (1998) *Audiences: A Sociological Theory of Performance and Imagination*. London: Sage.

Abercrombie, N. and Longhurst, B. (2007) *The Penguin Dictionary of Media Studies*. London: Penguin.

Albrecht, S. (2006) Whose voice is heard in online deliberation? A study of participation and representation in political debates on the Internet. *Information, Communication & Society* 9, 1: 62–82.

Albrow, M. (1996) *The Global Age*. Cambridge: Polity.

Albrow, M. and Washbourne, N. (1997) Sociology for postmodern organizers – working the 'net', pp. 135–51 in *Do Organisations have Feelings?*, by Martin Albrow. London: Routledge.

Alia, V. (2004) *Media Ethics and Social Change*. Edinburgh: Edinburgh University Press.

Allan, M. (ed.) (2007) *Reading CSI: Crime TV Under the Microscope*. London and New York: I.B. Tauris.

Allan, S. (1999) *News Culture*. Buckingham: Open University Press.

Allan, S. (2004) *News Culture* (2nd edn). Maidenhead: Open University Press.

Allan, S. (2006) *Online News: Journalism and the Internet*. Maidenhead: Open University Press.

Anderson, B. (1991) *Imagined Communities: Reflections on the Origin and Spread of Nationalism* (rev. edn). London and New York: Verso.

Anderson, P.J. and Weymouth, A. (1999) *Insulting the Public? The British Press and the European Union*. London and New York: Longman.

Ang, I. (1985) *Watching Dallas: Soap Opera and the Melodramatic Imagination*. London: Routledge.

Ang, I. (1991) *Desperately Seeking the Audience*. London and New York: Routledge.

Ang, I. (1996) *Living Room Wars: Rethinking Media Audiences for a Postmodern World*. London: Routledge.

Arsenault, A. and Castells, M. (2006) Conquering the minds, conquering Iraq: the social production of misinformation in the United States – a case study. *Information, Communication & Society* 9, 3: 283–307.

Atton, C. (2002) *Alternative Media*. London: Sage.

Atton, C. (2004) *An Alternative Internet: Radical Media, Politics and Creativity*. Edinburgh: Edinburgh University Press.

Atton, C. and Hamilton, J.F. (2008) *Alternative Journalism*. London and Los Angeles: Sage.

Bach, J. and Stark, D. (2004) Link, search, interact: the co-evolution of NGOs and interactive technology. *Theory, Culture & Society* 23, 3: 101–17.

Baker, C.E. (2007) *Media Concentration and Democracy: Why Ownership Matters*. Cambridge: Cambridge University Press.

Barkin, S.M. (2003) *American Television News: The Media Marketplace and the Public Interest*. Armonk, NY and London: M.E. Sharp.

Barnett, S. and Gabor, I. (2001) *Westminster Tales: The Twenty-first Century Crisis in Political Journalism*. London: Continuum.

Bauman, Z. (1999) *In Search of Politics*. Cambridge: Polity.

Beck, U. (1992) *Risk Society*. London: Sage.

Beetham, D. (2005) *Democracy: A Beginner's Guide*. Oxford: Oneworld.

Bell, D. (1999 [1973]) *The Coming of Post-industrial Society*. New York: Basic Books.

Bennett, W.L. (2005) *News: The Politics of Illusion* (6th edn). New York: Pearson Longman.

Bentley, C., Hamman, B., Littau, J., Meyer, H., Watson, B. and Welsh, B. (2007) Citizen journalism: a case study, pp. 239–60 in *Blogging, Citizenship and the Future of Media*, edited by M. Tremayne. New York and London: Routledge.

Bernt, J. and Greenwald, M. (2000) Enterprise and investigative reporting in metropolitan newspapers: 1980 and 1995 compared, pp. 51–79 in *The Big Chill: Investigative Reporting in the Current Media Environment*. Ames: Iowa State University Press.

Berry, D.M. (2008) *Copy, Rip, Burn: The Politics of Copyleft and Open Source*. London: Pluto.

Bhabha, H.K. (ed.) (1989) *Nation and Narration*. London: Routledge.

Billig, M. (1995) *Banal Nationalism*. London: Sage.

Birch, A.H. (1964) *Representative and Responsible Government*. London: George Allen & Unwin.

Blumler, J.G. and Gurevitch, M. (1995) *The Crisis of Public Communication*. London and New York: Routledge.

Boggs, C. (2000) *The End of Politics: Corporate Power and the Decline of the Public Sphere*. New York and London: The Guilford Press.

Bokhorst-Heng, W. (2002) Newspapers in Singapore: a mass ceremony in the imagining of the nation. *Media, Culture & Society* 24: 559–69.

Born, G. (2005) *Uncertain Vision: Birt, Dyke and the Reinvention of the BBC*. London: Vintage.

Brachman, J.M. (2006) High-tech terror: Al-Qaeda's use of new technology. *Fletcher Forum of World Affairs* 30, 2: 149–64.

Brandenburg, H. (2006) Pathologies of the virtual public sphere, pp. 207–22 in *The Internet and Politics: Citizens, Voters and Activists*, edited by S. Oates, D. Owen and R.K. Gibson. London and New York: Routledge.

Brooke, H. (2005) *Your Right to Know: How to use the Freedom of Information Act and Other Access Laws*. London: Pluto.

Brooker, W. and Jermyn, D. (eds) (2003) *The Audience Studies Reader*. London and New York: Routledge.

Brooks, L. (2003) Kid power: war broke out in Iraq and back in the UK something unexpected happened – thousands of children, previously thought to have no interest in politics came out on the street to protest. *Guardian*, 26 April: 40.

Brown, L.D. and Jacobs, L.J. (2008) *The Private Abuse of the Public Interest: Market Myths and Policy Muddles*. Chicago and London: University of Chicago Press.

Brown, W.J. (1945) *Everybody's Guide to Politics*. London: George Allan & Unwin Ltd.

Buckingham, D. (2000) *The Making of Citizens: Young People, News and Politics*. London and New York: Routledge.

Buckingham, D. (2005) *Media Literacy of Children and Young People: A Review of the Research Literature*. London: Ofcom.

Buckler, S. and Dolowitz, D. (2005) *Politics on the Internet: A Student Guide*. London and New York: Routledge.

Bunt, G. (2000) *Virtually Islamic: Computer-mediated Communication and Cyber Islamic Environments*. Cardiff: University of Wales Press.

Bunt, G. (2009) *iMuslims: Rewiring the House of Islam*. New York: Hurst.

Burn, A. and Parker, D. (2003) *Analysing Media Texts*. London and New York: Continuum.

Burnett, R. and Marshall, P.D. (2003) *Web Theory: An Introduction*. London and New York: Routledge.

Calcutt, A. (1999) *White Noise: An A–Z of the Contradictions of Cyberculture*. Basingstoke: Macmillan.

Calenda, D. and Mosca, L. (2007) Youth online: researching the political use of the Internet in the Italian context, pp. 82–96 in *Young Citizens in the Digital Age: Political Engagement, Young People and New Media*, edited by B.D. Loader. London and New York: Routledge.

Calhoun, C. (ed.) (1994) *Habermas and the Public Sphere*. Cambridge, MA and London: The MIT Press.

Caramani, D. (ed.) (2008) *Comparative Politics*. Oxford: Oxford University Press.

Castells, M. (1998–2004) *The Information Age* (2nd edn), Vols 1–3. Oxford: Blackwell.

Castells, M. (2001) *The Internet Galaxy*. Oxford: Blackwell.

Castells, M. (2009) *Communication Power*. Oxford: Oxford University Press.

Celis, K., Childs, S., Kantola, J. and Krook, M.L. (2008) Rethinking women's substantive representation. *Representation* 44, 2: 99–110.

Chadwick, A. (2006) *Internet Politics: States, Citizens and New Communication Technologies*. New York and Oxford: Oxford University Press.

Chaffey, D., Ellis-Chadwick, F., Mayer, R. and Johnston, K. (2009) *Internet Marketing: Strategy, Implementation and Practice* (4th edn), edited by D. Chaffey. Harlow: Prentice Hall/Financial Times.

Chand, V.K. (2001) *Legislating Freedom of Information: India in Comparative Perspective*. New Delhi: Commonwealth Human Rights Initiative.

Chang, J. and Halliday, J. (2007) *Mao: The Unknown Story*. London: Vintage.

Chapman, J. (2005) *Comparative Media History*. Cambridge: Polity.

Chester, J. (2007) *Digital Destiny: New Media and the Future of Democracy*. New York: The New Press.

Cheta, R. (2004) Dis@bled people, ICTs and a new age of activism: a Portuguese accessibility special interest group study, pp. 207–32 in *Cyberprotest: New Media, Citizens and Social Movements*, edited by W. Van de Donk, B.D. Loader, P. Nixon and D. Rucht. London and New York: Routledge.

Christiansen, T. (2005) European integration and regional cooperation, pp. 579–98 in *The Globalization of World Politics: An Introduction to International Relations* (3rd edn), edited by J. Baylis and S. Smith. Oxford: Oxford University Press.

Citizenship Foundation (2004) BBC dumps youth-focussed politics programmes, available at www.citizenshipfoundation.org.uk/main/news.php?n119 (accessed 29 October 2005).

Clayman, S. and Heritage, J. (2002) *The News Interview: Journalists and Public Figures on the Air*. Cambridge: Cambridge University Press.

Coates, T. (ed.) (2004) *The Hutton Inquiry*. London and New York: Tim Coates.

Cockerell, M. (1989) *Live from Number 10: The Inside Story of Prime Ministers and Television*. London and Boston: Faber & Faber.

Cohen, R. and Rai, S.M. (eds) (2000) *Global Social Movements*. London: Albury Press.

Coleman, S. (2007) How democracies have disengaged from young people, pp. 166–85 in *Young Citizens in the Digital Age: Political Engagement, Young People and New Media*, edited by B.D. Loader. London and New York: Routledge.

Coleman, S. and Blumler, J.G. (2009) *The Internet and Democratic Citizenship: Theory, Practice and Policy*. Cambridge: Cambridge University Press.

Collins, R. (2006) Internet governance in the UK. *Media, Culture & Society* 28, 3: 337–54.

Collins, T. and Kennedy, T. (2003) Demo pupils face charges. *Birmingham Evening Mail*, 21 November: 12.

Conboy, M. (2002) *The Press and Popular Culture*. London: Sage.

Conboy, M. (2006) *Tabloid Britain: Constructing a Community through Language*. London and New York: Routledge.

Conservatives (2008) Trust in politics: a programme for restoring public respect for the political system, available at www.conservatives.com/~/media/files/Down loadable%20Files/Trust%20in%20Politics.ashx?dl=true (accessed 2 January 2009).

Conway, M. (2006) Cybercortical warfare: Hizbollah's Internet strategy, pp. 100–17 in *The Internet and Politics: Citizens, Voters and Activists*, edited by S. Oates, D. Owen and R.K. Gibson. London and New York: Routledge.

Corner, J. (1999) *Critical Ideas in Television Studies*. Oxford: Clarendon Press.

Corner, J. (2003) Mediated persona and political culture, pp. 67–84 in *Media and the Restylisation of Politics*, edited by J. Corner and D. Pels. London: Sage.

Corner, J. and Pels, D. (2003) *Media and the Restylisation of Politics*. London: Sage.

Cotrim-Macieria, J. (2005) Change to win? The Brazilian Worker's Party 2002 general election marketing strategy, pp. 148–64 in *Political Marketing: A Comparative Perspective*, edited by D.G. Lilleker and J. Lees-Marshment. Manchester and New York: Manchester University Press.

Couldry, N. (2000) *Inside Culture: Re-imagining the Methods of Cultural Studies*. London: Sage.

Couldry, N. (2005) The extended audience: scanning the horizon, pp. 185–219 in *Audiences*, edited by M. Gillespie. Maidenhead: Open University Press.

Craig, D.B. (2000) *Fireside Politics: Radio and Political Culture in the United States 1920–40*. Baltimore and London: Johns Hopkins University Press.

Craig, G. (2004) *The Media, Politics and Public Life*. Crows Nest: Allen & Unwin.

Crick, B. (2003) *Democracy*. Oxford: Oxford University Press.

Crossley, N. and Roberts, J.M. (eds) (2004) *After Habermas: New Perspectives on the Public Sphere*. Oxford: Blackwell.

Cullingford, C. (1992) *Children and Society: Children's Attitudes to Politics and Power*. London: Cassell.

Cunningham, S. and Lavalette, M. (2004) 'Active citizens' or 'irresponsible truants'? School strikes against the war. *Critical Social Policy* 24, 2: 255–69.

Cushion, S. (2009) 'The truants take to the streets': young people, politics and citizenship in the UK. Published in Portuguese *Media and Jornalismo*, 11. Coimbra: Minerva Coimbra (English version supplied by the author).

Cushion, S. (forthcoming) Discouraging citizenship? Young people's reactions to news media coverage of anti-Iraq War protesting in the UK. *Nordic Journal of Youth Research*.

Dahl, R.A. (1989) *Democracy and its Critics*. New Haven and London: Yale University Press.

Dahl, R.A. (1998) *Democracy*. New Haven and London: Yale University Press.

Dahlgren, P. (2009) *Media and Political Engagement: Citizens, Communication and Democracy*. Cambridge: Cambridge University Press.

Dahlgren, P. and Olsson, T (2007) Young activists, political horizons and the Internet: adapting the net to one's purposes, pp. 68–81 in *Young Citizens in the Digital Age: Political Engagement, Young People and New Media*, edited by B.D. Loader. London and New York: Routledge.

Dale, I. (2001) *Directory of Political Websites*. London: Politico's.

Davies, N. (2009) *Flat Earth News: An Award-winning Reporter Exposes Falsehood, Distortion and Propaganda in the Global Media*. London: Vintage Books.

Davis, R. (1999) *The Web of Politics: The Internet's Impact on the American Political System*. New York and Oxford: Oxford University Press.

Delanty, G. (2000) *Citizenship in the Global Age*. London: Sage.

Della Porta, D. and Diani, D. (2000) *Social Movements: An Introduction.* Oxford: Blackwell.

Denver, D. (2003) *Elections and Politics in Britain.* Basingstoke: Palgrave Macmillan.

De Sousa Santos, B. (2006) *The Rise of the Global Left: The World Social Forum and Beyond.* London and New York: Zed.

Deuze, M. (2006) Participation, remediation, bricolage: considering principal components of a digital culture. *The Information Society* 22: 63–75.

De Wijs, S. (2008) *Presidentialization of a Parliamentary Democracy.* Berlin: VDM Verlag.

Diamond, E. and Bates, S. (1992) *The Spot: The Rise of Political Advertising on Television* (3rd edn). Cambridge, MA and London: MIT Press.

Doherty, B. (2006) Friends of the Earth International: negotiating a transnational identity. *Environmental Politics* 15, 5: 860–80.

Douglas, S.B. (1994) *Where the Girls Are: Growing up Female with the Mass Media.* London: Penguin.

Douglas, S.B. (2004) *Listening In: Radio and the American Imagination.* Minneapolis and London: University of Minnesota Press.

Dow, B.J. (1996) *Prime-time Feminism: Television, Media Culture, and the Women's Movement since 1970.* Philadelphia: University of Pennsylvania Press.

Doyle, G. (2002) *Understanding Media Economics.* London: Sage.

Drahos, P. and Braithwaite, J. (2002) *Information Feudalism: Who owns the Knowledge Economy?* London: Earthscan.

Drobny, S. (2004) *The Road to Air America: Breaking the Right-wing Stranglehold on our Nation's Airwaves.* New York: SelectBooks.

Dryzek, J.S. (1997) *The Politics of the Earth: Environmental Discourses.* Oxford: Oxford University Press.

Engelmann, R. (1996) *Public Radio and Television in America: A Political History.* Thousand Oaks, CA and London: Sage.

Ericson, R.V., Baranek, P.M. and Chan, J.B.L. (1987) *Visualizing Deviance: A Study of News Organization.* Milton Keynes: Open University Press.

Esser, F. and Pfetsch, B. (eds) (2004) *Comparing Political Communication: Theories, Cases and Challenges.* Cambridge: Cambridge University Press.

Evans, L. (2008) Barack Obama is rocking the youth vote, available at searchenginewatch.com/3629136 (accessed 4 December 2008).

Fabbrini, S. (2005) The semi-sovereign American Prince: the dilemma of an independent president in a presidential government pp. 313–35 in *The Presidentialization of Politics: A Comparative Study of Modern Democracies*, edited by T. Poguntke and P. Webb. Oxford and New York: Oxford University Press.

Feintuck, M. and Varney, M. (2006) *Media Regulation, Public Interest and the Law* (2nd edn). Edinburgh: Edinburgh University Press.

Ferguson, R. (2007) Chattering classes: the moderation of deliberative forums in citizenship education, pp. 158–65 in *Young Citizens in the Digital Age: Political*

*Engagement, Young People and New Media*, edited by B.D. Loader. London and New York: Routledge.

Flavian, C. and Gurrea, R. (2006) The choice of digital newspapers: influence of reader goals and user experience. *Internet Research* 16, 3: 231–47.

Flew, T. (2004) A medium for mateship: commercial talk radio in Australia, pp. 229–46 in *More than a Music Box: Radio Cultures and Communities in a Multi-media World*, edited by A. Crissell. New York and Oxford: Bergahn Books.

Foley, M. (2001) *The British Presidency: Tony Blair and the Politics of Public Leadership*. Manchester: Manchester University Press.

Foley, M. (2008) The presidential dynamics of leadership decline in contemporary British politics: the illustrative case of Tony Blair. *Contemporary Politics* 14, 1: 53–69.

Foot, K.A. and Schneider, S.M. (2006) *Web Campaigning*. Cambridge, MA and London: The MIT Press.

Fortier, A.-M. (2005) Diaspora, pp. 182–7 in *Cultural Geography: A Critical Dictionary of Key Concepts*, edited by D. Atkinson, P. Jackson, D. Sibley and N. Washbourne. London: I.B. Tauris.

Frady, M. (2006) *Martin Luther King, Jr: A Life*. New York: Lipper Penguin.

Franklin, B. (2004) *Packaging Politics: Political Communications in Britain's Media Democracy* (2nd edn). London: Arnold.

Franklin, B., Hamer, M., Hanna, M., Kinsey, M. and Richardson, J.E. (2005) *Key Concepts in Journalism Studies*. London: Sage.

Fraser, N. (1994) Rethinking the public sphere: a contribution to the critique of actually existing democracy, pp. 109–42 in *Habermas and the Public Sphere*, edited by C. Calhoun. Cambridge, MA and London: The MIT Press.

Freedman, D. (2006) Internet transformations: 'old' media resilience in the 'new media' revolution, pp. 275–90 in *Media and Cultural Theory*, edited by J. Curran and D. Morley. London: Routledge.

Freedman, D. (2008) *The Politics of Media Policy*. Cambridge: Polity.

Friedman, S. (2007) *Dilemmas of Representation: Local Politics, National Factors and the Home Styles of Modern US Congress Members*. Albany: State University of New York Press.

Friedman, T.L. (2006) *The World is Flat: The Globalized World in the Twenty-first Century*. London: Penguin.

Friel, H. and Falk, R. (2004) *The Record of the Paper: How the New York Times Misreports US Foreign Policy*. London and New York: Verso.

Friends of the Earth International (2009) Friends of the Earth International blog, available at www.foei.org/en/blog (accessed 15 January 2009).

Frith, S. (2000) Entertainment, pp. 201–17 in *Mass Media and Society* (3rd edn), edited by J. Curran and M. Gurevitch. London: Arnold.

Galindo, P.P. (2005) The re-launch of the Popular Revolutionary American Alliance: the use of political marketing in Peru's new political era, pp. 165–80 in *Political*

*Marketing: A Comparative Perspective*, edited by D.G. Lilleker and J. Lees-Marshment. Manchester and New York: Manchester University Press.

Gamble, A. (2000) *Politics and Fate*. Cambridge: Polity.

Gamson, J. (1999) *Freaks Talk Back: Tabloid Talk Shows and Sexual Nonconformity*. Chicago and London: Chicago University Press.

Gamson, W.A. (1995) *Talking Politics*. Cambridge: Cambridge University Press.

Gans, H.J. (2003) *Democracy and the News*. Oxford and New York: Oxford University Press.

Gardner, J.F. (1974) *Leadership and the Cult of Personality*. London: Everyman.

Garfield, S. (1998) *The Nation's Favourite*. London: Faber & Faber.

Garnham, N. (1994) The media and public sphere, pp. 359–76 in *Habermas and the Public Sphere*, edited by C. Calhoun. Cambridge, MA and London: The MIT Press.

George, C. (2005) The Internet's political impact and the penetration/participation paradox in Malaysia and Singapore. *Media, Culture & Society* 27, 6: 903–20.

Gerodimus, R. and George, J. (2007) Rethinking online youth civic engagement: reflections on web content analysis, pp. 114–26 in *Young Citizens in the Digital Age: Political Engagement, Young People and New Media*, edited by B.D. Loader. London and New York: Routledge.

Get out the Vote (2008) GetouttheVote.org: a voter empowerment and information source, available at www.getoutthevote.org/ (accessed 4 December 2008).

Gibson, R. and Ward, S. (eds) (2000) *Reinvigorating Democracy: British Politics and the Internet*. Aldershot: Ashgate.

Gibson, R., Ward, S.J. and Nixon, P. (2003) *Net Gain? Political Parties and the Impact of the New Information Communication Technologies*. New York and London: Routledge.

Gibson, R., Lusoli, W. and Ward, S. (2005) Online participation in the UK: testing a 'contextualised' model of Internet effects. *British Journal of Politics and International Relations* 7, 4: 561–83.

Giddens, A. (1990) *The Consequences of Modernity*. Cambridge: Polity.

Giddens, A. (2007) *Over to You, Mr. Brown*. Cambridge: Polity.

Gill, R. (2007) *Gender and the Media*. Cambridge: Polity.

Gillespie, M. (1996) *Television, Ethnicity and Cultural Change*. London: Routledge.

Gillespie, M. (ed.) (2005) *Audiences*. Maidenhead: Open University Press.

Gilroy, P. (1987) *There Ain't No Black in the Union Jack*. London: Unwin Hyman.

Ginsborg, P. (2008) *Democracy: Crisis and Renewal*. London: Profile Books.

Goldsmith, J. and Wu, T. (2006) *Who Controls the Internet? Illusions of a Borderless World*. Oxford: Oxford University Press.

Goode, L. (2005) *Jurgen Habermas: Democracy and the Public Sphere*. London and Ann Arbor: Pluto Press.

Graber, D.A. (2001) *Processing Politics: Learning from Television in the Internet Age*. Chicago and London: University of Chicago Press.

Graber, D.A. (2004) Mediated politics and citizenship in the twenty-first century. *Annual Review of Psychology* 55: 545–71.

Graber, D.A. (2006) *Mass Media and American Politics*. Washington, DC: CQ Press.

Greenberg, B.S. and Parker, E.B. (1965) *The Kennedy Assassination and the American Public: Social Communication in Crisis*. Stanford: Stanford University Press.

Greenstein, F.I. (1965) *Children and Politics*. New Haven and London: Yale University Press.

Guibernau, M. (1999) *Nations without States: Political Communities in a Global Age*. Cambridge: Polity.

Guo, B., Bricout, J.C. and Huang, J. (2005) A common open space or a digital divide? A social model perspective on the online disability community in China. *Disability & Society* 20, 1: 49–66.

Gurevitch, M. and Scannell, P. (2003) 'Canonization achieved? Stuart Hall's 'Encoding/Decoding', pp. 231–47 in *Canonic Texts in Media Research*, edited by E. Katz, J.D. Peters, T. Liebes and A. Orloff. Cambridge: Polity.

Gutstein, D. (1999) *e.con: How the Internet Undermines Democracy*. Toronto: Stoddart.

Habermas, J. (1989 [1962]) *The Structural Transformation of the Public Sphere: An Inquiry into a Category of Bourgeois Society*. Cambridge: Polity.

Haddon, L. (2006) The contribution of domestication research to in-home computing and media consumption. *The Information Society* 22: 195–203.

Hafez, K. (2007) *The Myth of Media Globalization*. Cambridge: Polity.

Halavais, A. (2009) *Search Engine Society*. Cambridge: Polity.

Hall, J. (2008) Online editions: newspapers and the 'new' news, pp. 215–23 in *Pulling Newspapers Apart: Analysing Print Journalism*, edited by B. Franklin. London and New York: Routledge.

Hall, S. (1980) Encoding/decoding, pp. 128–38 in *Culture, Media, Language: Working Papers in Cultural Studies 1972–1979*. London: Hutchison.

Hallin, D.C. and Mancini, P. (2004) *Comparing Media Systems: Three Models of Media and Politics*. Cambridge: Cambridge University Press.

Hannerz, U. (1992) *Cultural Complexity: Studies in the Social Organisation of Meaning*. New York: Columbia University Press.

Hannerz, U. (1996) *Transnational Connections*. London: Routledge.

Hansen, D.W. (2003) *The Dream: Martin Luther King, Jr, and the Speech that Inspired a Nation*, New York: ECCO.

Haynes, J. (2005) *Comparative Politics in a Globalizing World*. Cambridge: Polity.

Heffernan, R. and Webb, P. (2005) The British Prime Minister: much more than 'first among equals', pp. 26–62 in *The Presidentialization of Politics: A Comparative Study of Modern Democracies*, edited by T. Poguntke and P. Webb. Oxford and New York: Oxford University Press.

Held, D. and McGrew, A. (eds) (2002) *Governing Globalization: Power, Authority and Global Governance*. Cambridge: Polity.

Held, D. and McGrew, A. (2007) *Globalization/Anti-globalization: Beyond the Great Divide* (2nd edn). Cambridge: Polity.

Henderson, L. (2007) *Social Issues in Television Fiction*. Edinburgh: Edinburgh University Press.

Henn, M., Weinstein, M. and Forrest, S. (2005) Uninterested youth? Young people's attitudes towards party politics in Britain. *Political Studies* 53: 556–78.

Hetherington, M.J. (2005) *Why Trust Matters: Declining Political Trust and the Demise of American Liberalism*. Princeton, NJ: Princeton University Press.

Higgins, M. (2006) Substantiating a political public sphere in the Scottish press: a comparative analysis. *Journalism: Practice, Theory and Criticism* 7, 1: 25–44.

Higgins, M. (2008) *Media and their Publics*. Maidenhead: Open University Press.

Hill, S. (2002) *Fixing Elections: The Failure of America's Winner Take All Politics*. New York and London: Routledge.

Hix, S. (2008) The EU as a political system, pp. 573–601 in *Comparative Politics*, edited by D. Caramani. Oxford: Oxford University Press.

Holland, P. (2006) *The Angry Buzz: This Week and Current Affairs Television*. London and New York: I.B. Tauris.

Huggins, R. (2001) The transformation of the political audience, pp. 127–50 in *New Media and Politics*, edited by B. Axford and R. Huggins. London: Sage.

Humphrys, J. (2005) First do no harm, pp. 265–74 in *Television Policy: The MacTaggart Lectures*. Edinburgh: Edinburgh University Press.

Huntingdon, S. (2005) *Who Are We? America's Great Debate*. London: The Free Press.

Ingle, S. (2008) *The British Party System: An Introduction* (4th edn). London and New York: Routledge.

Iyengar, S. and McGrady, J.A. (2007) *Media Politics: A Citizen's Guide*. New York and London: W.W. Norton & Co.

Jamieson, K.H. (1988) *Packaging the Presidency: A History and Criticism of Presidential Campaign Advertising*. Oxford and New York: Oxford University Press.

Jamieson, K.H. (2000) *Everything you Think you Know about Politics: And Why you're Wrong*. New York: Basic Books.

Jamieson, K.H. and Campbell, K.K. (2006) *The Interplay of Influence: News, Advertising, Politics and the Internet* (6th edn). Belmont, CA: Thomson Wadsworth.

Jensen, J. (1990) *Redeeming Modernity: Contradictions in Media Criticism*. Newbury Park: Sage.

Johnson-Cartee, K.S. (2005) *New Narratives and News Framing: Constructing Political Reality*. Lanham: Rowman & Littlefield.

Jones, C.O. (2007) *The American Presidency: A Very Short Introduction*. Oxford: Oxford University Press.

Jones, J.P. (2005) *Entertaining Politics: New Political Television and Civic Culture*. Lanham: Rowman & Littlefield.

Jones, J.P. (2007) 'Fake' news versus 'Real' news as sources of political information: *The Daily Show* and postmodern political reality, pp. 129–50 in *Politicotainment: Television's Take on the Real*, edited by K. Riegert. New York: Peter Lang.

Jones, S. (2000) The bias of the web, pp.171–82 in *World Wide Web and Contemporary Cultural Theory*, edited by A. Herman and T. Swiss. New York and London: Routledge.

Judge, D. (1999) *Representation: Theory and Practice in Britain*. London and New York: Routledge.

Judge, D. (2005) *Political Institutions in the United Kingdom*. Oxford: Oxford University Press.

Judge, D. and Earnshaw, D. (2008) *The European Parliament* (2nd edn). Basingstoke: Palgrave Macmillan.

Kaid, L.L. and Postelnicu, M. (2007) Credibility of political messages on the Internet: a comparison of blog sources, pp. 149–64 in *Blogging, Citizenship and the Future of Media*, edited by M. Tremayne. New York and London: Routledge.

Karpf, A. (2006) *The Human Voice*. London: Bloomsbury.

Kasbekar, A. (2006) *Pop Culture India! Media, Arts, and Lifestyle*. Santa Barbara, CA and Oxford: ABC CLIO.

Katz, R. (2007) *Political Institutions in the United States*. Oxford and New York: Oxford University Press.

Katz, R. (2008) Political parties, pp. 293–317 in *Comparative Politics*, edited by D. Caramani. Oxford: Oxford University Press.

Keeter, S., Horowitz, J. and Tyson, A. (2008) Young voters in the 2008 election, available at www.pewresearch.org/pubs/1031/young-voters-in-the-2008-election (accessed 4 December 2008).

Kelly, M., Mazzoleni, G. and McQuail, D. (eds) (2004) *The Media in Europe: The Euromedia Handbook*. London: Sage.

Kennedy, C. (2001) *The Future of Politics*. London: HarperCollins Publishers.

Kennedy, P. (2007) *The Parliament of Man: The United Nations and the Quest for World Government*. Penguin: London.

Kersbergen, K. and Manow, P. (eds) (2008) *Religion, Class Coalitions and Welfare State Regimes*. New York: Cambridge University Press.

Kilborn, R. and Izod, J. (1997) *An Introduction to Television Documentary: Confronting Reality*. Manchester and New York: Manchester University Press.

Kitty, A. (2005) *Outfoxed: Rupert Murdoch's War on Journalism*. New York: Disinformation.

Klein, N. (2000) *No Logo: Taking Aim at the Brand Bullies*. London: Flamingo.

Klinenberg, E. (2007) *Fighting for Air: The Battle to Control America's Media*. New York: Metropolitan Books.

Knuckey, J. and Lees-Marshment, J. (2005) American political marketing: George W. Bush and the Republican Party, pp. 39–58 in *Political Marketing: A Comparative Perspective*, edited by D.G. Lilleker and J. Lees-Marshment. Manchester and New York: Manchester University Press.

Kohli, V. (2003) *The Indian Media Business*. New Delhi: Response Books.

Kohli-Khandekar, V. (2006) *The Indian Media Business* (2nd edn). New Delhi: Response Books.

Kumar, R. and Best, M.L. (2006) Impact and sustainability of e-government services in developing countries: lessons learned from Tamil Nadu, India. *The Information Society* 22: 1–12.

Kundra, S. (2005) *Media Laws and the Indian Constitution*. New Delhi: Anmol Publications.

Lacey, C. and Longman, D. (1997) *The Press as Public Educator: Cultures of Understanding, Cultures of Ignorance*. Luton: University of Luton Press.

Ladd, E.C. (1999) *The Ladd Report: Startling New Research Shows How an Explosion of Voluntary Groups, Activities, and Charitable Donations is Transforming Our Towns and Cities*. New York: Free Press.

Lakoff, G. (2004) *Don't Think of an Elephant! Know your Values and Frame the Debate*. White River Junction, VT: Chelsea Green Publishing.

Lally, E. (2002) *At Home with Computers*. London: Berg.

Laufer, P. (1995) *Inside Talk Radio: America's Voice or Just Hot Air?* New York: Birch Lane Press.

Laughey, D. (2006) *Youth Culture and Popular Music*. Edinburgh: Edinburgh University Press.

Laughey, D. (2007) *Key Themes in Media Theory*. Maidenhead: Open University Press.

Law, A. (2001) Near and far: banal national identity and the press in Scotland. *Media, Culture & Society* 23: 299–317.

Lazarsfeld, P.F. and Field, H. (1946) *The People Look at Radio*. Chapel Hill: University of North Carolina Press.

Leadbeater, C. (2009) *We-Think: Mass Innovation, Not Mass Production*. London: Profile Books.

Lechner, F.J. and Boli, J. (eds) (2008) *The Globalization Reader* (3rd edn). Oxford: Blackwell.

Ledbetter, J. (1997) *Made Possible By . . .: The Death of Public Broadcasting in the United States*. London: Verso.

Lederer, A., Plasser, F. and Scheucher, C. (2005) The rise and fall of populism in Austria: a political marketing perspective, pp. 132–46 in *Political Marketing: A Comparative Perspective*, edited by D.G. Lilleker and J. Lees-Marshment. Manchester and New York: Manchester University Press.

Lees, C. (2005) Political marketing in Germany: the case of the Social Democratic Party, pp. 114–31 in *Political Marketing: A Comparative Perspective*, edited by D.G. Lilleker and J. Lees-Marshment. Manchester and New York: Manchester University Press.

Lees-Marshment, J. (2001) *Political Marketing and British Political Parties*. Manchester and New York: Manchester University Press.

Lees-Marshment, J. (2004) *The Political Marketing Revolution: Transforming the Government of the UK*. Manchester and New York: Manchester University Press.

Lees-Marshment, J. (2008) *Political Marketing and British Political Parties* (2nd edn). Manchester and New York: Manchester University Press.

Lees-Marshment, J. (2009) *Political Marketing: Principles and Applications*. London and New York: Routledge.

Lees-Marshment, J., Rudd, C. and Stromback, J. (forthcoming) *Global Political Marketing*. London and New York: Routledge.

Lemish, D. and Gotz, M. (2007) *Children and Media in Times of War and Conflict*. Creskill: Hampton Press.

Lerner, D. (1958) *Passing of Traditional Society: Modernizing the Middle East*. Glencoe, IL: The Free Press.

Levitt, P. (2001) *The Transnational Villagers*. Berkeley, CA: University of California Press.

Lewis, J. (2002) *Constructing Public Opinion: How Political Elites Do What They Like and Why We Seem to Go Along With It*. New York: Columbia University Press.

Lewis, J. (2004) The meaning of real life, pp. 288–302 in *Reality TV: Remaking Television Culture*, edited by S. Murray and L. Ouellette. New York and London: New York University Press.

Lewis, J., Inthorn, S. and Wahl-Jorgensen, K. (2005) *Citizens or Consumers? What the Media tell us about Political Participation*. Maidenhead: Open University Press.

Liberal Democrats (2009) Home, available at www.libdems.org.uk (accessed 20 January 2009).

Liebes, T. and Katz, E. (1990) *The Export of Meaning: Cross-cultural Readings of Dallas*. New York: Oxford University Press.

Lilleker, D. and Lees-Marshment, J. (eds) (2005a) *Political Marketing: A Comparative Perspective*. Manchester and New York: Manchester University Press.

Lilleker, D. and Lees-Marshment, J. (eds) (2005b) Conclusion: towards a comparative model of party marketing, pp. 205–28 in *Political Marketing: A Comparative Perspective*, edited by D.G. Lilleker and J. Lees-Marshment. Manchester and New York: Manchester University Press.

Lindley, R. (2002) *Panorama: 50 Years of Pride and Paranoia*. London: Politico's.

Ling, O.G. and Shaw, B.J. (2004) *Beyond the Port City: Development and Identity in 21st Century Singapore*. Singapore: Pearson Prentice Hall.

Livingstone, S. (2005) On the relation between audiences and publics: why audiences and public? London: LSE Research Online, available at eprints.lse.ac.uk/archive/00000437 (accessed 11 December 2008).

Livingstone, S. (2008) Audiences and interpretations. London: LSE Research Online, June 2008, available at eprints.lse.ac.uk/5646/ (accessed 20 November 2008).

Livingstone, S. and Lunt, P. (1994) *Talk on Television*. London: Routledge.

Livingstone, S., Van Couvering, E. and Thumim, N. (2005) *Adult Media Literacy: A Review of the Research Literature*. London: Ofcom.

Lloyd, J. (2001) *The Protest Ethic: How the Anti-globalisation Movement Challenges Social Democracy*. London: Demos.

Lloyd, J. (2004) *What the Media are Doing to our Politics*. London: Constable.

Loader, B.D. (ed.) (2007) *Young Citizens in the Digital Age: Political Engagement, Young People and New Media*. London and New York: Routledge.

Lobo, M.C. (2005) The presidentialization of Portuguese democracy?, pp. 269–87 in

*The Presidentialization of Politics: A Comparative Study of Modern Democracies*, edited by T. Poguntke and P. Webb. Oxford and New York: Oxford University Press.

Lunt, P. and Stenner, P. (2005) The *Jerry Springer Show* as an emotional public sphere. *Media, Culture & Society* 27, 1: 59–81.

Lusoli, W. and Ward, S. (2006) Hunting protestors: mobilisation, participation and protest online in the Countryside Alliance, pp. 59–79 in *The Internet and Politics: Citizens, Voters and Activists*, edited by S. Oates, D. Owen and R.K. Gibson. London and New York: Routledge.

McChesney, R.W. (2000) So much for the magic of technology and the free market: the World Wide Web and the corporate media system, pp. 5–37 in *World Wide Web and Contemporary Cultural Theory*, edited by A. Herman and T. Swiss. New York and London: Routledge.

McChesney, R.W. (2004) *The Problem of Media: US Communication Politics in the 21st Century*. New York: Monthly Review Press.

McChesney, R.W. (2007) *Communication Revolution: Critical Junctures and the Future of Media*. New York and London: The Free Press.

McGough, S. (2005) Political marketing in Irish politics: the case of Sinn Fein, pp. 97–113 in *Political Marketing: A Comparative Perspective*, edited by D.G. Lilleker and J. Lees-Marshment. Manchester and New York: Manchester University Press.

McGuigan, J. (1992) *Cultural Populism*. London: Routledge.

McNair, B. (2000) *Journalism and Democracy: An Evaluation of the Political Public Sphere*. London: Routledge.

McNair, B. (2003) *News and Journalism in the UK* (4th edn). London: Routledge.

McNair, B. (2007) *An Introduction to Political Communication* (4th edn). London and New York: Routledge.

Madon, S. (2005) Book review: IT experience in India: bridging the digital divide (edited by K. Keniston and D. Kumar). *The Information Society* 21: 391–2.

Malik, S. (2002) *Representing Black Britain: Black and Asian Images on Television*. London: Sage.

Mankekar, P. (1999) *Screening Culture, Viewing Politics: An Ethnography of Televising Womanhood, and Nation in Postcolonial India*. Durham and London: Duke University Press.

Mansbridge, J. (1999) Should blacks represent blacks and women represent women? A contingent 'Yes', available at www.hks.harvard.edu/wappp/research/working/mansbridge99.pdf (accessed 13 June 2007).

Manuel, P. (1993) *Cassette Culture: Popular Music and Technology in North India*. Chicago and London: University of Chicago Press.

March, L. (2006) Virtual parties in a virtual world: the use of the Internet by Russian political parties, pp. 136–62 in *The Internet and Politics: Citizens, Voters and Activists*, edited by S. Oates, D. Owen and R.K. Gibson. London and New York: Routledge.

Margolis, M. and Resnick, D. (2000) *Politics as Usual: The Cyberspace 'Revolution'*. Thousand Oaks, CA: Sage.

Mathiason, J. (2009) *Internet Governance: The New Frontier of Global Institutions*. London and New York: Routledge.

Mathijs, E. and Jones, J. (eds) (2004) *Big Brother International: Formats, Critics and Publics*. London: Wallflower Press.

Melucci, A. (1996) *Challenging Codes*. Cambridge: Cambridge University Press.

Meraz, S. (2007) Analyzing political conversation on the Howard Dean candidate blog, pp. 59–82 in *Blogging, Citizenship and the Future of Media*, edited by M. Tremayne. New York and London: Routledge.

Mesch, G.S. and Coleman, S. (2007) New media and new voters: young people, the Internet and the 2005 UK election campaign, pp. 35–47 in *Young Citizens in the Digital Age: Political Engagement, Young People and New Media*, edited by B.D. Loader. London and New York: Routledge.

Michels, R. (1964) *Political Parties*. New York: Free Press.

Miller, D. and Slater, D. (2001) *The Internet: An Ethnographic Approach*. London: Berg.

Modood, T. (2007) *Multiculturalism: A Civic Idea*. Cambridge: Polity.

Moe, H. (2006) Dissemination and dialogue in the public sphere: an argument for public service online, paper given at the Media Change and Social Theory CRESC Annual Conference, 6–8 September, Oxford.

Morley, D. (1980) *The* Nationwide *Audience: Structure and Decoding*. London: British Film Institute.

Morley, D. and Brunsdon, C. (1999) *The* Nationwide *Television Studies*. London: Routledge.

Mosley, I. (ed.) (2000) *Dumbing Down: Culture, Politics and the Mass Media*. Thorverton: Imprint Academic.

Mossberger, K., Tolbert, C.J. and McNeal, R.S. (2008) *Digital Citizenship: The Internet, Society and Participation*. Cambridge, MA and London: The MIT Press.

Munice, J. (2001) *Youth and Crime: A Critical Introduction*. London: Sage.

Nagel, J. (1997) *American Indian Ethnic Renewal: Red Power and the Resurgence of Identity and Culture*. New York and Oxford: Oxford University Press.

Nash, K. (2000) *Contemporary Political Sociology: Globalization, Politics and Power*. Oxford: Blackwell.

Naylor, R., Driver, S. and Cornford, J. (2000) The BBC goes online: public service broadcasting in the new media age, pp. 137–49 in *web.studies: Rewiring Media Studies for the Digital Age*, edited by D. Gauntlett. London: Arnold.

Negrine, R. (1996) *The Communication of Politics*. London: Sage.

Negrine, R. (2008) *The Transformation of Political Communication: Continuities and Changes in Media and Politics*. Houndmills, Basingstoke: Palgrave Macmillan.

Newman, B.I. (ed.) (1999) *Handbook of Political Marketing*. Thousand Oaks, CA: Sage.

Newton, K. and van Deth, J.W. (2005) *Foundations of Comparative Politics*. Cambridge: Cambridge University Press.

Norris, P. (2001) *Digital Divide: Civic Engagement, Information Poverty, and the Internet Worldwide*. Cambridge: Cambridge University Press.

Oates, S. (2008) *Introduction to Media and Politics*. London: Sage.

Oates, S. and Gibson, R.K. (2006) The Internet, civil society and democracy: a comparative perspective, pp. 1–19 in *The Internet and Politics: Citizens, Voters and Activists*, edited by S. Oates, D. Owen and R.K. Gibson. London and New York: Routledge.

Obama, B. (2008) *The Audacity of Hope: Thoughts on Reclaiming the American Dream*. Edinburgh: Canongate Books.

O'Keefe, A. (2006) Planet saved? Why the green movement is taking to the streets, available at www.newstatesman.com/200611060014 (accessed 6 February 2007).

Osler, F. and Hollis, P. (2001) *The Activist's Guide to the Internet*. London: Pearson Education.

Outhwaite, W. (1994) *Habermas: A Critical Introduction*. Cambridge: Polity.

Paglen, T. and Thompson, A.C. (2007) *Torture Taxi: On the Trail of the CIA's Rendition Flights*. Thriplow: Icon Books.

Painter, A. and Wardle, B. (eds) (2001) *Viral Politics: Communication in the New Media Era*. London: Politico's.

Paletz, D. (1999) *The Media in American Politics: Contents and Consequences*. London: Longman.

Paletz, D. (2002) *The Media in American Politics: Contents and Consequences* (2nd edn). New York and London: Addison-Wesley.

Parekh, B. (2008) *A New Politics of Identity: Political Principles for an Interdependent World*. London: Palgrave Macmillan.

Parry-Giles, T. and Parry-Giles, S.J. (2006) *The Prime-time Presidency: The West Wing and US Nationalism*. Chicago: University of Illinois Press.

Paterson, D., Willoughby, D. and Willoughby, S. (2001) *Civil Rights in the USA, 1863–1980*. Oxford: Heinemann.

Pendakur, M. (2004) All India Radio, pp. 35–7 in *The Museum of Broadcast Communication Encyclopedia of Radio*, edited by C.H. Sterling. New York and London: Fitzroy Dearborn.

Peters, J.D. (1993) Distrust of representation: Habermas on the public sphere. *Media, Culture and Society* 15, 4: 541–72.

Pew (Research Centre for People and the Press) (2007) What Americans know: 1989–2007: public knowledge of current affairs little changed by news and information revolution, available at people-press.org/reports/pdf/319.pdf (accessed 11 December 2007).

Phillips, A. (1991) *Engendering Democracy*. Cambridge: Polity.

Phillips, A. (1998) Introduction, pp. 1–22 in *Feminism and Politics*, edited by A. Phillips. London and New York: Oxford University Press.

Pinder, J. and Usherwood, S. (2007) *The European Union*. Oxford: Oxford University Press.

Pitcher, G. (2002) *The Death of Spin*. London: John Wiley & Sons.

Pitkin, H.F. (1967) *The Concept of Representation*. Berkeley, CA: University of California Press.

Pittock, M. (2008) *The Road to Independence: Scotland Since the Sixties*. London: Reaktion Books.

Poffenberger, T. and Poffenberger, S. (1971) *Reaction to World News Events and the Influence of Mass Media in an Indian Village*. Ann Arbor: University of Michigan.

Poguntke, T. and Webb, P. (2005) The presidentialization of politics in democratic societies: a framework for analysis, pp. 1–25 in *The Presidentialization of Politics: A Comparative Study of Modern Democracies*, edited by T. Poguntke and P. Webb. Oxford and New York: Oxford University Press.

Postman, N. (1988) *Amusing Ourselves to Death: Public Discourse in the Age of Show Business*. London: Methuen.

Power (2006) *Power to the People: The Report of Power: An Independent Inquiry into Britain's Democracy*. London: The Power Inquiry.

Preston, P. (2009) *Making the News: Journalism and News Cultures in Europe*. London and New York: Routledge.

Price, S. (1997) *Presidentialising the Premiership*. London: Macmillan.

Putnam, R. (2000) *Bowling Alone: the Collapse and Revival of American Community*. New York: Simon & Schuster.

Reigert, K. (ed.) (2007) *Politicotainment: Television's Take on the Real*. New York: Peter Lang.

Rogers, E.M., Singhal, A. and Thombre, A. (2004) Indian audience interpretations of health-related content in *The Bold and the Beautiful*. *International Journal for Communication Studies* 66, 5: 437–58.

Rosenkrands, J. (2004) Politicizing *Homo economicus*: analysis of anti-corporate websites, pp. 57–76 in *Cyberprotest: New Media, Citizens and Social Movements*, edited by W. Van de Donk, B.D. Loader, P. Nixon and D. Rucht. London and New York: Routledge.

Ruddock, A. (2007) *Investigating Audiences*. Los Angeles and London: Sage.

Rutigliano, L. (2007) Emergent communication networks as civic journalism, pp. 225–38 in *Blogging, Citizenship and the Future of Media*, edited by M. Tremayne. New York and London: Routledge.

Saccamano, N. (1991) The consolation of ambivalence: Habermas and the public sphere. *Modern Language Notes* 106: 685–98.

Sanders, V. (2006) *Race Relations in the USA: 1863–1980* (3rd edn). London: Hodder Education.

Sassatelli, R. (2007) *Consumer Culture: History, Theory and Politics*. London: Sage.

Scammell, M. (2003) Citizen consumers: towards a new marketing of politics, pp. 117–36 in *Media and the Restylisation of Politics*, edited by J. Corner and D. Pels. London: Sage.

Scannell, P. (1996) *Radio, Television and Modern Life*. Oxford: Blackwell.

Scannell, P. and Cardiff, D. (1991) *A Social History of British Broadcasting, Vol. 1*. Oxford: Blackwell.

Schudson, M. (1994) Was there ever a public sphere?, pp. 143–63 in *Habermas and the Public Sphere*, edited by C. Calhoun. Cambridge, MA and London: The MIT Press.

Scott, D.T. (2007) Pundits in muckrakers' clothing: political blogs and the 2004 presidential election, pp. 39–58 in *Blogging, Citizenship and the Future of Media*, edited by M. Tremayne. New York and London: Routledge.

Scruton, R. (2007) *A Dictionary of Political Thought* (3rd edn). London: Palgrave.

Sen, A. (2007) *Identity and Violence: The Illusion of Destiny*. New York and London: W.W. Norton.

Shukra, K. (1998) *The Changing Pattern of Black Politics in Britain*. London: Pluto.

Siapera, E. (2006) Multiculturalism online: the Internet and the dilemmas of multicultural politics. *European Journal of Cultural Studies* 9, 1: 5–24.

Silverstone, R. (2007) *Media and Morality: On the Rise of the Mediapolis*. Cambridge: Polity.

Slevin, J. (2000) *The Internet and Society*. Cambridge: Polity.

Sloboda, J. and Dardagan, H. (2005) The Iraq Body Count project: civil society and the democratic deficit, pp. 219–37 in *The Iraq War and Democratic Politics*, edited by A. Danchev and J. Macmillan. Abingdon and New York: Routledge.

Smulyan, S. (1994) *Selling Radio: The Commercialization of American Broadcasting 1920–1934*. Washington and London: Smithsonian Institution Press.

Spender, D. (1995) *Nattering on the Net: Women, Power and Cyberspace*. North Melbourne: Spinifex.

Spink, A., Jansen, B.J., Kathuria, V. and Koshman, S. (2006) Overlap among major web search engines. *Internet Research* 16, 4: 419–26.

Squires, J. (2005) Common citizenship and plural identities: the politics of social difference, pp. 109–38 in *Exploring Political Worlds*. edited by P. Lewis. Edinburgh: Edinburgh University Press/Open University.

Stanyer, J. (2007) *Modern Political Communication: Mediated Politics in Uncertain Times*. Cambridge: Polity.

Starkey, G. and Crisell, A. (2009) *Radio Journalism*. London: Sage.

Starr, P. (2004) *The Creation of the Media: Political Origins of Modern Communications*. New York: Basic Books.

Stein, S. (2003) *Politics of the Web: A Student Guide*. Harlow: Prentice Hall.

Stevenson, N. (2003) *Cultural Citizenship: Cosmopolitan Questions*. Maidenhead: Open University Press.

Stewart, J., Karlin, B. and Javerbaum, D. (2005) *America, the Book: A Citizen's Guide to Democracy Inaction*. London: Penguin Allen Lane.

Stoker, G. (2006) *Why Politics Matters: Making Democracy Work*. London: Palgrave Macmillan.

Straubhaar, J.D. (2007) *World Television: From Global to Local*. Los Angeles and London: Sage.

Street, J. (1997) *Politics and Popular Culture*. Cambridge: Polity.

Street, J. (2001a) The Transformation of political modernity?, pp. 210–24 in *New Media and Politics*, edited by B. Axford and R. Huggins. London: Sage.

Street, J. (2001b) *Mass Media, Politics and Democracy*. Houndmills: Palgrave.

Street, J. (2003) The celebrity politician: political style and popular culture, pp. 85–98 in *Media and the Restylisation of Politics*, edited by J. Corner and D. Pels. Sage: London.

Street, J. (2004) Celebrity politicians: popular culture and political representation. *British Journal of Politics and International Relations* 6: 435–52.

Street, J., Hague, S. and Savigny, H. (2008) Playing to the crowd: the role of music and musicians in political representation. *British Journal of Politics and International Relations* 10: 269–85.

Subiamaniam, V. (2006) Unshackle community radio: media for, and by, the people, pp. 211–23 in *The Indian Media: Illusion, Delusion and Reality – Essays in Honour of Prem Bhatia*, edited by A. Mathur. New Delhi: Rupa and Co.

Subrahnsanyam, K. (2006) Media and strategy in the globalising world, pp. 98–106 in *The Indian Media: Illusion, Delusion and Reality – Essays in Honour of Prem Bhatia*, edited by A. Mathur. New Delhi: Rupa and Co.

Such, E., Walker, O. and Walker, R. (2005) Anti-war children: representations of youth protests against the war in the British national press. *Childhood* 12, 3: 301–26.

Sunstein, C.R. (2007) *Republic.com 2.0*. Princeton and Oxford: Princeton University Press.

Sussman, G. (2005) *Global Electioneering: Campaign Consulting, Communication and Corporate Financing*. Lanham, MD: Rowman & Littlefield.

Talkingcock (2009) Singapore's premier satirical humour website, available at www.talkingcock.com/html/index.php (accessed 20 January 2009).

Tapscott, D. and Williams, A.D. (2008) *Wikinomics: How Mass-collaboration Changes Everything*. London: Atlantic Books.

Tarrow, S. (2005) *The New Transnational Activism*. Cambridge: Cambridge University Press.

Taylor, P. and Curtis, D. (2005) The United Nations, pp. 405–24 in *The Globalization of World Politics: An Introduction to International Relations* (3rd edn), edited by J. Baylis and S. Smith. Oxford: Oxford University Press.

Tewkesbury, D. (2005) The seeds of audience fragmentation: specialization in the use of online news sites. *Journal of Broadcasting & Electronic Media*. 49, 3: 332–48.

Thomas, A.O. (2005) *Imagi-nations and Borderless Television: Media, Culture and Politics across Asia*. New Delhi, Thousand Oaks and London: Sage.

Thomas, E. (2009) *'A Long Time Coming': The Inspiring, Combative 2008 Campaign and the Historic Election of Barack Obama*. London: Public Affairs Ltd.

Thompson, J.B. (1985) *Critical Hermeneutics: A Study in the Thought of Paul Ricoeur and Jurgen Habermas*. Cambridge: Cambridge University Press.

Thompson, J.B. (1995) *The Media and Modernity: A Social Theory of the Media.* Cambridge: Polity.

Thompson, J.B. (2000) *Political Scandal: Power and Visibility in the Media Age.* Cambridge: Polity.

Tremayne, M. (ed). (2007) *Blogging, Citizenship and the Future of Media.* New York and London: Routledge.

Tully, M. (2006) Broadcasting in India: an under-exploited resource, pp. 285–92 in *The Indian Media: Illusion, Delusion and Reality – Essays in Honour of Prem Bhatia,* edited by A. Mathur. New Delhi: Rupa and Co.

Tunstall, J. (2008) *The Media were American: US Mass Media in Decline.* New York and Oxford: Oxford University Press.

Turner, G. (1992) *British Cultural Studies: An Introduction.* London and New York: Routledge.

Van Zoonen, L. (1998) One of the girls? The changing gender of journalism, pp. 33–46 in *News, Gender and Power,* edited by C. Carter, G. Branston and S. Allan. London: Routledge.

Van Zoonen, L. (2004) Desire and resistance: *Big Brother* in the Dutch public sphere, pp. 16–24 in Big Brother *International: Formats, Critics and Publics,* edited by E. Mathijs and J. Jones. London: Wallflower Press.

Van Zoonen, L. (2005) *Entertaining the Citizen: When Politics and Popular Culture Converge.* Lanham: Rowman & Littlefield.

Varma, P.K. (2005) *Being Indian: The Truth About Why the 21st Century will be India's.* London: Heinemann.

Vibert, F. (2007) *The Rise of the Unelected: Democracy and the New Separation of Powers.* Cambridge: Cambridge University Press.

Vilanilam, J.V. (2005) *Mass Communication in India: A Sociological Perspective.* New Delhi, Thousand Oaks and London: Sage.

Viswanath, K. and Karan, K. (2000) India, pp. 84–117 in *Handbook of Media in Asia,* edited by S.A. Gunaratna. New Delhi, Thousand Oaks and London: Sage.

Wachbroit, R. (2004) Reliance and reliability: the problem of information on the Internet, pp. 29–42 in *The Internet in Public Life,* edited by V.V. Gehring. Lanham, MA: Rowman & Littlefield.

Walter, D. (2003) *The Strange Rebirth of Liberal England.* London: Politico's.

Ward, S. and Gibson, R. (2003) On-line and on message? Candidate websites in the 2001 general election. *The British Journal of Politics and International Relations* 5, 2: 188–205.

Ward, S. and Vedel, T. (2006) Introduction: the potential of the Internet revisited. *Parliamentary Affairs* 59, 2: 210–25.

Washbourne, N. (1999) *Information Technology and Social Transformation in the Global Environmental Movement.* Unpublished doctoral thesis, University of Surrey.

Washbourne, N. (2001) Information technology and new forms of organising? Translocalism and networks in Friends of the Earth, pp. 129–41 in *Culture and*

*Politics in the Information Age: A New Politics?*, edited by F. Webster. Routledge: London.

Washbourne, N. (2005) Globalisation and globality', pp. 161–8 in *Cultural Geography: A Critical Dictionary of Key Concepts*, edited by D. Atkinson, P. Jackson, D. Sibley and N. Washbourne. London: I.B. Taurus.

Washbourne, N. (2006) Media context of public relations and journalism, pp. 62–77 in *Exploring Public Relations*, edited by R. Tench and L. Yeomans. Harlow: Pearson Education.

Washbourne, N. (2009) Media context of public relations and journalism (revised), pp. 68–81 in *Exploring Public Relations* (2nd edn), edited by R. Tench and L. Yeomans. Harlow: Financial Times Prentice Hall.

Webb, P. (2000) *The Modern British Party System*. London: Sage.

Webb, P. and Poguntke, T. (2005) The presidentialization of contemporary democratic politics: evidence, causes and consequences, pp. 336–56 in *The Presidentialization of Politics: A Comparative Study of Modern Democracies*, edited by T. Poguntke and P. Webb. Oxford and New York: Oxford University Press.

Webster, J.G. (2005) Beneath the veneer of fragmentation: television audience polarization in a multi-channel world. *Journal of Communication* 55, 2: 366–82.

Whitby, K.J. (2007) Dimensions of representation and the congressional black caucus, pp. 195–211 in *African American Perspectives on Political Science*, edited by W.C. Rich. Philadelphia: Temple University Press.

White, J. (1999) *The Politico's Guide to Politics on the Internet*. London: Politico's.

Wilhelm, A.G. (2000) *Democracy in the Digital Age: Challenges to Political Life in Cyberspace*. New York and London: Routledge.

Wilkinson, R. and Pickett, K. (2009) *The Spirit Level: Why More Equal Societies Almost Always Do Better*. London: Allen Lane.

Williams, B. (2004) *Truth and Truthfulness: An Essay in Genealogy*. Oxford and Princeton: Princeton University Press.

Wilmer, F. (1997) First Nations in the USA, pp. 186–201 in *The Ethnicity Reader: Nationalism, Multiculturalism and* Migration, edited by M. Guibernau and J. Rex., Cambridge: Polity.

Wilson, B. (2005) *The Laughter of Triumph: William Hone and the Fight for the Free Press*. London: Faber & Faber.

Wong, P.-K. (2003) Global and national factors affecting e-commerce diffusion in Singapore. *The Information Society* 19: 19–32.

Wright, S. (2006) Design matters: the political efficacy of government-run discussion boards, pp. 80–99 in *The Internet and Politics: Citizens, Voters and Activists*, edited by S. Oates, D. Owen and R. K. Gibson. London and New York: Routledge.

Wyn, J. and Harris, A. (2004) Youth research in Australia and New Zealand. *Research on Youth and Culture* 12, 3: 271–89.

Xenos, M. and Bennett, W.L. (2007) Young voters and the web of politics: the promise and problems of youth-oriented political content on the web, pp. 48–67 in *Young Citizens in the Digital Age: Political Engagement, Young People and New Media*, edited by B.D. Loader. London and New York: Routledge.

YMCA (2006) Young people get political at the Lib Dem party conference, available at www.ymca.org.uk/pooled/articles/BF_NEWSART/view.asp?Q=BF_NEWS-ART . . . (accessed 29 October 2006).

# Index

# Related books from Open University Press

Purchase from www.openup.co.uk or order through your local bookseller

## NEWS CULTURE 3e

### Stuart Allan

*News Culture* offers a timely examination of the forms, practices, institutions and audiences of journalism. Having highlighted a range of pressing issues confronting the global news industry today, it proceeds to provide a historical consideration of the rise of 'objective' reporting in newspaper, radio and television news.

It explores the way news is produced, its textual conventions, and its negotiation by the reader, listener or viewer as part of everyday life. Stuart Allan also explores topics such as the cultural dynamics of sexism and racism as they shape news coverage, as well as the rise of online news, citizen journalism, war reporting and celebrity-driven infotainment.

Building on the success of the bestselling previous editions, this new edition addresses the concerns of the news media age, featuring:

- An expanded chapter on news, power and the public sphere
- A chapter-length discussion of war journalism, tracing key factors shaping reportage from the battlefields of Vietnam to the current war in Iraq
- A chapter on citizen journalism in times of crisis, including a number of examples where ordinary individuals have performed the role of a journalist to bear witness to tragic events

This book is essential reading for students of journalism, cultural and media studies, sociology and politics.

### Contents

*Series Editor's foreword – Introduction: The culture of news – News, power and the public sphere – The rise of 'objective' newspaper reporting – The early days of radio and television news – Making news, reporting truths – The cultural politics of news discourse – News, audiences and everyday life – The gendered realities of journalism – Racial diversity in the news – War reporting – Citizen journalism in times of crisis – Good journalism is popular culture – References – Index.*

2010   384pp
978–0–335–23565–0 (Paperback)

## ONLINE NEWS
## JOURNALISM AND THE INTERNET
## Stuart Allan

> If the promises of online news are to be fulfilled, books like this deserve the widest possible readership
>
> Paul Bradshaw, University of Central England, UK

In this exciting and timely book Stuart Allan provides a wide-ranging analysis of online news. He offers important insights into key debates concerning the ways in which journalism is evolving on the internet, devoting particular attention to the factors influencing its development. Using a diverse range of examples, he shows how the forms, practices and epistemologies of online news are gradually becoming conventionalized, and assesses the implications for journalism's future.

The rise of online news is examined with regard to the reporting of a series of major news events. Topics include coverage of the Oklahoma City bombing, the Clinton-Lewinsky affair, the September 11 attacks, election campaigns, and the war in Iraq. The emergence of blogging is traced with an eye to its impact on journalism as a profession. The participatory journalism of news sites such as Indymedia, OhmyNews, and Wikinews is explored, as is the citizen journalist reporting of the South Asian tsunami, London bombings and Hurricane Katrina. In each instance, the uses of new technologies – from digital cameras to mobile telephones and beyond – are shown to shape journalistic innovation, often in surprising ways.

This book is essential reading for students, researchers and journalists.

### Contents
*Introduction – The rise of online news Brave new media worlds: BBC News – Online, the Drudge Report, and the birth of blogging – Covering the crisis: online journalism on September 11 – Sensational scandals: the new(s) values of blogs – Online reporting of the war in Iraq: bearing witness – Participatory journalism: IndyMedia, OhmyNews and Wikinews – Citizen journalists on the scene: the London bombings and Hurricane Katrina – New directions*

2006   216pp
978-0-335-22121-9 (Paperback)      978-0-335-22122-6 (Hardback)

# MEDIATIZED CONFLICT

## Simon Cottle

We live in times that generate diverse conflicts; we also live in times when conflicts are increasingly played out and performed in the media. *Mediatized Conflict* explores the powered dynamics, contested representations and consequences of media conflict reporting. It examines how the media today do not simply report or represent diverse situations of conflict, but actively 'enact' and 'perform' them.

This important book brings together the latest research findings and theoretical discussions to develop an encompassing, multidimensional and sophisticated understanding of the social complexities, political dynamics and cultural forms of mediatized conflicts in the world today. Case studies include:

- Anti-war protests and anti-globalization demonstrations
- Mediatized public crises centering on issues of 'race' and racism
- War journalism and peace journalism
- Risk society and the environment
- The politics of outrage and terror spectacle post 9/11
- Identity politics and cultural recognition

This is essential reading for Media Studies students and all those interested in understanding how, why, and with what impacts media report on diverse conflicts in the world today.

### Contents

*Series editor's foreword – Acknowledgements – Mediatized conflict in the world today – Getting a fix on mediatised conflict: Paradigms and perspectives – Reporting Demonstrations and protest: Public Sphere(s), public screens – From moral panics to mediatised public crises: Moving stories of 'race' and racism – War journalism: Disembodied and embedded – Peace journalism and other alternatives: On hopes and prayers – Media, 'risk society' and the environment: A different story? – From 'terrorism' to the 'global war on terror': The media politics of outrage – Identity politics and cultural difference: On mediatised recognition – Mediatized conflict: Conclusions – References – Index.*

2006   232pp
978–0–335–21452–5 (Paperback)      978–0–335–21453–2 (Hardback)